BUDDHIST BUBBLEGUM

BUDDHIST BUBBLEGUM

Esoteric Buddhism in the creative process of
Arthur Russell

Matt Marble

coolgrove press

Coolgrove Press, an imprint of
Cool Grove Publishing, Inc. New York.
512 Argyle Road, Brooklyn, NY 11218
All rights reserved under the International and
Pan-American Copyright Conventions.

www. coolgrove. com
For permissions and other inquiries write to info@coolgrove. com

ISBN: 978-1-887276-30-6
Library of Congress Control Number: 2020945377

Front cover photos of Arthur Russell:
Kind courtesy of the Allen Ginsberg Estate.

The background image of the book cover:
Postcard designed by Tom Lee for "Arthur Russell and The Singing Tractors"
performance March 7, 1982 at the Experimental Intermedia Foundation,
224 Centre St, NY NY.

Coolgrove Press is a member of
Community of Literary Magazines and Presses [CLMP]
and a past receipient of their Face Out Re-grant for marketing.

This book is distributed to the trade by Ingram Spark

Book font: Iowan Old Style

Media alchemy by Kiku

Coolgrove Press

ACKNOWLEDGEMENTS

I would like to thank the Department of Music Composition at Princeton University for their support and assistance in preparing this manuscript—especially my advisors, Dan Trueman and Dmitri Tymoczko. I am indebted to Steve Knutson, of Audika Records, and Tom Lee for their support and for allowing me years of access to Arthur Russell's extant archive. I want to thank all of Arthur's friends and collaborators whom lent their time to share their memories and thoughts with me through in-person interviews, and telephone or email correspondences: Alan Abrams, Mustafa Ahmed, Beth Anderson-Harold, Bob Blank, Joyce Bowden, Ernie Brooks, Andrew Franck, Tej Hazarika, V.K. "Keisho" Leary, Ronald Kuivila, Elodie Lauten, Paul Nagy, Bill Ruyle, and Peter Zummo. I am grateful for and indebted to the prior work and research of Tim Lawrence and Matt Wolf, both of whom laid a strong foundation for my own research--and to Tim especially for his correspondence and feedback. I want to thank my dear friend Joseph Bradshaw, who first introduced me to the music of Arthur Russell. Thanks also to my parents, A.C. Marble Jr. and Diene Harper, Emma Lipp and all the Lipps and Barrys for their constant love and support. Rest in Peace, Elodie Lauten, V.K. "Keisho" Leary, and Barbara "Ladybear" Sue, all three of whom passed away during the process of my writing this work.

TABLE OF CONTENTS

LIST OF IMAGES

CHAPTER 5

CHAPTER 6

I.

MISTER MYSTERY

Exploring, fusing, and transcending musical styles as diverse as disco, North Indian classical music, country, hip-hop, and avant-guard composition, Arthur Russell (1951-1992) has remained—both during his life and after—as mysterious and ignored as he has been accessible and revered. Musician and author, David Toop once said of his work, "No style is higher or lower" (35). And from his adolescence until his premature death by AIDS in 1992, Russell would forever seek to fuse the conceptual and intellectual "highs" of avant-garde art with the "lowly" play and pleasure of popular music.

But for Russell the breaking down of music's stylistic walls was not only aesthetic, but spiritual. For he also sought to join the cosmic heights of spiritual enlightenment with the terrestrial day-to-day. The thread connecting all of these highs and lows—and Russell's stylistically diverse output— is found in his lifelong Buddhist practice. After studying Hindu and Hare Krishna spiritual traditions, the Beatles' George Harrison once expressed that his aim was "to spiritually infiltrate popular culture" through music (Prabhupada, 15)—Russell had the same agenda. Applying *mantra*, meditation, numerology, astrology, and ritual directly to his music, Russell sought to project spiritual illumination to the masses through techniques drawn from esoteric Buddhist philosophy. Buddhism shaped Russell's life; it was at the core of his creative process. With his crisscrossing of genres and constant revisions, Russell's work could seem haphazard and disjointed to many. But, through the lens of Buddhism, we see Russell's underlying aims to be clear, unified, and unwavering throughout his life. Russell's close friend, neighbor, and renowned poet Allen Ginsberg succinctly echoed these aims in a eulogy he gave following Russell's death:

> His ambition seemed to be to write popular music, "bubblegum" music, but "Buddhist bubblegum"—to transmit the *dharma* through the most elemental form, or to transmit some sense of illumination. That was [his] constant preoccupation (Wolf, 2009).

Buddhist Bubblegum is an in depth exploration of the influence of Vajrayana Buddhism upon the life and music of the late Arthur Russell—cellist, singer, songwriter, composer, and producer. It offers an overview of Russell's creative process, informed by unreleased notebooks and scores from Russell's archives, musical transcriptions and personal interviews made by the author, as well as the historical and contextual backgrounds of the Buddhist lineages that Russell embraced and applied to his music.

Largely ignored during his lifetime, Russell has received a renaissance of renewed interest from a younger generation since Soul Jazz records released the compilation album, *The World of Arthur Russell*, in 2004. Since then, a series of new releases and re-releases have followed—pioneered by Steve Knutson via Audika Records—as well as a biography, a video documentary, conferences, festivals, dance parties, tribute albums, and numerous covers by contemporary artists. Tim Lawrence's biography (*Hold On to Your Dreams*) and Matt Wolf's video documentary (*Wild Combination*) offer the most comprehensive portraits of the artist to date. And while Russell's Buddhism is addressed in these works, the direct influence of Buddhism upon Russell's creative process remained vague. At the same time Russell's actual compositional documents—his notations and scores—have been given similarly little attention. Augmenting these works,

Buddhist Bubblegum dives deeper into Russell's notations and scores, his compositional mind, and shows how Buddhism directly influenced the artist's creative process.

Following a biographic introduction to Russell, chapter two begins by looking extensively into the three primary traditions of Buddhism that Russell followed at various points throughout his life: Shugendo, Shingon, and various branches of Tibetan Buddhism. At Kailas Shugendo, Neville Warwick had uniquely combined several esoteric practices. At the core was the ascetic Japanese folk Buddhist tradition of Shugendo, which had revered mountains and focused on physical acts of meditation, or *sadhana*. To this tradition Warwick added aspects of Tibetan Lamaism, largely through the teachings of Lama Govinda. After a falling out with Warwick, Russell began private study with Yuko Nonomura, and became more deeply acquainted with Shugendo's parent lineage, Shingon. His studies then focused on meditation, as well as reflection upon the sutras, or holy scriptures. After moving to New York Russell's Buddhist practice became more private, but he appeared to have been drawn largely to Tibetan Buddhist traditions, which he encountered through local organizations and friends, as well as in the writings of controversial *tantra* teacher, Chögyam Trungpa. Trungpa's conception of "first thought, best thought" resonated deeply with Russell, and guided his performance practice, as well as his compositional approach.

Through engaging these various traditions that Russell embraced, we'll gain a deeper understanding of the Buddhist concepts and practices that Russell applied in his music. Chapter two, then, extends the scope of these esoteric spiritual influences to include Russell's study of North Indian music and his relationship with astrology and numerology.

Chapter three has us diving into Russell's notebooks and

scores, primarily those made during his last years in California and his first years in New York. Considerable time is given to some of Russell's earliest compositions and to a series of unreleased text scores from what I call Russell's "black notebook." In his earliest compositional efforts, Russell was applying aspects of observation and found materials, Buddhist meditation and ritual, comedy, conceptual discipline, mathematics, and the fusion of popular and high art music. Through addressing an array of these techniques and concepts, we trace the early formation of Russell's general creative process and the emergence of a unique compositional system.

Through an extended look at one of his most ambitious works, *Instrumentals Vol. 1 & 2* (1974-1978), we see Russell's creative process mature in Chapter four. *Instrumentals* began as a suggestion of his Buddhist teacher, Yuko Nonomura, who encouraged Russell to compose music for Nonomura's cloud photography. Russell got started immediately, carrying the project from California, where it found its' first performance, to New York, where it would be performed numerous times. To compose *Instrumentals*, Russell devised a laborious and imaginative compositional system—I call it the "matrix system"—which functioned as both a musical and spiritual discipline, inspired by Russell's experience with Shingon Buddhism.

After analyzing the matrix system, I then show direct compositional paths from this system to specific portions of *Instrumentals*. But as we'll see, this matrix system—only alluded to in previous publications—was an extensive and critical part of Russell's creative process. Beyond *Instrumentals*, this system would go on to inform a vast majority of the works we'll be looking at, spanning over a decade of Russell's short career. Chapter four shows how Russell applied his matrix system in different ways to subsequent works, including his aborted orchestral collaboration with theatre director Robert Wilson (*Medea/Tower of Meaning*, 1981), his experimental disco opus (*24>24 Music*, 1980), and his scored improvisation work under the monicker of Singing Tractors (throughout the 1980s). These works show Russell expanding and experimenting with his matrix system, while generating very different musical styles.

Chapter seven offers a study of one of Russell's most highly regarded albums, *World of Echo* (1985). *World of Echo* showcases Russell's maturing solo performance practice—one he had been developing throughout the early 80s—featuring his voice, accompanied by amplified cello and effects. For this project Russell largely discarded the matrix system. Instead he developed a less rigid and more conceptual compositional approach. One aspect of this approach involved the role of echo, reverb, and other effects—what Russell called the "world of echo P.A. System." In addition, Russell intentionally obscured the delivery of his lyrics. Mumbled, whispered, and drenched in effects, the language is abstracted and, often repeated, approached as mantra. More broadly Russell's concept concerned fusing pop and high art musics while treating song as meditation. This involved an approach to brainstorming ideas, lyrics, and notations for the the album, using what he called "parenthetical ideas" or, as he often abbreviated it, "p-ideas." Here are some brief examples from Russell's notebooks:

> P-Idea: (the construction of structure which can be abandoned at any moment and that is transparent--WOE)
>
> P-Idea: (the creation of a system which accepts any musical input)
>
> P-idea: (improvisation which is based on time and space limitations and composition which is not properly concerned with

limitations, including long list of impossible things, and the integration of the two.)

P-idea: (different kinds of echo co-existing, like plants growing within plants) (like delay and reverb)

Russell's grand conception of *World of Echo* was as a space of free and constant mutability, a place in which "any input" was welcome. Just as with these "P-ideas," lyrics, chord progressions, melodies, entire songs, studio effects, cello techniques, musings and observations—everything was approached modularly. Any one element could be altered, contracted or expanded, combined or superimposed—everything was mutable and endlessly collaged. It was this attraction towards mutability or flux and this fusion of logic and intuition, all rooted in Buddhist philosophy and practice, that had driven Russell since his adolescence. "Seeing analysis as freeze frame of phenomena," Russell mused in the late 1980s, "investigate altering flows of thought" (Russell, N). Russell's aim was always to bring attention back to spontaneous "first" thoughts, to moments of fresh inspiration. He had attempted to do this musically through a number of his works. But he was perhaps nowhere more successful in sonifying these "first thoughts" than in *World of Echo*. Stripped down and saturated in reverb and echo, *World of Echo* offers the most refined distillation of Russell's diverse influences—North Indian raga, disco, folk, minimalist composition, experimentalism, blues, gospel, heavy metal, Buddhist chant and mantra. The songs of *World of Echo* are nothing less than abstract genre-bending hymns and the essence of Arthur Russell.

While other posthumously released works by Russell will be addressed—*Another Thought* (1994), *Calling Out of Context* (2004), *Love Is Overtaking Me* (2008), and various E.P.'s—the works noted in the paragraphs above were chosen for their distinctness, their completion during Russell's lifetime, and their ability to best represent the specific techniques of Russell's creative process that we will be addressing. I have had no intention of de-mystifying Russell's music, nor of "systematizing" it. Though the "matrix system" is fascinating as a self-made compositional tool, Russell's creative process would never reduce itself to simply following the rules of a system, even one of his own design. But that was where Russell's voice was clearest and most itself: within a system, without rules (or vice versa). In a Point Music video promo for Russell's *Another Thought*, Philip Glass noted: "It is the mystery of the creative process. It's the mysterious thing that does not submit to formula, but which subverts the formula" (Russell, AT). Russell seemed to find some transcendence and joy in the contradictory position between discipline and pleasure, intelligence and intuition—between the everyday mind and a cosmic imagination.

A Brief Introduction to Arthur Russell

Born on May 21, 1951, Charles Arthur Russell, Jr. was raised in Oskaloosa, Iowa—where Russell's father, Charles Sr., would later become mayor. Shy, ponderous, and with a face covered by severe acne, Russell was an outcast as a child. He took to the cello—his mother had played it at home—and began performing and soon composing for high school productions. In his teens Russell was actively absorbing all manner of music, poetry, spiritual and philosophical texts, finding special interest in the *Tibetan Book of the Dead*, the writings of the Beats (Kerouac, Ginsberg), as well as the music of John Coltrane and John Cage. He also began experimenting with L.S.D. and other drugs. It was after his father scolded him for possession of marijuana that Russell ran away from home. He moved from Oskaloosa, to Iowa City, and ultimately to America's counter-culture hub, San Francisco. Russell was then arrested for marijuana possession and released to the custody of an obscure Bay Area Buddhist commune, Kailas Shugendo, lead by a controversial guru, Neville Warwick.

Russell joined the community on Valentine's Day in 1969. Warwick's philosophy was an amalgam of an ascetic mountain tradition, Shugendo, an obscure subsidiary of Shingon Buddhism, and Tibetan Lamaism, via the teachings of Warwick's guru, Lama Anagarika Govinda. Russell was lost and Kailas Shugendo offered him sanction and discipline as he continued to work on music and rebuild his strength. There he played and sang in the Shugendo Mantric Sun Band, a mixture of bluegrass, folk, and Buddhist chant. He spent time hiking and reciting mantra in the neighboring mountains. And he performed the fire rituals (fire meditation and fire-walking), which the commune was becoming publicly known for. But internal politics, Warwick's abusive behavior, and the attempt to separate Russell form his cello would compel Russell to part ways with the commune after almost two years in attendance.

Meanwhile, during Russell's time at the commune, he also attended the San Francisco Conservatory where he took cello lessons with Margaret Rowell and Andor Toth, and composition courses with William Allaudain Mathieu, a sympathetic composer with experimental and spiritual affinities. While Russell's cello studies with Toth were more straightforward, his studies with Rowell were closer to the visualization and sadhana techniques he was learning through Vajrayana Buddhism. As one of Rowell's students, Irene Sharp, recalls the teacher would use highly unorthodox techniques to develop the students' physical and emotional relationship with their instrument.

One day when I couldn't get the feel of the bow, Margaret said, "Think of a paint brush," and had me get up and pretend to be painting her wall. When she wanted a "poured tone" she took me to the kitchen to fill a pitcher and a cup so that I could get the actual feeling of pouring. When I insisted on gripping the three-ounce bow in a deathlike grasp, Margaret got her most beautiful bone china tea cup and saucer and had me manipulate them up and down and around. "Was there any danger that you would drop them?" she asked. And so I realized the feeling of an easy clinging hold to the cup, nothing like the vise-like grip that I had been using on the bow (Sharp, 1984).

Russell would also commute to Berkeley to study Hindustani music at the recently formed Ali Akbar College of Music. There Russell extended his experience of mantra and spiritual folk music to include the North Indian devotional song traditions of *bhajan, kirtan,* and *dhrupad,* as well as Hindu philosophy. He spent a great deal of time playing with classmates, learning various *ragas* and *talas,* and becoming obsessed with the spiritually guided musical practice of *riaz.*

Allen Ginsberg met Russell during one of Kailas Shugendo's public events in Berkeley. Ginsberg championed Russell's esoteric Buddhist interest as well as his budding homosexuality. Following a sexual fling they would become close friends, and eventually neighbors. Throughout the years they would continue to perform Buddhist *sutras* as well as Ginsberg's musical settings of the poetry of William Blake. Ginsberg would also expose Russell to the teachings of Tibetan *tulku* Chögyam Trungpa, whose ideas of "first thought, best thought" and "crazy wisdom" would continue to influence Russell. Ginsberg was skeptical of Russell's teacher, Warwick; and Russell's own skepticism was growing. Russell was being verbally and physically abused by Warwick, who also threatened to take Russell's cello away. It didn't take long for the young cellist to take his exit from Warwick's dysfunctional community.

After breaking from the commune, Russell would continue studying privately with a Shingon Buddhist priest, Yuko Nonomura. It was largely Nonomura, balancing his life as a Buddhist priest with his daily life as an insurance salesman, who gave Russell the confidence that he could pursue popular music while maintaining his Buddhist practice. Russell's aim to "make it" in New York was, in part, to sustain himself and his career through the music he loved; but it was also a hope to channel any financial rewards toward the construction of a Buddhist temple being planned by Nonomura.

Russell moved to New York in 1973. He scheduled a brief meeting with John Cage for his first day in the city. Within his first year, at the age of 20, he was curating The Kitchen, one of Manhattan's earliest and most prominent venues for avant-guard music and performance art, and working with established composers such as Christian Wolff and Philip Glass. Alongside Wolff, David Behrman, Garrett List, and Jon Gibson, Russell performed Wolff's *Exercises* and *Songs*; while Glass scored his soundtrack to Samuel Beckett's *Cascando* specifically for Russell's cello. He would go on to add cello and/or vocals to the works of Jon Gibson, Elodie Lauten, Peter Zummo, Peter Gordon, and many others. He was also continuing his academic studies, taking linguistics courses at Columbia University, while studying composition (with an unsympathetic Charles Wuorinen) and electronic music (with a sympathetic Elias Tannenbaum) at the Manhattan School of Music. But, more than a performer of others' works, Russell aspired to be a composer.

Russell's early compositions, some of which were devised in California, were frequently performed with friends, during his first years in New York, at the Manhattan School. These works often involved settings of Buddhist sutras, folk-like melodies, the use of Cagean/Zen-inspired chance operations, and a Fluxus-like sense of humor. Composed and performed during his time at the Manhattan School, *City Park* was an amalgam of bizarre textual instructions and musical notations, which Russell felt could be listened to in variable ways, with people tuning in and out at their leisure. Wuorinen, a conservative icon of 12-tone, serialist composition thought it "the most unattractive thing I've ever heard" (Lawrence, *Hold On* 53).

The same year he moved to New York, Russell's criss-crossing of popular and experimental musics culminated in an ongoing series of works called *Instrumentals*, a varying blend of avant-guard and popular idioms scored for rock and orchestral ensembles. This work was inspired by Nonomura, who proposed that Russell score music for Nonomura's nature photography, featuring clouds, flowers, and mountain landscapes, revered symbols in the Shingon Buddhist tradition.

It was for this work that Russell developed a unique compositional system that I call the "matrix system." Using the matrix system, Russell continued re-working and performing *Instrumentals* for several more years. And he would continue using his matrix system in numerous other works that followed, including *24 > 24 Music, Tower of Meaning*, and his work with the Singing Tractors.

At the same time as Russell was becoming a force in the avant-garde of New York, he had equal energy applied to popular music. He was sought out by acclaimed Columbia record producer John Hammond, who thought he could be "the next Bruce Springsteen." When Russell showed up at the studio with an ensemble and arrangements, Hammond-- who wanted another solo guitar strumming singer-songwriter--became frustrated and canceled their plans after a making a few recordings. During his first years in New York Russell participated in many pop and rock ensembles, recording with the Talking Heads, and working in numerous bands, including The Necessaries, Bright and Early, Turbo Sporty, and the

Flying Hearts, the latter formed with Ernie Brooks, former bass player for The Modern Lovers. Notably, Russell also played drums in Laurie Anderson's first band, Fast Food; he played keyboards in a short-lived trio with Catherine Christer Hennix and Henry Flynt; and was the resident cellist of Peter Gordon's Love of Life Orchestra. He would also offer his cello playing on recordings of numerous rock and pop bands, including Thick Pigeon, Powerman, and Jill Kroesen. His curation at the Kitchen was somewhat controversial and pioneering for incorporating pop/rock bands, like the Modern Lovers and the Talking Heads, alongside the more common fare of avant-guard artists, such as Cornelius Cardew, Alvin Curran, and Phill Niblock. And while Russell would incorporate numerous popular genres into his work—including country, rock, pop, folk, dixieland, gospel, jazz, and new wave—it was disco and hip-hop, dance music that would gain the upper hand and redefine Russell's musical trajectory during the second half of the 1970's.

After attending a party at The Gallery in 1976, Russell would go on to fall in love with Manhattan's underground disco scene, situated in the independent venues of The Loft, the Gallery, Paradise Garage, and other venues. He found a spiritual affinity in the dance culture that was developing, which itself began as seated psychedelic listening parties, "with the Buddha," Mancuso notes, "always positioned between my two speakers" (Lawrence, *Love Saves* 10). Russell began working towards making a hit single, while also incorporating dance into his experimental compositional practice. In 1978, under the numerologically derived moniker, Dinosaur L, Russell gathered high profile session musicians to record his single, "Kiss Me Again," with producer Nicky Siano. Featuring the masterful rhythm and bass duo, the Ingram Brothers, with David Byrne on guitar and Myriam Valle on vocals, "Kiss Me Again" was a hit at local clubs and sold well in the New York area. It was during this time that Russell also co-founded, with Will Socolov, Sleeping Bag Records. Their first release, in 1978, was *24>24 Music*. But due to personal conflict between Russell and Socolov, Russell was fired from the label after two years.

As with Dinosaur L, Russell's dance music would continue to develop under various pseudonyms, including Loose Joints, Felix, Indian Ocean, and Killer Whale. Going into the 80s, Russell would release numerous dance singles, such as "Is It All Over My Face" (1980), "Pop Your Funk" (1980), "School Bell/Treehouse" (1985), and "Let's Go Swimming" (1986). The strangeness of these works exemplified a style of dance music that would come to be known as "mutant disco." Even as Russell found himself immersed in the late night ecstasies of New York dance clubs, Buddhism remained his guiding force. Dance works like, "In The Light of the Miracle," "Let's Go Swimming," "Go Bang," and many others effectively merge symbols at once sexual, natural, spiritual, and cosmic. From the beginning, Russell was tuned into the spiritual origins of disco that were expressed at David Mancuso's groundbreaking Loft venue. As Rhys Chatham recalls, "I have a recollection of Arthur describing disco clubs as 'temples of music' and evocatively describing the bass frequencies coming out of the subwoofers" (Lawrence, *Hold On* 164).

After a slew of turbulent relationships in New York, in 1978 Russell met the person that would become his life partner, Tom Lee. In 1980 Lee moved into the East Village "poet's building," where Russell had lived since moving to New York—they lived two floors above Allen Ginsberg, who also supplied their electricity. Russell's relationship with Lee was suffused with mutual love and support. Moreover, as a screen-printer and frame shop owner, Lee provided financial support to Russell over the years, allowing Russell to work on his music without interruption. And he provided the cover art for several of Russell's releases, including the album cover for "24>24 Music," the "Pop Your Funk" and, more recently, "Let's Go Swimming" EPs, not to mention promotional postcards for Russell's concerts. Lee would also become a muse and central figure for many of Russell's songs. Before Lee's move, Russell's apartment had been devoted entirely to music and Buddhist practice. As Lee recalls:

> When I first met him, he was doing more meditation, so he had this scrim and he had a platform he found on the street—a little meditation area. I would come in at the planned time and would find him meditating. That sort of ended at a certain time, though [...] I think he saw Buddhism and meditation as a way of being. He was very kind, one of those people who would never kill an insect. He was a meek person in many ways. We would have conversations about religion, and he always felt I was too knee-jerk about being anti. But I never learned from him that Buddhism wasn't trying to be religion. To him it was pretty personal. We spent 10 years living together, but he really held that inside himself. He had certain objects, fetishes—he always had a packet of scented dust that he kept in his pocket (Lee, "Q&A").

Russell's cosmic altar—compiling deity figures, incense, and other symbolic objects—was removed or internalized to make room for Lee. However, Russell continued his meditation practice until his death. In New York Russell found himself in a community of artists with explicit interests in Buddhism, including Andrew Franck, Elodie Lauten, Steven Hall, Philip Glass, and numerous others. From the mid 70's and throughout the 80's Russell would regularly visit and/or perform at various Buddhist centers in the city, such as Yeshe Nying Po, the Tibet Center, and the Tibet House, the latter co-founded by Philip Glass. At the Tibet Center, Russell also volunteered as a janitor. At Yeshe Nying Po, Russell met and befriended Tej Hazarika, whom would play music occasionally with Russell and Steven Hall, while exploring the meanings of sutras and guru teachings in late night conversation. While Russell's Buddhist practice seems to have become more private as he aged, his music, lyrics, and journals from this time show the persistence of lifelong spiritual concerns.

1980 was a significant year for Russell. It was through Philip Glass that renowned avant-garde dramaturge Robert Wilson had sought out Russell to compose an orchestral score for his adaptation of the Greek tragedy, *Medea*. The collaboration began developing rapidly and with mutual admiration. It would have been a breakthrough project for Russell—as it had been for Glass with the latter's work on Wilson's *Einstein on the Beach*. But due to increasing disagreements between the artists, Russell was booted from the project after nearly a year of work—Russell would be replaced by British composer Gavin Bryars. Nevertheless, the recording of the rehearsal for this production would be reconfigured by Russell as an album of abstract orchestral music, *Tower of Meaning*, which would be released by Chatham Square Productions in 1983.

Following his rejection from the *Medea* project, Russell's involvement in ensemble composition all but disappeared, aside from smaller scale projects with friends like the Singing Tractors. The Singing Tractors were a group of Russell's closest musical comrades (Elodie Lauten, Peter Zummo, Mustafa Ahmed, and various guests), who freely blended scored composition and free improvisation, as well as popular and experimental sensibilities.

Throughout the 1980's Russell continued recording dance works, but increasingly focused on solo performance and recording, with his voice and cello often embellished by a premeditated p.a. set up, including echo, reverb, and other effects. This latter approach was distilled and captured on Russell's 1985 album, *World of Echo*, released by Upside/

Rough Trade in 1986/1987. *World of Echo* featured Russell alone, his voice accompanied by cello and an effects set-up. Rarely using the matrix system by this time, Russell devised a conceptual process for creating *World of Echo*. This included a "World of Echo P.A. System" (Russell's application of his effects), and what Russell called "parenthetical ideas," which outline the collage-like and Buddhist inflected approach that formed the basis of the project. While receiving high praise from critics, *World of Echo*, failed to sell and find its audience upon its release.

Shortly after the release of *World of Echo*, Russell was diagnosed with H.I.V. He continued performing live and recording for the next several years. However, much of Russell's later recordings wouldn't be released until after his death. *Another Thought*, an album following in the style of *World of Echo*, but incorporating synthesizers and drum machines, was posthumously released by Philip Glass on his label Point Music. Russell continued performing with the Singing Tractors, and began to perform extensively with New York dancers— including Ishmael Houston-Jones, Daniel McIntosh, Diane Madden, Alison Salzinger, and others.

Russell kept performing until his health made it impossible. As dementia and throat cancer set in, Russell's voice devolved into a low muffled whisper and his performances into quiet train wrecks. It is in this regard that he has been notably remembered as having "vanished into his music" (Lawrence, *Hold On* 337). During the last months of his life he was visited regularly by friends and family. Allen Ginsberg was a frequent visitor and he would bring Tibetan lama, Gehlek Rimpoche, as well as numerous visitors, to Russell's bedside. Russell passed away on April 4, 1992. Giving his remains to the ocean, his family scattered his ashes off the coast of Bar Harbor Maine. Immediately following his death, there were memorial concerts and in 1994 Philip Glass' label, Point Music, released the album, *Another Thought*. After the release of *Another Thought*, Russell received scarce to no attention until a compilation of his music, *The World of Arthur Russell*, was released by Soul Jazz records in 2004. Since then he has become a highly regarded icon and influence in contemporary music.

I first discovered Russell's music when Audika Records re-released *World of Echo* in 2005. I had never heard a voice—nor cello—played so delicately or virtuosically, and certainly not amplified and drenched in reverb, echo, and other effects. The lyrics were strange and often unintelligible—it felt like a spell was being cast or a mystery revealed through Russell's soft melismas. I was absolutely captivated. I immediately dove into what David Toop called Russell's "floating world." As more and more came out on the artist, I devoured every piece of music or information I could find. And with each release, the identity of Russell's persona and music became—not more clear, but--more enigmatic and fascinating. Simply wanting to steep myself in the nuances of his melodies, I took to transcribing *World of Echo* in my free time while in my second year of graduate school at Princeton University. I began playing Russell's songs in bars in New York City. With Russell's close friend and collaborator, Ernie Brooks, and a large ensemble of New York musicians, I performed one of Russell's *Instrumentals* at The Stone in Manhattan. In 2009 I wrote an essay on *World of Echo*; and I didn't want to stop there. I began contacting Russell's collaborators, while Steve Knutson and Tom Lee allowed me access to Russell's archives.

When I told Russell's friend and collaborator Phill Niblock that I was writing a book on his late friend, he replied with a chuckle, "didn't someone just do that?" Indeed, Niblock was referring to Tim Lawrence's biography, *Hold On to Your*

Dreams, published by Duke University Press in 2009, which we've mentioned. For further biographical inquiry the reader is directed to Lawrence's book, and Matt Wolf's intimate video documentary, *Wild Combination* (2009). Through these works, Russell's personal life and his extended role in New York's "downtown" scene are laid out in unsurpassable depth. Nevertheless, I left these works with more questions than answers. Upon meeting Steve Knutson and beginning research in Russell's extant archive, it was clear there was more to learn. It is in consultation with the archive, under Knutson's direction, through personal interviews with Russell's friends and collaborators, and by my own musical transcription and performance of Russell's works that the following text came to be. With much owed to the work of Lawrence and Wolf, and with much gratitude to Steve Knutson, Tom Lee, and Russell's friends, *Buddhist Bubblegum* offers itself as a focused study on Russell's compositional work and creative process. Here, I have sought a deeper inquiry into the spiritual ideas and techniques that influenced and would ultimately unify Russell's diverse output, while also going deeper into his written reflections and notated scores. In the following chapters we will see how Russell strategically made the dharma "go pop."

II.

BUDDHIST BACKGROUNDS

Russell's attraction to Buddhism was of its time. He was one among many, from the "baby boomer" generation, who sought out cultural and spiritual alternatives as the counter-culture movement took shape during the late 1960s. Such alternatives were being widely embraced in the Bay Area, where Russell found himself in 1968 at the age of 17. For one independently seeking to learn and practice the Buddhist tradition, there are numerous cultural and philosophical schools of thought to choose from. Russell was notably drawn towards the esoteric and mystical branches of Buddhism, broadly named tantric or Vajrayana Buddhism. It was within this broader esoteric perspective that Russell would go on to study the sub-branches of Shugendo, Shingon, and Tibetan tantric Buddhism. While aspects of esotericism pervade all branches of Buddhist philosophy and practice, it was primarily through the Vajrayana (or "Diamond Vehicle") school, which developed in the second and third centuries, that the Buddhist perspective was refashioned into a formally esoteric style. These esoteric teachings focused on symbolism, guru transmission, artistic expression, and ritual. Such esoteric spiritual perspectives were in vogue with the youth culture of 1960's San Francisco, so much so that one of the most esoteric schools of Japanese Vajrayana Buddhism, the Shugendo tradition, found itself in San Francisco right around the time Russell had moved there.

The meaning of the term "esoteric," from the original Greek, concerns a sense of being "within" or "secret, hidden." This secrecy functions at every level of esoteric spiritual practice. Symbolism and codes purposefully confuse any singular rational meaning in both the language and content of the teachings, so that acquiring knowledge requires great effort and practice. Harnessing individual intuition and imagination, the ambiguities and riddles of Vajrayana teachings subjectively solicit a multiplicity of potential meanings and interpretations. Esoteric practices are generally performed in private settings, though often include public outreach and aid of some kind. Education in esoteric tradition may only be gained by entering the lineage, where knowledge is passed from person-to-person, often in the oral tradition of the guru/disciple format, and according to specific ritual practices. The teachings, concepts, symbols, and philosophy are otherwise hidden from public awareness and guarded secretly by the practitioners—it is only recently that esoteric Vajrayana teachings and practices are being exposed to the public, largely in order to sustain the lineage. Another primary difference between the Vajrayana school and other exoteric Buddhist schools—the other schools being Theravada and Mahayana, as well as their derivations—focuses on the experience and requisites of attaining enlightenment. In their discussion of the esoteric style of communication in Buddhist meditation and symbolism, Bucknell and Stuart-Fox articulate this distinction:

> The Vajrayana, later to become established as the dominant form of Buddhism in Tibet, represented a reaction against two aspects of the [previously dominant] Mahayana [school of Buddhism]: it's philosophical and doctrinal speculations, and its emphasis on the accumulation of merit. In opposition to these scholastic and popular pursuits, the Vajrayana was concerned with the *immediate* quest for enlightenment by means of meditative practices taught secretly by adept masters to their disciples (Bucknell, 33).

All esoteric or mystical traditions, whether formalized by tradition or idiosyncratic and informal, emphasize the non-dualist immediacy of a transcendental consciousness of the infinite, a union with the Divine, or cosmic consciousness. The core teachings of the Vajrayana tradition were laid out in the tantras of India, the ancestral home to all Buddhist thought. The term "tantra," in its original Sanskrit, refers to "loom, doctrine, system." It is within tantric teachings that the mystical "twilight language" was developed and manifested as a repository of meditative techniques, including the *chakras* (vital positions of the human body), *yoga* (breathing and physical exercises), *mudra* (symbolic hand gestures), *mithuna* (ritualized sex), *Dhyani yidam* (visualized identification with deity/ guru), *yantra* and *mandala* (visualization meditation), *mantra* (spiritually imbued sound and language), as well as the use of numerology, astrology, and symbolic and ritualized objects (e.g. the *vajra*, hand drum, lotus flower, etc).

Within and across various Buddhist lineages, certain authors have described the means of enlightened communication as the "twilight language" (*sandha-bhasa*), or "intentional language" (*samdha-bhasa*). The former developed gradually as "a purposely created mode of communication having a concealed meaning." The term "twilight" is used because the meaning of what is given is never considered by a singular perspective; instead all things may be explained both "by the light of day or by the darkness of night" (Bucknell, 12). The rich taxonomy of symbolic practices noted above is engaged—certainly through reading, recitation, listening, and dialogue—but more importantly through various personal meditative techniques and *sadhana*, a "set sequence of procedures to be followed by the meditator, carried out via visualization," or by physical act (Lopez, 13). A sadhana is then a technical ritual, a spiritual tool or instruction.

Visualization is often a major component of meditation, while also being one of the primary means of realizing or performing a sadhana. However, its range of expression may potentially engage any of the senses, alone or in combination, as well as physical action, and environmental or social inter- action, etc. And it is from this style of learning that one will begin to hear surprising stories of gurus giving their students a seemingly absurd task, such as Marpa demanding that Mi- larepa build and destroy three consecutive towers before the former would teach the latter. Tantric Buddhism is filled with such sadhanas and we'll be looking at some more closely as we continue. One of the primary aims in working with this sensually symbolic language, these illogical tasks and rituals, is to hone one's intuition, imagination, and intellect, through an engagement with ambiguity and contradiction.

> The *sandha-bhasa*... seeks... chiefly to project the yogin into the "paradoxical situation" indispensable to his training. The se- mantic polyvalence of words finally substitutes ambiguity for the usual system of reference inherent in ordinary language. And this destruction of language contributes, in its ways too, towards "breaking" the profane universe and replacing it by a universe of convertible and integrable planes. In general, symbolism brings about a universal "porousness," "opening" beings and things to transobjective meanings (Hess, 137).

It is through the techniques of meditation and the twilight language of Vajrayana Buddhism that Russell would form his earliest musical creations. Not relegated to youthful explo- ration, this Buddhist perspective would accompany Russell for the rest of his life, fusing itself to his music. The purpose of this chapter is to set the stage for the Buddhist concepts, symbols, and techniques that Russell applied to his music. In subsequent chapters, Russell's music takes the foreground and the connections between these esoteric teachings and Russell's music will become progressively clearer.

KAILAS SHUGENDO

In the last three years, the most single profound influence in a positive direction that I can see in my life [...] has been a conscious move in the direction of religious activity, with motives in the direction of an open mindedness [towards] people in general—so that things can become more harmonious in the world. And I've never seen more of that [...] than in [the] religious examples of a gift-giving life, a self-less life (Wolf, 2009).

Arthur Russell, cassette letter to parents

Russell's ability to post bail during his brief stint in police custody, following his arrest for marijuana possession, was aided by his willingness to join a disciplined spiritual community in the Bay Area. On Valentine's Day of 1969 Russell would leave jail to join the Kailas Shugendo commune, where he would remain a member for approximately two years. The community was founded by Dr. Neville G. "Ajari" Pemchekov-Warwick, a Russian émigré who would come to be known primarily as "Ajari" (Sanskrit, "a practitioner who is able to teach students"; Fischer-Schreiber, 5). According to Paul Nagy, one of Russell's Kailas Shugendo cohabitants, "Arthur lived with Warwick for a while. Arthur was 'out of it,' and Warwick was really taking care of him. Gradually Arthur became stronger and more confident, as he played his cello more and more" (Nagy, 2012). Warwick outlawed drug use by his disciples, and Russell practiced abstinence during this time. Russell came to Kailas Shugendo lost and vulnerable. He eagerly embraced the discipline, philosophy, and lifestyle that Warwick offered.

Warwick's philosophy was primarily a combination of the Tibetan Lamaist tradition, which he met through Mongolian

Image 1. Neville Warwick walks fired coals as Russell
(right) and others chant mantra (Leary, 2008).

Buddhists and shamans, and the Shugendo lineage of esoteric Shingon Buddhism. But he would also incorporate
aspects of his native Russian Old Believers and Russian
Orthodox Christianity, which he had encountered in his native Siberian upbringing. "Kailas" refers to the revered Mount
Kailas in Japan, and "Shugendo" refers to the ascetic mountain-based folk religion, one of the most obscure and esoteric
lineages in the history of Japanese Buddhism. Warwick had
absorbed Tibetan tantra (the Rimé tradition) via Mongolian
Buddhists and shamans. But his primary offerings of the
Tibetan perspective came form one man, Lama Anagarika
Govinda.

Tibetan Buddhism and Lama Govinda

Govinda, born Ernst Lothar Hoffman in Germany, began practicing Buddhism at the age of 18. By the orders of his senior, Tomo Geshe Rimpoche, Govinda later founded his own Buddhist order, Arya Maitreya Mandala. Govinda was inducted into the Drugpa Kagyu, Nyingma, and Sakyapa lineages of Tibetan Buddhism. Govinda's order focused on a particular deity, Maitreya, who was predicted to arrive on Earth when Buddhist beliefs had been forgotten or threatened. Maitreya represented ascetic spiritual ideals of loving kindness, the disowning of possessions and home, and the pursuit of meditative trance. Govinda was also a painter and poet, believing himself to be the reincarnation of the German poet and philosopher Novalis. His teachings and interpretations of Buddhist practice placed a strong emphasis on the practical use of the arts, especially painting and poetry, the influence of which was apparent in the activities of those at Kailas Shugendo and in Warwick's interpretation of the Shugendo tradition. Warwick studied under Govinda in India and sometime thereafter Govinda initiated Warwick, who was given the name "Vajrabodhi," into the Tibetan lineage. In a 1968 letter to Warwick, who was concerned with engaging "corporations" in America, Govinda corrects his thinking:

Our Order [Arya Maitreya Mandala] is based on personal relationship between each Member and the Line of Gurus, who have transmitted the living power of the Dharma... Our Order represents a spiritual hierarchy—not a democratic society, in which heads are counted irrespective of what is in them...A "Mandala" is not a collection of heterogeneous elements, but an organized unity of individuals grouped around and directed toward a common center, represented by the ideal and the active path of the Vajrayana, as the integration and culmination of all previous Schools of Buddhism (Power, xxxvii).

Govinda's *Way of the White Clouds* was treated as scripture at Kailas Shugendo. The book was a travelogue of Govinda's pilgrimage through Tibet during the 1940s. The symbolism of the cloud, as evidenced in the title, is a primary theme in the work.

> Just as a white summer-cloud, in harmony with heaven and earth freely floats in the blue sky from horizon to horizon, following the breath of the atmosphere—in the same way the pilgrim abandons himself to the breath of the greater life that wells up from the depth of his being and leads him beyond the farthest horizons to an aim which is already present within him, though yet hidden from his sight.
>
> In Tibetan Buddhism the symbol of the cloud is of far-reaching importance […] The figures of Buddhas, Bodhisattvas, saints, gods and genii manifest themselves from cloud-formations which surround their haloes. The cloud represents the creative power of the mind, which can assume any imaginable form. The white cloud especially is regarded as the ideal medium of creation for the enlightened mind, which manifests itself on the plane of timeless meditative vision.
>
> The "White Cloud" becomes a symbol of the Guru's wisdom and compassion, and therefore "the Way of the White Clouds" hints at the same time at the way of spiritual unfoldment, the way of a pilgrimage that leads to the realization of final completeness (*Way* xiv).

The propitious symbolism of the cloud was one of several Buddhist themes expressed in Russell's music. His large scale composition, *Instrumentals*, was inspired by his Buddhist teacher, Yuko Nonomura, who suggested Russell compose a work to accompany Nonomura's photographs of clouds. For Russell's song "Lucky Cloud," which would take numerous forms over time—the lyrics consistently meditate upon the fortuitous vision of a cloud in the sky and the ecstasies of a kiss.

Lucky cloud in your sky
A little rain, a lot of fun
One kiss, and I go overboard

I will find more to see
I will see more to find
It's a two-way street
The more I look ahead, the more I see behind.

Lucky cloud in your sky
A little rain, a lot of fun
One kiss, and I go overboard

What a day
As the sun peeps around
Around the cloud
That's in the way
Like a two-way, two-way street
The weather at a point will show me what you will say

Lucky cloud in your sky
A little rain, a lot of fun
One kiss, and I go overboard

I see you I touch my eyes
And then the rest is history
One kiss and I go overboard

Jigmé [Bhutanese, "having no fear"] was the name given to Russell by his friends, Terry ("Nona") and Lorna ("Jivaki") Mills, on the commune. It is likely that this name was derived from Lama Govinda's *Way of the White Clouds*, in which Govinda tells the story of a *tulku*, the traditionally ascribed persona attributed to a modern-day child. Tibetan monks believe that through oracular guidance past lamas can be found reincarnated in contemporary children. They are found through a series of esoteric techniques and tests and, upon identification, they are taken from their birth homes and groomed to become a lama. In Govinda's story, the tulku in question was reincarnated as the elder lama, Tomo Geshe. When the child's father called him "Pu-chung" ("little son"), the child corrected him, proclaiming that his true name was Jigmé ("the Fearless One"), which, it turns out, was the name that the oracle had prophesied for Tomo Geshe's reincarnated identity. Russell's relentless pursuit of unfiltered openness and infinite possibility within his own musical path, would, unquestionably, live up to the fearlessness attributed to his youthful commune name.

Warwick's incorporation of Govinda's Tibetan teachings into Shugendo tradition is not outlandish, though he likely distorted Govinda's teachings to suit his own. Both traditions prioritized a nomadic, ascetic, possessionless lifestyle with significant awareness of and interaction with nature, art, and physical activity, and a devout application of prayer, chanting, and meditation. Govinda's influence was minimal however compared to the role that the Shugendo tradition played in the commune's activities.

SHUGENDO BUDDHISM: The Ascetic Life

Rooted in the esoteric Shingon lineage, the Shugendo sect of Buddhism was founded in the seventh century by En no Gyôja, who was believed to possess magical powers. It began as a mountain-based ascetic religion evolving from an increasing number of spiritually-motivated hermits independently dwelling in the mountains—the unifying factor being their emphasis on man's relationship with nature and physical struggle through tantric practice. After having formed a distinct Buddhist philosophy, Shugendo reached its maturity in the twelfth and thirteenth centuries. Now there are only a few still carrying on the tradition, existing in small mountain areas, primarily in Japan and France (Asai, 25), while, as we noted, Warwick's commune would shift completely to

Russian Orthodoxy much later. Shugendo practitioners are also sometimes called *yamabushi*, (Japanese, "one who lies in the mountains"). It is said that En no Gyôja would dwell in mountain caves, treating the caves as symbolic spaces or 3-dimensional mandalas. He found a connected group of three caves in particular which he would ritualistically dwell in as the "Pure Realm," the "Womb Realm," and the "Diamond Realm" (Payne, 208). While their spiritual practices remained hidden in the mountains, the yamabushi were active in local villages where they functioned as priests or shamans, performing exorcisms, healing the sick, and offering propitious spells for ceasing rainfall and the like (Asai, 26).

The activities and methods that transpired in the mountain landscape were steeped in mystery, beyond the awareness of nearby civilians. Their practice was so mysterious to civilian culture, that the yamabushi began being dramatized as characters in village myths. In effect, the practitioners were taking part in rigorous physical rituals (*shugyo*), such as lengthy mountain hikes, standing beneath freezing waterfalls, or subsisting on a diet of pine needles. Earlier manuals of this practice involved more supernatural feats, rituals and spells in pursuit of invisibility, flying, walking on fire, stepping into cauldrons of boiling water, and climbing barefoot up ladders of swords. These more extreme feats are largely believed to have been symbolic rather than actual (Blacker, 220).

The reverence for sacred mountains—originally focused on Mt. Kailas in the Tibetan Highlands or Mt Kumano, Yoshino and Kimpu in Japan—formed the basis for all of the Yamabushi's esoteric Buddhist practice (*mikkyo*). The majority of rituals were focused on the mountains as a dwelling place of enlightenment (Asai, 28). In the history of Japanese culture and religion, the mountain is generally considered the dwelling place of the spirits of the dead [early Yamabushi considered themselves dead and would dress themselves in death's symbolic color, white, in recognition of this]. Mount Kailas is revered in both Hindu and Buddhist cultures, being geographically the meeting point of these two spiritualized civilizations (India and China). Govinda described Kailas as "[being] surmounted by the invisible temple of the highest transcendental powers, which to each devotee appear in the form that symbolizes to him the highest reality. Thus to Hindus Kailas is the seat of Shiva, while to Buddhists it represents a giant Mandala of Dhyani-Buddhas and Bodhisattvas" (*The Way* 198).

Much of Shugendo ritual, including the practitioners' relationship to the mountain, was rooted in a 10-tiered hierarchy of worlds (*jukkai shugyo*), beginning with *Jingku*, the practice of hell and ending with *Butsu*, the practice of a Buddha. The practitioner moves through each level, one at a time, by performing associated ritual actions (shugyo), such as abstaining from water, wrestling, and fire rituals. Advancing through these stages—as well as physically ascending the mountain in the process—the practitioner may reach Buddha-hood within their own lifetime.

Highly symbolic belief systems like the jukkai shugyo above were often combined with or functioned alongside other tantric techniques. For example, upon completion of the 10th and final level (the practice of a Buddha), the practitioner is taught the tantric techniques of *mudra* (symbolic hand gestures) and *mantra* (symbolic vocalizations). A wide array of these esoteric techniques developed in Shingon mikkyo practice. *Mudras, mantras, mandalas* and other multi-media techniques—which we'll go more into shortly—were incorporated into Shugendo worship. But it was their use of fire ceremonies that distinguished their Shugendo practice and brought them the most attention.

For Warwick the Shugendo tradition only entered gradually into Kailas Shugendo, which began sometime in 1966-67. He and his followers went through several incarnations and names: "The Mountain Yogis," "The Unreformed Buddhist Church of America" (Nagy, 2012), "The Shugen Church of America" (Leary, 2013), and the more enduring "Kailas Shugendo." During this nascent period the commune was integrated with other emerging communes in the Bay area. For example, those at Kailas would often go on mountain hikes—open to the public—with the followers of Samuel L. "Murshid" Lewis (a.k.a. "Sufi Sam").

Other gurus gaining prominence (and followers) in the Bay area during this time were Pir Vilayat Inayat Khan, son of the revered Hazrat Inayat Khan, A.C. Bhaktivedanta Swami Prabhupada, who founded the International Society for Krishna Consciousness in New York and then in San Francisco in 1967, Sivajy Subramuniya, who opened the Himilayan Academy and the first American Hindu temple, and D.T. Suzuki, who popularly imported Zen Buddhism into America. Suzuki remained the most universally revered gurus in the area and one could bump into any of the names mentioned above at Suzuki's Zen Center in San Francisco. In the realm of American art, awareness of Suzuki was amplified influentially when Beat writers (Allen Ginsberg and Jack Kerouac) and John Cage began study with him during the 1950's.

Warwick made a name for himself through his controversial personality and by embracing the fire ceremonies of Shugendo tradition. Curious individuals and media networks, would come from all over to watch Warwick's followers walk the coals themselves. Notably, it was Warwick himself that brought the phenomenon of fire walking to popular attention in America.

Fire Ceremonies: *Hiwatari and Goma*

Image 2. Warwick and his followers perform a goma ceremony on
Mt. Tamalpais (Leary, 2008)

Fire was a key ritual symbol amongst the yamabushi. Representing both fire and waterfalls, Fudo is a Shugendo deity associated with the power to overcome tribulations (Ashkenazi, 153). More generally, fire symbolized purification, the burning away of defilements and bad karma. There were two primary fire rituals in Shugendo practice: *hiwatari* and *goma*. Hiwatari is the practice of walking over fired coals. Such rituals were performed to "assert [the practitioners'] power and ability to subdue danger" as well as their ability to call upon divine powers associated with fire (Reader, 118). At Kailas Shugendo, hiwatari was performed frequently.

Once a week they did a purification, or hiwatari, for which Ajari donned his priestly garb: baggy Indian trousers, a short gown and an oversize white skullcap on the front of which was a large woolly bobble. Four more bobbles adorned his waistcoat and he held the usual Buddhist beads. He chanted while his followers, dressed in traditional Japanese outfits—also with bobbles—sang or played instruments. Then they would approach a large pit, about six feet long and filled with burning logs, and Ajari would lead the others in walking 108 times across hot coals while chanting mantras (Miles, 87).

Below, author of *Roots of Consciousness*, clinical psychologist Dr. Jeffrey Mishlove recalls his *hiwatari* experience with the commune:

> The ceremony was modest—simply a six-foot pit of flaming logs that we walked over dozens of times, quite briskly, generally stepping once with each foot [while the others chanted throughout]. The flames rose up and singed the hair on my legs, although I felt no pain and suffered no burns. I had complete confidence in Ajari who asked that I follow him across the pit. Microphone in hand, I recorded my impressions on tape as we went over the flames. I must admit that I actually felt protected in some way. It was a totally uplifting experience (Mishlove, 232).

Firewalking wasn't introduced until a year or so before Russell arrived, but this would become one of the primary rituals practiced by members of the commune. Traveling out to Ocean Beach about once a week, each participant would take two steps over the coals.

Another Shugendo fire ritual used by the commune was the goma ceremony. In Shugendo tradition this ritual involves the illumination of a large bonfire to which offerings are made. Fudo is invoked, and mantra is chanted. During these rituals, prayers and requests are made as those praying unify their consciousness with that of Fudo. At Kailas Shugendo this began somewhat meagerly with Warwick chanting mantra while lighting a large pile of matches in his San Francisco apartment on Hemlock and Ward St. As the fire went out, others would throw matches into the fire to keep it going, all the while chanting mantra. They eventually worked with larger pieces of wood and larger bonfires (Nagy, 2012). Writer, gallery owner, and friend of Ginsberg, Barry Miles recalls seeing goma paraphernalia in Russell's commune dwelling.

> One room [at the Kailas Shugendo commune] was so full that the student who slept there could hardly use it during the day; he had made a narrow corridor between stacked music stands and storage boxes leading to his bed. There were speakers, amps, a cello case and fire-making equipment, including a huge cauldron in the fireplace (Miles, 88).

Warwick was combining numerous spiritual techniques and interests together, and would apply them with greater frequency than they would be applied in their indigenous traditions (Nagy, 2012). Other spiritual groups in the Bay area began refining their interests, while individual gurus sought to gain more followers. Warwick would gain increasing guru status as he came to focus primarily on the fire rituals of Shugendo tradition. At Kailas Shugendo they did not eat pine needles as their elder Japanese practitioners were alleged to have done, but they subsisted off of rice with minimal supplements, embracing a drug-free vegetarian lifestyle—Russell was on a self-disciplined macrobiotic diet. Common rituals became hiking through the mountains while meditatively chanting mantra, painting or sewing mandalas, with great attention given to the fire ceremonies. Many of these rituals overlapped, and nearly all were accompanied by the chanting of mantra.

Mantra Meditation

> Words can be many things at once, like a mantra [...] People can understand a phrase on a visceral level, and it would mean the same thing that they understand on a spiritual level (Lawrence, *Hold On* 111).
>
> Arthur Russell

Image 3. Kailas Shugendo members gather to recite the Hannya Shingyo, or Heart Sutra (Leary, 2008)

The "A-syllable" is considered one of the core symbols of Shugendo and its parent Shingon philosophy. In the Sanskrit language the A-syllable is, literally, the first stroke of every written syllable. It is viewed as the primal human sound, the sound made when the mouth first opens. From this perspective the A-syllable represents both birth and transformation. But the ultimate exposition of enlightenment comes upon contemplating the A-syllable as containing all syllables—in essence, "the one containing the all." "One syllable embraces a thousand truths, manifesting universal reality in this very body" (Yamasaki, 119). Esoteric Shingon then emphasizes that all Buddhist teachings are only secondary to experiencing this abstraction of language and voice, sometimes called the "A-syllable gate," offering a portal into the infinitude of cosmic consciousness. Russell was sensitive to the symbol and more generally to the role of Sanskrit language in his own Buddhist practice, as he he reported in a letter to his parents:

> I found out where Sanskrit came from, what it's based on, and the relationships of the various places of the body to sound. In Sanskrit, words are not pronounced only on the tongue, lips, and teeth, but deep in the deepest part of your lungs and diaphragm. This is true of all languages of course, but particularly Sanskrit. They had certain sounds that were based solely on diaphragmatic vibration. And this is [...] the beginning of all music, because it's when singing started—and it's very close to poetry. Particularly the way the meaning (poetry) [and] sound (music) intertwine to form either a message or a sense of beauty and unity.
>
> [Sanskrit] provides a deeper understanding of those traditions of which I have been involved with for the last several years [...] It is the most commonplace language which most Buddhist scriptures are written in. Consequently [I've been] in the position of reading a lot of Sanskrit, while [...] with friends lately. And often times I'd be mispronouncing things and misunderstanding the true meaning of Sanskrit words. So it's a great thing to be able to do it right—and I *really* do wanna do things right... and not settle for a funny little half-assed method, by which one can be deceived into believing he's in the main stream of oriental thought without deeply considering it (Wolf, 2009).

Language would continue to be a primary interest of Russell's and he would eventually find his song lyrics evolving into an abstract singing practice by the time of *World of Echo*. Regardless, beyond the A-syllable gate, there are numerous such highly specific and detailed meditation rituals in the Shingon tradition, most derived from the Vajrayana tantras and older sources.

Originating in the Vedic traditions of India, mantra literally means "an instrument or tool of thought." Across all of its applications, mantra is always a speech act: "the linguistic utterance itself performs an act. The classical example in speech act theory was the statement 'I baptize.' In this case not only is something said, but uttering the words also performs the act of baptizing" (Wilke, 406). Many mantras are based on "seed syllables" (*bijas*) such as the most familiar and most are basic: *AUM* or *Om*. While some mantras have evolved into elaborate and lengthy recitations, derived from these syllables, which themselves originally corresponded to the syllables of the Sanskrit alphabet.

> Kukai also asserts that language is, above all, letters, "which are none other than differentiation," which is diametrically opposed to identity, essence, and constancy. A thing is recognized as distinct not because of its substance but because of the difference in its pattern from other things. Therefore, even voices are letters, in the sense that they are patterns inscribed in air.

> According to Kukai, all Sanskrit syllables originate in the syllable A, which as a negative prefix is a semiotic manifestation of the originally non-arising. All other syllables posit themselves as differences from the syllable A, the origin of no origin, making the Sanskrit syllabary a semiotic network of emptiness (Abé, 396).

Such syllabic mantras are often imbued with particular meanings or symbolisms, including associated colors and deities, but these will often vary from religion to religion and sect to sect. Richard King writes on the meaning of the well known mantra, *AUM,* from a Vedantic perspective:

> The letter "A" of "A-U-M" corresponds to the waking state of consciousness, "U" to the dream state, and "M" to the state of deep sleep. Meditation upon these letters and their intrinsic connection with the various states of consciousness will lead the aspirant to an understanding of the nature of their complex inter-relationship and the "fragmentary" view that these states provide. It is only upon realization of the whole, that is, *OM* or *turiya,* that reality can be properly understood (King, 147).

Japa is a long-standing Hindu tradition of the repetitive chanting of a mantra. Some believe more repetitions of a mantra equals a greater attainment of enlightenment, but there are numerous interpretations of the significance of mantra repetition. One is the goal of attaining *ajapa-japa*, essentially a state of constant remembrance, having spiritually digested the mantra through ongoing meditation.

As Kukai spread Shingon Buddhism, he also spread an awareness of mantra. Shingon esotericism prioritized a poetic logic for which mantra was the core: "Mantra indicates words that contain within themselves numerous meanings." Every letter takes on a wide spectrum of possible interpretations. As Kukai affirms "a mantra is supra-rational" (Hakeda, 79). Russell explicitly addresses this when speaking of the role of lyrics in popular music, "Words can be many things at once, like a mantra [...] Also, people can understand a phrase on a visceral level, and it would mean the same thing that they understand on a spiritual level" (Lawrence, *Hold On* 111).

The linguistic and cultural sources of various manifestations of mantra (e.g. in Sanskrit, Japanese, or Tibetan tongues) are often revered as being culturally definitive. At the same time, Lama Govinda and other teachers would emphasize, the intentionality underlying the mantric act, received through initiation. "[T]he power and the effect of a mantra depend on the spiritual attitude, the knowledge and the responsiveness of the individual. The *sabda* or sound of the mantra is not only a physical sound (though it may be accompanied by such a one) but a spiritual one [...]. The mantra has power and meaning only for the initiated, i.e., for one who has gone through a particular kind of experience connected with the mantra" (Govinda, *Foundations* 27). Mantras can also be expressed as visual forms, such as inscribing the mantra's written syllables upon a stone; or, as in the goma ceremony, the seed syllable is imprinted on the kindling used to make a fire.

In his five methods of mantric recitation Kukai uses imaginative visualizations to guide the practitioner (Yamasaki, 117):

Voice-Bearing Recitation: The practitioner visualizes a conch shell above a lotus within his mind, and recites so that his voice issues as though from the conch.

Lotus Recitation: He recites so that his voice can be heard only in his ears.

Vajra Recitation: The lips and teeth are held together and only the tip of the tongue moves slightly in recitation.

Samadhi Recitation: Without moving even the tongue, the practitioner recites only within the mind.

Light Recitation: While the practitioner recites, whether silently or out loud, he constantly visualizes light streaming from his mouth.

One unique use of mantra at Kailas Shugendo was its application to mountain hiking—on Mt. Tamalpais, Mt. Diablos, Mt. Shasta or other neighboring inclines around the Bay Area. Hiking or "walking meditation" (*kaihogyo*) was a daily ritual at Kailas Shugendo. Paul Nagy, who was at the commune the same time as Russell, recalled that when they hiked a mountain, a different mantra was used for the ascent and descent. The mantra invoking the wrathful deity, Mahakala, was used on the ascent:

OM SHRI MAHAKALA HUNG PHAT

The mantra invoking the peaceful deity, Maitreya, was used on the descent:

MAITRI MAITRI MAHA MAITRI SVAHA

Through a concerted invocation of these deities via mantra and visualization, one might then take on the associated qualities of that deity for themselves, mentally aspiring to

Image 4. Members of Kailas Shugendo chant mantra as they hike up
Mt. Tamalpais (Leary, 2008).

these qualities, assisting oneself in attaining Buddha-hood.
Other mantras that were used on the commune were tak-
en from the esoteric sutras common to Shugendo and other
Buddhist teachings, e.g. the Lankavatara Sutra and the Heart
Sutra, often in D.T. Suzuki's translation (Nagy, 2012). The
former emphasizes consciousness as the only reality, and that
all things in the world are only ephemeral and illusory projections of mind. One's spiritual practice, through meditation
upon this sutra, then lies in developing a constant recognition
of this fact. "There is nothing heard," Suzuki writes, "nothing hearing" (*Studies* 84). The latter reinforces this focus on
an all-pervading mind that nullifies the location of perceptions in the individual alone, emphasizing a tranquility of
emptiness and selflessness. Such was the focus of meditation
during these hikes. Another member V.K. Leary recalls that
"periodic stops," during these hiking meditations, "included
sutra recitation and Dharma talks" (Leary, 2013).

Another mantra that was regularly recited and which would be lastingly influential upon Russell is the "Perfection of Wisdom" mantra from the Heart sutra: **GATE, GATE, PARAGATE, PARASAMGATE, BODHI, SVAHA!** ("Gone, gone, gone to the other shore, landed at the other shore"). The "other shore" of this mantra is compared to a state of consciousness that is beyond any conception of birth and death, beyond any distinction of self, other, or world (Suszuki, *Studies* 100). It is from this perspective that one's flaws and personal attributes are dissolved into a broader awareness, and it is believed that through mantric repetition and meditation that a meditator can achieve enlightenment.

From 1971 onward, Russell would frequently accompany Allen Ginsberg in concert. In the early 70s Ginsberg was setting the poetic texts of William Blake, while forging his own musical poetry dealing explicitly with politics, sexuality, and Buddhism. Russell was largely responsible for the musical arrangements of the songs and would accompany

Image 5. Allen Ginsberg, Samuel Lewis, and Neville Warwick (Leary, 2008).

Image 6. Padmasambhava mantra, found in "Allen Ginsberg" folder in Russell's archive (Russell, AG)

Ginsberg, alongside other poets, as well as Ed Sanders, from the Fugs, and Bob Dylan, to record at Pacific High Studios in San Francisco and with John Hammond in New York City. Russell gained a taste for the city during the trip to New York, while the connections he made with Hammond and others would serve him in the future. And with the poems of Blake and Ginsberg himself, Ginsberg would also incorporate the singing of mantras and bhajans, a broad family of devotional songs including mantra, kirtan, and dhrupad—though Ginsberg would focus on simple forms of mantra often blended with his own take on the American blues style (the latter as taught to him by Russell and Bob Dylan). Bhajan is a general category used to describe various kinds of devotional music, reflective love-infused songs often connecting directly to Vedic texts and the praising of deities. As noted by Andrew Schelling, in his eulogy upon the death of Allen Ginsberg:

OM AH HUM VAJRA PADMA SIDDHI HUM. This was a mantra performed by Ginsberg with Russell and the Shugendo Mantric Sun Band, which may be heard on Russell's *Ballad of the Lights* released by Audika Records in 2010.

Rhythm and meter are deemphasized here to foreground a free-flowing chant, while various instruments sustain the pitches by any means necessary (continuous breathing, strumming, etc), creating a rich sonic texture or drone. But perhaps most interesting is the syllable-to-pitch relationship, as each syllable of the mantra is associated with a single pitch (and key signature). Through Shingon Buddhism Russell learned to hear a single sound both as an idea or concept as well as an act of prayer. We will see this syllabic or mantric approach to music composition again and again in Russell's compositions.

The Vajra Guru mantra, as it is also called, was a personal favorite of Ginsberg and is traditionally chanted for the purpose of engendering communion with body, speech, and mind ("the three vajras"), invoking the embodiment of Padmasambhava (also known as "Guru Rimpoche," said to be a second Buddha in the ancient Tibetan Nyingma lineage). In the liner notes to Russell's *Ballad of the Lights*, a recording featuring Ginsberg and Kailas Shugendo Mantric Sun Band, Ginsberg reflects on the significance of mantra in general:

> Mantra chanting can be an extension of shaking your ass or raising your voice in joyful exaltation. With no fundamental associations, it's sheer joy to sing, a good way to loosen one's heart in the world. The first main mantra I sang in the 60's was "Hare Krishna," I got really good at that. I exercised such a repertoire of monochordal variations beginning with that one tune that I got invited to sing at Charles Mingus' wedding. "Om Ah Hum Vajra Guru Padma Suddhi Hum" refers to Padma Sambhava founder of Nyingma, the Tibetan Buddhist old sect. It translates as "Body Speech Mind Diamond Teacher Lotus Power Amen" (or "Tough Teacher Tender Teaching"). When I first met Trungpa he said I shouldn't be singing this publicly giving audience a buzz, because there are complex meditation practices and visualization that go with it. I don't know if it's proper to put this out on the record, actually. Listeners are forewarned that it's here for the beauty of music sound not vanity of mystic consciousness.

In his own works Russell was constantly thwarting a clear narrative or abstracting language into pure sound. Though often, and intentionally, resting on the border of linguistic recognition, his voice would obscure the sound, opening it to potentially infinite interpretations and prioritizing a raw sonic expression. As friend and percussionist Mustafa Ahmed recalls Russell relaying to him during a taxi ride, "Arthur told me how he came up with his lyrics. He had this mantric alphabet, starting with just syllables. And that's how he developed his vocal parts" (Ahmed, 2013). Russell's mantric approach to language and voice would continue throughout his life. However, at Kailas Shugendo the use of mantra was not relegated solely to ritual incantation, but found a social and musical form of expression as well.

As community outreach in the Bay Area and to generate funding, the members of Kailas Shugendo engaged in all manner of public service. They maintained an ambulance rescue service and manufactured traditional Japanese mattresses and meditation cushions (Hiss, 29). Until his death Warwick would own and run the storefront, Golden Nagas, for these products on Geary St. in San Francisco. Warwick collected a massive amount of money, certainly not only by selling mattresses, but often through independent donations, e.g. from one of the members who was an early Apple developer (Nagy, 2012). Another means of engaging the local community was through entertainment. Warwick himself was also a musician, and, shortly after Russell's arrival, he lead the Shugendo Mantric Sun Band involving several members of the commune, including Russell on cello. The band has been described as a country and bluegrass band, but, as noted, would also incorporate mantric chanting and bhajan repertoire. They would regularly perform in the Bay Area, alongside other spiritually-oriented acts, as well as popular counter-culture performers such as Allen Ginsberg and the Grateful Dead. In 1971, a symposium titled "Naturally High" brought Allen Ginsberg, the Kailas Shugendo Mantric Sun Band, Yogi Bhajan Ashram, and the Integral Yoga Institute together "for a day of meditation and chanting" (Morgan, 144).

Meanwhile, Russell would play in the womb-like intimacy of his closet—Warwick had given Russell the sadhana of confining his cello playing within a closed closet, where he would play for hours a day. But as Russell's strength and confidence returned, he grew irritated, mistrustful, and critical of Warwick. Ginsberg himself said that he felt Warwick was a "charlatan." And Russell was coming to agree. By his second year at the commune, the two stubborn minds of Warwick and Russell were often in confrontation.

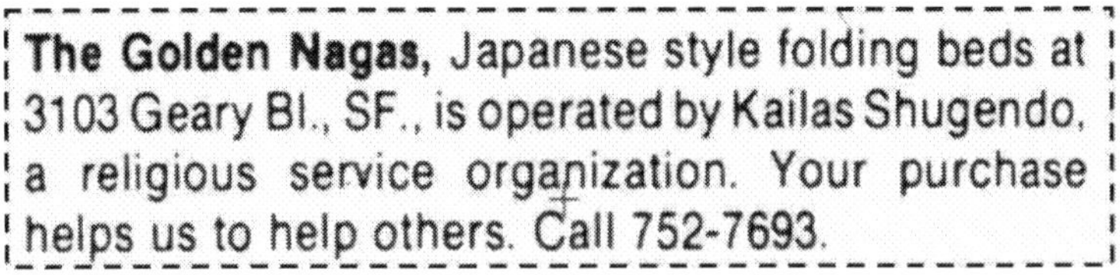

The Golden Nagas, Japanese style folding beds at 3103 Geary Bl., SF., is operated by Kailas Shugendo, a religious service organization. Your purchase helps us to help others. Call 752-7693.

Image 7. An advertisement for Golden Nagas in a 1971 Berkeley Barb newspaper ("Other Offerings" 12).

> The most active [student] was a younger, more energetic cello-playing adept called Jigmé, whose real name was Arthur Russell. Arthur was very shy, probably because he had suffered a bad attack of *acne vulgaris* when he was an adolescent, which left his cheeks badly scarred [...] Jigme had been at Kailas Shugendo for more than two years but was beginning to resent Ajari's authoritarianism. He had obviously gone along with it at the beginning but by the time we met him they were at loggerheads. Ajari would demand something and Jigme would ask why, and question the reasons. This infuriated Ajari, who roared and bellowed and leapt across the room to hit Jigme in the head, or to sometimes only pretend to do so. It was done in a playful, half-joking way but in reality both sides were deeply serious (Miles, 88).

Russell's composition teacher at the SF Conservatory, W.A. Mathieu, recalled, "Dr. Warwick had a public persona of great beneficence and Jupiterean generosity, but actually he had a very mean streak, and he liked to dominate people. He was a male dominatrix—very tortured inside and very powerful outside. The people who lived on the commune were his slaves, and Arthur was totally caught up in the life of the rooming house. He told me stories of subjugation and humiliation that were sad and anger-making to me." Mathieu continues, "I mistrusted Ajari Warwick enormously. He had tremendous power and had probably aggrandized his Buddhist studies in order to accrue power, or so it seemed to me at the time. You'd see this deadness in the eyes of the disciples, and after a while, that happened to Jigmé. I tried to get him out of there" (Lawrence, *Hold On* 32). After Russell left

Kailas Shugendo, V.K. Leary recalls "Dr. Ajari's story is that Ginsberg followed Jigme into the bathroom and awakened Jigme's homosexuality, which then led to Jigme's departure several months later" (Leary, 2012).

Russell had come to Warwick during a time of personal struggle and so was vulnerable and susceptible, readily acquiescing to Warwick's leadership early on. In a cassette letter to his family in Iowa, Russell reflects on his own reasons for leaving Kailas Shugendo:

> [Shingon] is not necessarily rooted in dogmatic philosophy. Although you know while I was at Kailas Shugendo [...] that was more of a dogmatic thing. It was rooted in the idea of personal conquest, and personal attainment, and personal... Self. [P]eople were attached to their ideas about things... about their religious involvement... and believed that they were right in insisting that other people take upon themselves the burdens which Kailas Shugendo took upon itself. But, be this as it may [...] I can't follow this course (Wolf, 2009).

Nevertheless, the commune's approach opened Russell to a regular esoteric practice of performing songs with a focus on mantric chanting, meditation, visualization, and the symbolic role of lyrics, imagery, ritual, and environment. But Russell was still looking for a more open-minded context for his spiritual practice. Of course all throughout this period Russell was exploring and attending various spiritual venues, such as the Tibetan Buddhist Centre in Kensington, California. But ultimately, after leaving Warwick's bondage, Russell found the next spiritual teacher that he needed in Yuko Nonomura, a Japanese priest of Shingon Vajrayana Buddhism.

SHINGON BUDDHISM: A Portable Dharma

I learned a lot more after coming back [from monastic life to American culture] and having to deal with the nitty-gritty. It's comparatively easy to be a monk in a quiet monastery, but the bodhisattva tries to engage with all the noise of the world (Seager, 134).

Robert Thurman

Russell first met Yuko Nonomura when Warwick had asked him to lecture at Kailas Shugendo. Little is known of Nonomura beyond what his students have conversationally shared. Russell's recollections are slim to none, save for comments in a grant application. Russell's friend Alan Abrams, however, recalls Yuko Nonomura as follows: "He was an amazing presence, and was the perfect example of the adaptability of Vajrayana practice. He came to America to teach as a Buddhist priest, but lost his offered position because he was interned in a camp during WWII. I believe he met his wife there and when they were released he became an insurance salesman, continuing to practice Vajrayana as a "householder" [a Buddhist term for non-monastic or laity practitioners of Buddhism]. I found a San Francisco Directory from both 1961 and 1963 that lists a "Rev Yuko Nonomura" as the "pastor" at the Gedatsu Church of America ("Gedatsu Church of America"). The Gedatsu church preached an emerging Japanese religion, Gedatsu-kai. It sprang from a vision that founder Seiken Okano (or, Gedatsu Kongo) experienced at the age of 48 in 1929. Gedatsu-kai is known to have combined Shinto and Shingon Buddhist traditions, giving primary attention to the deity, Mahavairocana. Like the Rimé tradition that Warwick imported, Gedatsu remained open to all religious views. Little else, however, is known of Nonomura.

Russell was most inspired in how Nonomura fused his esoteric spiritual practice with his day-to-day work life. "This was particularly inspiring to Arthur and all of us," Alan Abrams recalls, "as far as being able to be a dharma practitioner while [being, in Russell's case] part of the club and music scene in New York." Nonomura, unbeknownst to himself, gave Russell permission to be himself, to leave the ascetic life he had been living. He could re-enter the world; the dharma was not in the mountains, not locked in a closet—it was portable. As regards Russell's longing to make it big in New York, a practical perspective Russell began to take having left the commune to pursue music, Abrams continues, "Arthur's goal in making pop disco records was in being able to give money to Yuko (he was particularly interested in redeeming himself with Yuko's wife whom he felt thought he was a nuisance) for [the construction of] a temple" (Abrams, 2012).

Terry and Lorna Mills, known as Nona and Jivaka at Kailas Shugendo, were also students of Murshid Samuel Lewis ("Sufi Sam") and Nonomura. They would also host meetings, classes, and lectures at their home in Tam Valley Junction in Marin County, California. Nonomura lectured there regularly and would generally talk about the history of Shingon practice with focused attention given to interpreting the Heart Sutra (Sanskrit, *Prajnaparamita*, "perfection of wisdom"), which Russell had already engaged via Warwick and Ginsberg, and which he would continue to meditate upon throughout his life (Abrams, 2012). Russell's study with Nonomura was informal, but they met often from 1970-1973. Their study was largely made through dialogue and personal practice, rather than collective ritual and physical discipline. It lacked the clutter of the complicated personality and theatrics of Warwick and the self-centered pursuits of others which Russell had encountered at Kailas Shugendo. Nonomura also introduced Russell to the foundational Shingon text, *Kukai: Major Works*, which I previously referenced.

Shingon philosophy and Nonomura's teaching and friendship would lay the foundation and driving force for Russell's most labored and loved project, *Instrumentals*. It was Nonomura that suggested Russell compose music about clouds to accompany a slide show of Nonomura's own nature photography. This would set Russell off into an excited frenzy of creativity, enduring for years—chapter 5 explores this work in depth. Just prior to beginning his *Instrumentals*, Russell had been explicitly incorporating various Buddhist sutras into musical performance works, notably those (from Chapter 25, *Kannon Gyo*) of the lotus sutra, as well as those from the Heart Sutra (Japanese, *Hannya Shingyo*). These works were scored or at least conceived for chanting, for "gamba ensemble," as well as for trumpet and "cello section." These and other pieces could still be found in Russell's initial compositional efforts during his first few years in New York, which we'll look more into in chapter three.

Beyond the imagery provided by Nonomura for *Instrumentals*, Russell was constantly applying to his music various natural, animal, and cosmic symbols with strong connotations in Shingon tradition. In his song lyrics Russell frequently refers to oracular readings of the environment, such as the meditation on clouds in "Lucky Cloud," which we noted in relation to Lama Govinda. In another song, "Home Away From Home," Russell sings of finding insight by looking to the sky: "By looking up when you need to know. You will see that from looking, looking up. By looking up when you need to need to know. You will be able to do it again." In his "Ballad of the Lights, Part 2" Russell meditates an upward gaze again, "he sees the lights and he wonders if they are talking to each other, and he wonders if they are talking to him. And he asks if they are." From looking up to the sky to looking down into the ocean, in "Platform on the Ocean," he depicts an oracular reading of fish tales: "I looked down. I saw the fish and which way its tail was pointing and why." Elsewhere, Russell paints a mystical realm in the Iowan cornfield in "Hiding Your Present." In "Home Away From Home" he invites others to join him in his home "up in the treetops." The construction of such imaginary or metaphysical spaces, as well as the oracular reading of nature are both common in esoteric Buddhist practice and they pervade Russell's music. Always attending the oracle, Russell saw himself through the eyes of the prophetic Buddha, Maitreya. "Alone I wonder a thousand miles," Govinda quotes Maitreya, "and I ask my way from the white clouds" (Govinda, *The Way* 43).

During Russell's first year in New York he met others with Buddhist interests, including Andrew Franck, a composer and writer, with whom Russell would attend Elias Tannenbaum's electronic music course at the Manhattan School of Music. Franck would perform with The Flying Hearts, which lead to some performances at The Ear Inn. He performed in other works of Russell's as well, such as performances for Charlotte Moormon's Avant-Garde Festivals. Back in California, Russell would write songs "about the wind blowing in his hair, or the experience of passing through a town, or the sight of insects splattering onto the windshield of the car" as he road passenger in his girlfriend Yuko Fujii's VW Beetle (Lawrence, *Hold On* 42). In New York, Franck recalls that "we often sat around improvising/composing cello and vocal duets about street life, *bodhisattvas*, the cold weather" (Franck, 2010). Around this time Russell also met, through Ginsberg, fellow Buddhist musician, Steven Hall. Hall recalls, "when I first met him, Arthur and I would talk about using Buddhism as some kind of force in pop music [...] We wanted to write songs that used these ideas. Arthur was really passionate about this." Elodie Lauten, another friend who Russell met through Ginsberg, recalls, "He wanted to write Buddhist pop music, because he felt it would be karmically better to reach out to as many people as possible. I think he was hoping to make some money with it too" (Lawrence, *Hold On* 226). For Russell this Buddhist philosophy was primarily drawn from the Shingon tradition.

As it was the parent lineage of Shugendo philosophy, we have already imbibed a great deal of Shingon philosophy in our look at Shugendo beliefs, above. The symbolism of fire, mountains, and other natural phenomena are core components of Shingon philosophy. While the names of deities may differ between Shugendo and Shingon, the practitioner's interaction with these deities remain, in both disciplines, one of meditative union. The discussion of Shugendo mantra, above, stems directly from Kukai's conception of mantra, which is at the heart of Shingon philosophy. Similarly, our look into mandala and other visualization meditation techniques, below, are, equally applicable to both Shugendo and Shingon disciplines.

Russell was drawn to Nonomura and to Shingon in part because of its historical relationship to the teachings of Shugendo. But he was also drawn to it because Nonomura's personal teaching style contrasted so starkly with the messy politics and volatile drama of Warwick's commune. Russell began to see that devout Buddhist practice doesn't need to be divorced from the practicalities of modern culture and day-to-day life. The Shingon aim of merging one's inner self with the Universal self, developing cosmic consciousness, did not require one to hide in the mountains. The shugyo of Shugendo and the sadhana of Shingon were being channeled directly into his musical practice, liberated from Warwick's limitations, as Russell continued traditional Shingon meditation

Image 8. The Womb Realm (Jap., Taizokai) mandala, hanging scroll with colors on silk, late 9th century. Tō Temple, Kyoto, Japan. 1.83 x 1.54 meter. Photography by Benrido Co., Ltd., Tokyo (Benrido)

practices. One of the primary techniques for bringing about this realized perspective of cosmic consciousness, is that of mandala meditation.

Mandala Meditation

Following his return from China, Kukai brought back to Japan two primary mandalas which offer a visual taxonomy of Shingon deities and doctrines: the Diamond Realm mandala and the Womb Realm mandala (shown in **image 8**) are first met by students in an initiation ceremony. New Shingon practitioners are blindfolded and placed before a mandala, drawn upon the ground. They are given a flower and told to toss the flower into the air, and whichever deity in the mandala that the flower lands on determines the deity to which that student will devote their practice (Green, 2003). And from that point on, mandala meditation pervades an individual's practice.

In earlier traditions one might physically enter the mandala, drawn or sculpted on the ground. We noted earlier how En no Gyôja used actual caves for his mandala meditations. More commonly, a *mandala* (Sanskrit, "circle") is a drawing or painting, depicting deities and other symbols in a geometrically organized image. The mandala is then visualized in the mind, through which one meditates upon the deities, and seeks to unify oneself with these deities. In addition, mandala meditation often entails a nested body of rituals, including mantra, mudra, and/or other techniques. Yamasaki however emphasizes that mental visualization of mandala meditation is not purely symbolic.

> It is easy to view mandalas only as symbols of transcendent, universal Buddha-hood, which, as symbols of the universe, they indeed are. This universe, however, is not apart from the self. The deities in the mandala are symbols of the self as well as of

the universe. Shingon considers mandalas to be both mirrors of the mind and patterns of the manifold, ever-evolving activities of consciousness and of phenomena. The same patterns are equally applicable to all humanly conceivable levels of vision, macrocosmic and microcosmic. The innate Buddha is both the true self and the deity of the mandala, and both are the universe (128).

This cosmic perspective was further developed by Kukai through a spiritual system he called the "Body of Wisdom" (*chishin*). This system contains five core teachings, each symbolized by one of the five Buddhas depicted in the Diamond Realm mandala.

> **1. Wisdom That Perceives the Essential Nature of the World of Dharma**: the eternal source of gnosis.
>
> **2. Mirror-like Wisdom**: the wisdom that reflects reality as it is without distortion.
>
> **3. Wisdom of Equality**: the wisdom that perceives the fundamental identity of all phenomena as issuing forth from the One Reality and that recognizes the absolute equality of all beings as to their intrinsic value.
>
> **4. Wisdom of Observation**: the wisdom that observes the objects of mind free from discriminations and subjective calculations
>
> **5. Wisdom of Action**: the wisdom that is manifested as actions to help bring all sentient beings to spiritual maturity and, finally, to enlightenment (Hakeda, 83-4)

Many of the Buddhist concepts that form Shingon philosophy are implicit in Kukai's "Body of Wisdom." For example, many of the tantric techniques mentioned above were synonymous with sadhana, which functions as a technical ritual, a spiritual tool or map, for an action to be carried out. This Shingon concept of ritual is related to the Shugendo concept of shugyo. While inclusive of sitting meditation, shugyo primarily emphasizes more physical rituals performed outdoors (Dukes, 76). Both shugyo and sadhana however are believed, as Kukai alludes in the 'Wisdom of Action,' above, not only to assist the individual in attaining enlightenment, but also to assist every other person, creature, and thing in the entire universe to attain enlightenment. The sadhanas are largely laid out in the tantras and sutras, and they can often be quite cumbersome to execute. But this cumbersomeness is intentionally designed to maintain one's focus. "The entire process [of tantric meditation] is regulated by rules, that is, the process of time is punctuated by prescribed activities so that the student will not lose himself in timelessness; step by step he returns from unconscious imitating to his conscious self by counting beats, striking a hand bell, and so forth" (Hakeda, 99). Some common Shingon sadhana performed regularly are *sosokukan* (breath-counting meditation), *gachirinkan* (meditation on the image of the full moon), *gojigonjingan* (meditation on the five elements as located within one's own body), and *ajikan* (meditation on the "A-syllable"). It is important to remember that many rituals, such as these, are involved in Shingon mandala meditation. We'll look more at gachirinkan meditation, but first we'll look into the Shingon Womb Realm mandala.

At the center of a Womb Realm mandala one finds Mahavairocana (a.k.a. Dainichi Nyorai, or "Great Sun, Thuscome one"), the most revered Shingon deity, representing the utmost embodiment of wisdom. He is surrounded by other deities and bodhisattvas, each with their own conceptual identities and associations. Kukai characterized the deities and outlined the Womb mandala according to a philosophy of "essential mind" (*shinno*), which consists of five levels:

1. The essential mind of the central deity embraces all subsidiary minds in the One Consciousness (*isshiki*).

2. The eight major deities—the four Buddhas which are the major manifestations of Dainichi Nyorai, and the four Bodhisattvas which are their secondary manifestations—embrace all subsidiary minds, forming the eighth level of consciousness.

3. The central deity and eight major deities together embrace all subsidiary minds and form the ninth level of consciousness.

4. The numberless subsidiary minds of all the deities in the surrounding sections of the mandala are embraced in a single consciousness called the All-Embracing One Mind Consciousness (*issai isshin shiki*). This, joined to the ninth level, results in the tenth level of consciousness.

5. There are innumerable Minds and Consciousnesses. These result when innumerable subsidiary minds are added to the tenth level of consciousness (Yamasaki, 136).

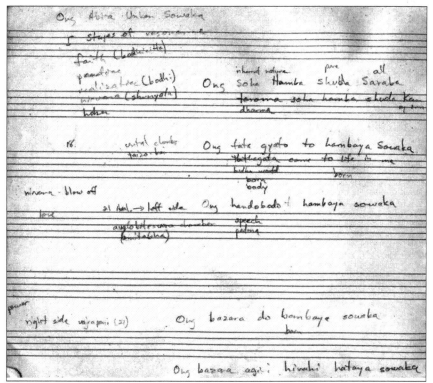

Image 9. Russell's notes on mandala meditation (Russell, SN)

Based on the notebook it was found in, **image 9** appears to have been written during the mid to late 1980's. Noting the use of Japanese text and the meaningful content that it depicts (mantras, deity names, and philosophical concepts), here Russell is reinforcing his meditation on the Shingon Womb Realm mandala (Japanese, *Taizokai*). Russell notes the deities Taizokai, Vajrapani, and Amitabha, and notes their locations in the mandala, with Taizokai in the center chamber—there are 409 deities in the twelve "halls" of the Womb Realm mandala. Each deity is an expression of this mandala's primary focus: compassion. This is also expressed through the symbols of the lotus blossom and the vajras and pervades mantras and sutras used in meditation.

In Russell's notes above he refers to what he calls the "5 stages of resonance." This categorization aligns itself with the numerous quintal philosophies of mandala consciousness, such as Kukai's five forms of "essential mind," and what are known as the "five transformations." The "five transformations," as described by Yamasaki below, explain the spiral-like process of meditating upon the womb mandala.

> The lotus of the central dais portrays a distinct movement. The northern lotus petal (to the left), seat of Tenkuraion, is the beginning of a counterclockwise movement that proceeds through Muryoju, Kaifuke-o, and Hodo. This spiral progression represents a deepening of consciousness that eventually reaches its greatest depth with Dainichi Nyorai in the very center.

> This spiral development is defined by the five transformations (*goten*), the stages by which the innately enlightened mind unfolds to its highest development in the activity of skillful means. The five stages are also related to the five wisdoms and the five Buddhas, and are considered an unfolding of the Dharma Gate of the Three Phrases. In the form of the five-fold A-syllable (A AH AN AKU ANKU) they are used as a mantra in the Taizo Mandala practice.

> The first stage is the awakening mind, which is called
> cause (*in*). This includes both innately enlightened mind and the
> realization of that mind. The second stage is that of correct prac-
> tice (*gyo*) leading to realization of enlightened mind. The third
> stage is the "proof" (*sho*) of enlightened mind. The fourth stage
> is nirvana (*nehan*), which is enlightenment in the aspect of truth.
> The fifth stage is the ultimate activity of skillful means (*hoben*),
> which is the creative flowering of the enlightened mind (136-
> 137).

The Japanese mantras that Russell wrote down correspond with various deities and the five transformations.
**ONG SOHA HAMBA SHUDA SARABA TARAMA SOHA
HAMBA SHUDO KAN** is also known as the "Purification
of the Three Karmic Actions." The mantra is recited during
the goma ceremony and this mantric recitation is one in a
long series of ritual steps of goma, which involve other mantras and mudras, rituals with water, oil, rice, lotus flowers,
grains, incense, and other materials. In preparation for this
mantra, the *gyoja*, or Shugendo practitioner, first forms his
hands in the "Lotus Bud" mudra, cupping his palms, with fingers touching, and holding them close to his heart. He then
recites the mantra five times. The mantra translates into En-
glish as, "all the attributes are pure in nature. I am also pure
by nature" (Kolhatkar, 57). With each of the five recitations
of the mantra the reciter "imagines going to the five points
of his body, viz., forehead, right shoulder, left shoulder, chest
and throat" (58). The goma ceremony as a whole is considered to be a three-dimensional mandala, with the cauldron of
fire in Dainichi Nyorai's central position.

Mandala meditation is one of the more complexly organized visual meditations in esoteric Buddhism. We will likely never know the extent to which Russell meditated using
mandalas, but we know for a fact he did. And it is clear that,
if not influencing him directly, mandala meditation offers
insights into Russell's creative process. His construction—

conceptually, lyrically, compositionally—of imaginary realms, his use of symbolism in lyrical imagery, his complexly nested compositional systems, and his ability to take on other identities as his own—these were all nascent in the mandala meditation he exercised through Shugendo and Shingon traditions. However, there are numerous other forms of Shingon

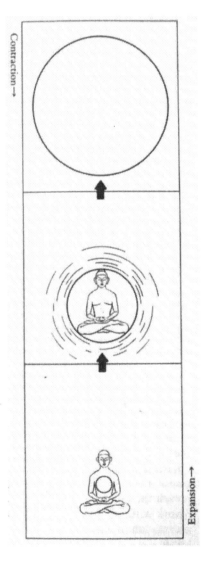

Image 10. Expansion and contraction technique in gachirinkin meditation- (Bottom) The practitioner visualizes his mind in the shape of a moon disk. (Center) Self becomes moon disk. (Top) Moon disk expands to the size of the Universe (Yamasaki, 157).

meditation based in visualization, as we noted above. Two in particular are explored by Russell directly through his own music. We'll briefly look at these below.

Other Visualization Meditations:
The Moon Disc & the Nectar of Immortality

For the practice of gachirinkan, one meditates on the white disc of the full moon, with external visual aids or mentally. The Heart Sutra describes one practice of this visualization as follows: Having visualized oneself as a deity surrounded by other supportive deities, one "next visualizes the goddess Prajnaparamita seated on a moon disc, surrounded by buddhas and bodhisattvas. Moving to an even smaller scale, the meditator imagines that there is a moon disc in the center of her heart, upon which stands the letter ĀḤ. At an even more minute level, the officiant is instructed to visualize the letters of the Heart Sutra standing upright around the edge of the mantra, but the entire sutra, for the entire sutra functions as a mantra in this ritual. The letters of the sutra radiate both light and their own sound, serving as offerings to the buddhas and bodhisattvas, who in turn alleviate the sufferings and purify all sentient beings as the officiant contemplates the meaning of "emptiness" (Lopez, 222). As we'll continue to recall, Russell would record on nights of the full moon and edit on nights of the new moon, feeling it gave his work more favor.

Lunar imagery would feature in many of Russell songs. He may well have had the gachirinkan meditation in mind in this excerpt from his "Some Imaginary Far Away Type Things, AKA Lost in the Meshes," from the World of Echo period:

> It's an unfamiliar sight.
> In an unfamiliar place.
> Outside the mirror.

By the moon that goes with what we're thinking now.
Laugh about the things that we are doing now

The moon would feature in several other works by Russell, including "Big Moon," "This Is How We Walk On The Moon," "Love Comes Back," "Ballad of the Lights, Pt. 1." As we'll go into in the following chapter, this lunar symbolism was also related to Russell's personal study of astrology. One interpretation of the gachirinkan meditation experience has it that "the mind/heart of the practitioner [is] visualized as progressively filling with light, often identified with the light of the full moon. Objectives of such exercises included an enhanced ability to recollect the past, greater powers of memorization, and—in the most literal sense—enlightenment" (LaFleur, 66). This infusion of light is found in numerous visualization exercises, for example, in the visualization of *amrita*, another sadhana meditation used by Russell.

Having been playing with composer Ron Kuivila in the mid-80's, Russell would reflectively fixate in his notebooks on the sounds that Kuivila was using during their playing with reference to another Tantric visualization/meditation practice. In a few places Russell relates a particular sound of Kuivila's to a ritual drink with strong Buddhist symbolism: "Visualize Ron's sample [an audio sample they were improvising with] as amrita. First, Kuivila describes his sample as follows:

> [T]his was using a homemade delay line where the output taps could run at completely different rates from the inputs. This could be like a harmonizer or, by doubling speed, a funny sped up playing where if you stayed in synch with the delay you could play live with articulations at double your performed rate. [One of Kuivila's keyboard studies on his album "Fidelity" is based on this]. So, I made some funny popish lines using that technique as well as large scale processing (Kuivila, 2011).

The result is a coarsely fuzzy pulsation, moving in and out of sync with itself, whipping pitch into highly elastic directions. Russell heard something special in Kuivila's sound, which he felt worth ritualizing as amrita. In Buddhist thought amrita [Sanskrit for "deathlessness"] is a symbol of immortality, often visualized as a luminescent liquid or nectar. Rooted in mahamudra meditation, one traditional esoteric ritual involving amrita asks that one focus their mind on a given object (for example, "ron's audio sample") and internally visualize that object as a radiant light, like a glowing nectar dripping from above, entering and purifying one's body and spirit. This visualization would be accompanied by mantric recitation, such as the Vajrasattva "Purification" mantra (aka "the 100 syllable mantra"). Russell's primary experience with amrita would have likely been in the drinking rituals occurring before every meal and other important rituals (such as the goma fire ritual) at Kailas Shugendo. It's unclear how Russell's interest in Kuivila's sound may have manifested though most likely it arose during a Singing Tractors performance or rehearsal. The concept of amrita was the particular way Russell heard Kuivila's sound, i.e. listen to this sound as a light filling your soul with overflowing bliss. From his early works, incorporating Buddhist sutras, in California to the Shingon-inflected *Instrumentals*, and beyond, Russell was always exploring the relationship between music and meditation. Musical scribblings in his notebooks, for example, are found paired with explicit personal reflections such as, "how, or how not to, mix a meditative and non-meditative approach" (Russell, N).

TIBETAN VAJRAYANA:
"First Thought, Best Thought"

First thought is best
Then you compose
Composition's what you compose —
In terms of what? (*First Thought* 18)

Chögyam Trungpa

Encountering one another accidentally, when both were hailing the same cab in Manhattan, Allen Ginsberg met and befriended reincarnated Tibetan lama, Chögyam Trungpa. Ginsberg would go on to co-found the Naropa Institute, a college integrating Buddhist practice and the arts, with Trungpa, William Burroughs, and Anne Waldman in Boulder, Colorado. It was through Ginsberg that Russell came to discover Trungpa's unique perspective within the Kagyu lineage of Tibetan Buddhism. Russell and his friends, notably Elodie Lauten and Steven Hall, found Trungpa's writing in *The Myth of Freedom* and *Cutting Through Spiritual Materialism* to be deeply inspiring. Hall had even studied at Naropa just before meeting Russell through Ginsberg. Russell's relationship with Trungpa's Shambhala vision was not extensive, but Trungpa's Beat-inflected emphasis on "first thought, best thought" and "crazy wisdom" (Tibetan, *yeshe cholwa*, literally "wild or uncontainable wisdom that has always been there") was of some appeal to Russell. While Russell's study of Tibetan Vajrayana would largely be pursued beyond Trungpa's philosophy, Trungpa was such an enormous influence in the reception of Tibetan philosophies in America and upon the work of numerous friends of Russell that he warrants some significant attention.

At 2 years old Trungpa was determined by Buddhist elders to be a reincarnated Lama, or tulku. Understanding the situation, he adjusted his teachings to the American audience. Through the Tibetan lineages of Kagyu and Nyingma Buddhist traditions, Trungpa sought to reach the masses. Trungpa's unique and often controversial teaching style, in large part brought these traditions to a popular audience. Much of the controversy revolved around Trungpa's application of the Tibetan Buddhist concept of "crazy wisdom," which he described as follows:

> In the case of primordial craziness of crazy wisdom, we do not permit ourselves to get seduced by passion or aroused by aggression at all. We relate with these experiences as they are, and if anything comes up in the midst of that complete ordinariness and begins to make itself into a big deal, *then we cut it down* [author's italics]—without any special reference to what is good and what is bad. Crazy wisdom is just the action of truth (*Crazy Wisdom* 12).

Nothing is taboo in the realm of crazy wisdom. The primary goal is squelching the negative force of anxiety. One is simply trying to cut through delusions, inhibitions, habitual understanding, and spiritual materialism. Trungpa's aim was to shatter delusion by any means necessary. He was known for his alcoholism and sexual promiscuity with his students. Others recollect his "crazy wisdom" tactics in the midst of his lectures: "On the night of the Vajrayana transmission he rambled from subject to subject in a series of blazing non sequiturs... waited until we were dozing off and then shouted "Fat!" or "Fuck You!" into the microphone loud enough to burst our eardrums" (Urban, 233). And in one instance Trungpa forcibly demanded that an attendee to one of his gatherings undress themselves—after which Trungpa's reputation met strong criticism.

Analogous to the behavior of the "trickster" character

found in various folk mythologies, crazy wisdom techniques rely on shock/surprise, humor, de-contextualization, and absurdity to attain their effect of immediately cutting through the mind's habits and crutches. For Trungpa this was also related to the Vajrayana concept of upayana (the "vehicle of many methods"), which essentially encourages a teacher to adapt their teachings uniquely to a particular student or situation, adjusting the teaching according to aspects of temperament, mood, etc (Goodman, 2005). While Russell might have been inspired by Trungpa's living out the concept of "crazy wisdom" and while aspects of Russell's music might have reflected a similar intention—pieces might involve the sudden loud clattering of a bundle of sticks dropped onto the floor or a recitation on the spiritual merits of Bugs Bunny—Russell was ultimately too shy or was simply inclined towards a gentler and less theatrical approach. While Russell, primarily through Ginsberg and other friends, would become familiar with Trungpa and inspired by his writings, Russell was ultimately critical and dismissive of Trungpa's indulgent theatrics. His friend Tej Hazarika recalls: "[Russell] was scandalized by [Trungpa]. He would say, 'What is this shit?! I told Allen [Ginsberg] to stay away from him!'" (Hazarika, 2013).

Largely because of his "crazy wisdom" antics, by the 1970's Trungpa was one of the most popularly known Buddhist teachers in America and abroad. He went on to found over a hundred meditation centers throughout America as well as, in 1975, the first Buddhist University, the Naropa Institute in Colorado, for which he asked Ginsberg, William Burroughs, Anne Waldman and other poets to pioneer a spiritually based school of poetics—Ginsberg and Waldman would found the Jack Kerouac School of Disembodied Poetics. And he was the first to take the secret Vajrayana teachings and offer these teachings to America and to the layman.

Trungpa would teach numerous celebrity-artists, such as, Ginsberg, Peter Orlovsky, Anne Waldman, Peter Lieberson, David Bowie, Thomas Merton, Leonard Cohen, and Joni Mitchell, while he would interact with numerous others at the Naropa Institute (e.g. William Burroughs, John Cage, Marianne Faithful). Distrustful of his behavior and his popular veneration, Russell would never study with Trungpa, but the idea of "first thought, best thought" resonated deeply with Russell.

Asking Ginsberg why he relied on the written page, rather than trusting in his heart and spontaneously poetizing from there, Trungpa encouraged Ginsberg to emulate the improvisatory practice of Buddha/singer Milarepa.

> I was writing a spontaneous chain poem with Chögyam and he said, and we finally agreed, "First thought is best thought." That is to say, the first thought you had on your mind, the first thought you thought before you thought, yes, you'd have a better thought, before you thought you should have a more formal thought—first thought, best thought. If you stick with the first flashes, then you're all right. But the problem is, how do you get to that first thought—that's always the problem. The first thought is always the great elevated, cosmic, non-cosmic shunyata ["empty"] thought. And then, at least according to the Buddhist formulation, after that you begin imposing names and forms and all that. So it's a question of catching yourself at your first open thought (Midal, 377).

Trungpa says of "first thought, best thought": "'First thought, best thought' is not necessarily a chronological event. Quite possibly, the first thought might be the worst thought, chronologically speaking. In this case, first thought refers to that thought which is fresh and free" (*True Perception* 10). But "first thought, best thought" wasn't purely a Buddhist phenomenon; it was an American interpretation of Buddhism, which originated out of natural affinities. This was largely through a community of poets, beginning with the Beats and extending into the New American poetry in downtown New York. Inspired both by Vajrayana Buddhism and the high energy improvisatory jazz stylings of bebop, Jack Kerouac championed an unedited mind; and it was he that coined the phrase "first thought, best thought."

While Trungpa became the spokesman for this message of spontaneous mindfulness, both Kerouac and Ginsberg had encountered a similar spirit through American poetic channels in the work of William Carlos Williams. In fact, when Ginsberg introduced young musician Steven Hall to Russell for the first time he told Hall that Russell was "like William Carlos Williams, but he sings" (Wolf, 2009). Ginsberg is specifically referring in the Williams reference to Russell's transcendental poetics of "everyday life." Aside from incorporating raw observation, Williams, who was an extraordinary influence on Ginsberg and via him, upon Russell as well, had developed a manner of writing which he called the "variable foot" or writing "by breath."

> The grammar of the term, variable foot, is simply what it describes itself to be: a poetic foot that is not fixed but varies with the demands of the language, keeping the measured emphasis as it may occur in the line (Hudson, 63).

Though easily viewed as a variant of "free verse," Williams' "variable foot" was a manifestation of his insistence that "no verse can be free, it must be governed by some measure." But while such a measurement appears rational upon the surface, Williams clarifies that "[w]e have no measure by which to guide ourselves except a purely intuitive one which we feel but do not name" (Williams, 408). Like Russell, Williams was quick to contradict the rationale of his process.

A Sort of a Song

Let the snake wait under
his weed
and the writing
be of words, slow and quick, sharp
to strike, quiet to wait,
sleepless.
— through metaphor to reconcile
the people and the stones.
Compose. (No ideas
but in things) Invent!
Saxifrage is my flower that splits the rocks (Williams, 46).

Evident in this "sort of a song," we can see Williams, in his consistent style, breaking up the line, fragmenting or sequencing words in an idiosyncratic speech-form. In one of his later works, *Asphodel*, Williams stated that his aim was "to break up the usual metric pattern. In order to get away from the conventional thing, dividing it by breath, by inflection" (Terrel, 328). Ginsberg had sought to follow in the style of William's "variable foot," respiratory poetics, and a guided intuitive approach:

> I was working with my own neural impulses and writing impulses. See, the difference is between someone sitting down to write a poem *in* a definite preconceived metrical pattern and filling in that pattern, and someone working with his physiological movements and arriving at a pattern, and perhaps even *arriving* at a pattern which might have a name (Hudson, 63).

All of this was reinforced by Trungpa, whom would have a massive influence on the poets of New York and "New American Poetry," similar to the influence of Pandit Pran Nath on New York composers of the minimalists of the Downtown scene. Trungpa taught numerous poets, such as Ginsberg, Anne Waldman, Diane Di Prima, John Giorno, and others.

Allen Ginsberg considered poet Anne Waldman, another teacher at Naropa and a student of Trungpa, to be his "spiritual wife" (Waldman, *Disembodied* xlix). Waldman was a pioneering figure in the downtown poetry scene. She directed the Poetry Project at St. Mark's Church from 1968-1978. And just as Russell and his cohorts began bringing popular artists into the avant-guard music scene at The Kitchen, at the same time Waldman was doing this for poetry at St. Marks, where she brought in artists like Patti Smith, Jim Carroll, and Ed Sanders (of The Fugs). Through Ginsberg, Waldman would meet Russell at the Pacific High Studio Mantras in 1971. Like other Buddhist oriented artists from the New York poetry scene, Waldman's poetry dynamizes repetition with an effulgent almost ecstatic Buddhist intentionality. In her "Makeup on Empty Space," which she claims was "inspired by a talk Trungpa gave on the feminine principle," she takes the enculturated female ritual of make-up application and projects it upon the void.

> I am putting makeup on empty space
> all patinas convening on empty space
> rouge blushing on empty space
> I am putting makeup on empty space
> pasting eyelashes on empty space
> painting the eyebrows of empty space
> piling creams on empty space
> painting the phenomenal world (Midal, 432)

Waldman was also an admirer of Russell. In a recent interview she was asked about the relationship between poetry and music in underground [arts] culture. Waldman thought of Russell as an example:

[Y]es, thank god for that, all the hybrids and experiments, and passionate originality that's not so caught up in the difficult economics of the materialist fame-money-machine. The work of someone like Arthur Russell comes to mind. The relationship has always been there back many centuries. Shaking a gourd. And there's always this more interesting work going on at the margins, in the interstices (Rogers, 2011).

Trungpa's own poetry—as in the first few lines of his "KÜNGA GARMA" below—sits easily next to Ginsberg, Waldman, Williams, as well as the lyrics of Russell. All of these poets reflected the art of the everyday, intuitive heart-driven spontaneity, as well as Williams' variable foot and writing "by breath."

> Jalapeños are good to eat
> Antelope has slanted eyes
> There comes a rocket
> Alice is magnificent
> She's courageous
> Fun-fair
> Jalapeños seem to be good (*First Thought* 45)

All of the poets mentioned above had a deep interest in the form of their expression, preferring an ephemeral or variable form, one closer to live speech, one that could adapt to the consciousness of the moment. Ginsberg was supportive and critical of Russell's writing, saying supportively that "[s]taying with the real... is a rare art you have" (Lawrence, *Hold On* 56). Russell would not only take all of these things to heart in his lyric writing, but in nearly every aspect of his work. As we will see, this maintenance of "the real" and a steady stroll with a "variable foot" would influence Russell's stylistic take on song form, on meter and rhythm, on melodic development, as well as his manner of studio recording and large-scale orchestration.

Singer/songwriter Bob Dylan, who would go on to embrace Christianity, and later Judaism, in the 1980's, was one of the many celebrities that regularly flowed through Ginsberg's social scene. It was Kerouac's Buddhist-infused *On*

The Road that was "like a Bible" for the young Dylan (Dylan, 57). Reciprocally, Ginsberg recalls: "[Dylan] taught me three chords so I got down to blues. Right after Trungpa suggested I start improvising, I began improvising and Dylan heard it, and encouraged it even more" (Chowka, 1976).

This spontaneity, this "freshness," this engagement with one's immediate surroundings—these were artistic affinities, spiritual affinities, lifestyle affinities for Dylan, Ginsberg, Kerouac, Russell, Williams, Trungpa and many others. Trungpa himself explained this core synthesis of the arts and pedestrian life in his Buddhist philosophy, emphasizing the significance of the mundane moment, before our mind evaluates it. Meditation itself, Trungpa says, is an art.

> The art of meditative experience might be called genuine art. Such art is [...] a perpetually growing process in which we begin to appreciate our surroundings in life, whatever they may be—it doesn't necessarily have to be good, beautiful, and pleasurable at all. The definition of art from this point of view, is to be able to see the uniqueness of everyday experience. Every moment we might be doing the same things [...]. But that seeming repetitiveness becomes unique every day. A kind of intimacy takes place with the daily habits that you go through and the art involved in it. That's why it is called art in everyday life (*The Essential* 96).

Meanwhile, Trungpa was aware that American identity, born by the rugged pragmatics of individualism, had evolved into the 1960's reactionary version of personal growth and self-discovery. For Trungpa this focus upon the self often involved what he called "spiritual materialism," the process of turning spiritual imagery, ideas, and symbols into personal "status" symbols and self-glorification. Russell met such spiritual materialism at Kailas Shugendo. In response to this phenomenon, drawing from Western analogies in psychology and philosophy, Trungpa's teachings focused on untangling this self-centered perspective [Lama Govinda did this as well, often citing Aldous Huxley, Nietzsche, the Bible]. Regardless, most Buddhist techniques were rendered precisely for this re-adjustment of individual psychology. Tantra, with its sensual media of color, sound, and symbol, was his primary vehicle of teaching, and was catalyzed through artistic expression.

Trungpa was the first representative of Tibet to place tantric thought in the minds of the American masses [note: Pierre Bernard would introduce tantra in America around 1905]. He would make an effort to recall its Indian and Chinese origins, as well as the influence of their visual and symbolical cultures. But he knew that in order to engage an American audience, he had to teach beyond these specific cultural symbols, either through generalization, contemporary contexts, or through more familiar American references. Trungpa speaks to this in the following passage, where he offers a unique yet clear definition of symbolism which opens itself up indeterminately to the American situation.

> On the whole, understanding the vividness of the energy of the universe in terms of symbolism, in terms of patterns, colors, shapes, is not a matter of imagination or hallucination for the real tantric practitioner. It is real. It is similar to a person hearing music that is very moving to him and feeling that he could almost carve statues out of it, that he could almost hold it, handle it. Sound becomes almost a solid object, almost a color or shape. If a person is able to see the energies of the universe as they are, then shapes and colors and patterns suggest themselves; symbolism happens. That is the meaning of *mahamudra*, which means "great symbol." The whole world is symbol—not symbol in the sense of a sign representing something other than itself, but symbol in the sense of the highlights of the vivid qualities of things as they are (*Myth* 195).

Mahamudra, Dzogchen, Ngondro

Engaging the dualistic teachings of *samatha-vipasana* meditation, the muhamudra (lit. "great symbol/seal"), is a body of Tibetan teachings emphasizing a particular practice of advanced meditation. Such teachings were found in subgroups of Tibetan Kagyu lineages, as well as other schools of thought, including Japanese Shingon, both of which Russell studied and practiced. The *samatha muhamudra* technique primarily involves the body, focusing on sitting posture and breathing. The *vipassana muhamudra* technique involves a series of "pointing-out" things to the mind through focused concentration on an object, or upon the mind itself. Focusing on the mind, for example, the practitioner goes through five points of attention: the settled mind, the moving or thinking mind, the mind reflecting appearances, the relation of mind and body, and the settled and thinking mind together. Each point involves a series of questions related to each point's topic. After going through each point, and its associated questions, the practitioner then goes over each point once more, this time asking themselves with each point only, "What is it?" Perhaps this is what Russell is referring to when he writes in his journal: "Did you ask yourself? In order to clarify, examine moment of fixture of schedule. Letter to myself: a reminder to think. Before asking, penetrate again the span of moments, what is this I am asking for? Color, time, and thought converging: may the bright symbol stand out, (in this unique moment) unobstructed throughout all time." Or, again, in the experimental disco work, "Go Bang"--in which Russell lyrically merges the cosmic explosion of social and erotic union--the mahamudra's question returns: "Thank you for asking the question. Thank you for asking the question. You showed us the face of delusion. To uproot the cause of confusion [...] I wanna see all my friends at once. I'd do anything to get the chance to go bang."

The infinite openness of mahamudra meditation is probably the most pervasive and enduring Buddhist concept in Russell's life and work, for it is potentially so open that it extends one's view beyond what they think they should see, eradicating all mental restrictions and barriers, conjoining it to the cosmos. When Milarepa met Tilopa, a wondering yogi and teacher of Mahamudra, Tilopa would describe mahamudra as an active void: "When mind has no place where it can stop (and become limited) the mahamudra [lit. 'The Great Attitude'] is present. By cultivating such an attitude one attains supreme enlightenment" (Govinda, *The Way* 150).

All Tibetan lineages of Buddhism focus on a core meditation practice, passed down orally by teachers. These are often used, in combination with yoga, as the preliminary teachings to new students, but remain core disciplines throughout one's spiritual development, and often extend into advanced tantric practices. While each branch of Tibetan Vajrayana prioritizes one or more core practices, students of one school are welcome and often seek to learn the methods of other schools through guru-disciple teachings. All of these teachings, essentially being variations on preliminary training, subsist upon the belief that "enlightenment is not a distant goal to strive toward, but an immanent reality that must be recognized in the present moment. Effort and agendas only serve to obscure the true nature of mind. Once this nature has been recognized, however, problems and negativity automatically dissolve, leaving the open space of pure awareness, in which the qualities of enlightenment spontaneously unfold" (Dahl, 5). The aim in all of these meditation practices prioritizes the realization of *bodhicitta*. Bodhicitta [Sanskrit, "awakening mind"] is a sudden experience of manifesting compassion for all sentient beings.

While, as noted above, mahamudra was a core practice in Kagyu traditions, within Nyingma traditions the teachings and practices of *dzogchen* (Sanskrit, "great perfection") and *ngondro* (Tibetan, "that which goes before") were of similar central importance. Dzogchen [pronounced "Zog-chen"] refers to the natural condition of mind; and over time various meditative practices were developed to aid achievement of this natural condition. Within dzogchen an emphasis is placed upon attaining rigpa, a subtle form of self-reflective knowledge. The Dalai Lama describes the Nyingma tradition, for example, by their method of practice: "Those who practice the Nyingma system of meditation do not rely on actions for penetrating vital points of the vajra-body. They follow, instead, a guideline instruction for manifesting clear light mind by relying solely on meditation on a non-conceptual state."

> The dzogchen system emphasizes two main points in connection with the hidden path of tantra: (1) meditation on a correct view presented in terms of what has a devoid nature—namely, meditation on primordial clear light of mind, known in dzogchen terminology as rigpa, pure awareness—and (2) understanding all appearances as the play of clear light (Dalai Lama, *The Gelug/ Kagyu* 125).

While dzogchen focuses on a purely mental meditation upon emptiness, Nyingma tradition also prioritizes the practice of ngondro meditation, which uses various ritual, physical, and meditative techniques honing one's intelligence, loving compassion, and familiarity with the pantheon of Shingon deities. Ngondro [pronounced "nun-dro"], an analog to dzogchen, is the foundational or preliminary practice of Nyingma Tibetan Buddhism. Ngondro practice is often paired with samatha and vipassana yoga as the foundation for all Vajrayana practices. The ngondro practice is typically organized according to a five-part structure:

Part One: The Four Methods for Reversing One's Thoughts From Samsara.

Part Two: Taking refuge in the Buddha, dharma, and sangha, and then in gurus, deities, and dakinis.

Part Three: Developing bodhichitta, a special teaching of the mahayana, which is the beneficial thought of caring more for others than yourself.

Part Four: The mandala offering, which is particularly connected with accumulating merit and wisdom.

Part Five: The practice of Buddha Vajrasattva, who is a special deity of buddha of the vajrayana tradition (Sherab, 77).

Each offers a guided meditation rooted in a particular intention or perspective. Repetition within these activities is crucial. Ngondro practice has participants chanting mantras and performing prostrations up to and beyond 100,000 times. According to Trungpa, the full duration of carrying out the five methods and all their repetitions can take from 3-5 years. As we have already looked at mantra and mandala meditation, we should take a moment here to note the nature of prostration, which is another key technique in ngondro practice. As recounted by Dilgo Khyentse Rimpoche, the prior head of the Nyingma school of Tibetan Buddhism, prostration is performed as follows:

> To do prostrations properly, you touch the ground with five points—the forehead, the two hands, and the two knees. Another method, used by the Kadampas, is to fling yourself forward, letting the hands hit the ground before the knees. This is known as the full or extended prostration and is the most secret way of purifying impairments or the samaya. Before we begin the prostration, first we join the palms of our hands together at the level of the heart. The hands should not be held pressed flat against each other, but with an empty space in between them, so that they resemble a lotus bud about to burst into bloom. This symbolizes the blossoming of our bodhicitta. Then we raise our two joined hands to our forehead, consider that we are prostrating to the body aspect of all the buddhas, and pray:

May all the obscurations of my body be dispelled and

May I receive the blessing of realizing the body of all the buddhas!

Then we place our hands at the level of the throat, consider that we are prostrating to the speech aspect of all the buddhas, and pray:

May all the obscurations of my speech be purified and

May I receive the blessing of realizing the speech of all the buddhas!

Finally, we place our hands at the level of our heart and pay homage to the heart, or mind, aspect of all the buddhas, praying:

May all the obscurations of my mind be clarified and

May I receive the blessing of realizing the mind of all the buddhas! (Rinpoche, 44).

In 1976 the Yeshe Nying Po center, a Tibetan Nyingma Buddhist meditation facility, was founded on West 16th Street in Manhattan. Russell was friends with poet and Buddhist John Giorno, whom had also played a significant role in getting the center founded. Up through the early 1980's Russell would attend workshops, such as for the practicing of ngondro, which was offered by the center. It was at one such ngondro session in the Shrine Room, in 1979, that Russell would meet Tej Hazarika. Hazarika is the son of renowned Assamese singer Bhupen Hazarika. Having lived with his mother in Africa during his childhood, Hazarika moved to New York at the age of 17, in 1969. He developed a deep interest in Mahayana and Vajrayana Buddhism and began formal study under Dudjum Rimpoche. After meeting Hazarika and discovering his interest in music, Russell invited Hazarika to play some of Russell's songs, alongside friends Steven Hall and Kent Goshorn. After only a few rehearsals they even managed to have an audition with the President of Columbia records, Clive Davis, but as Hazarika recalls, "nothing much came of that." Reflecting on their collective pursuit Hazarika says, "we had one foot in the Mudd Club and the other in the Shrine Room, and [we were] trying to bridge the current from one to the other" (Hazarika, 2013).

As far as the relationship between music and Buddhist practice, Hazarika—like Russell—was focused on their integration. "It was work," Hazarika emphasizes, "because you're dealing with a lot of information... that has to be—first of all, understood—before you can start integrating it all. But there's an intuition that lets you know... it's all connected. It's definitely connected. Integration, you do it all the time. That's what keeps you alive!" (Hazarika, 2013). Hazarika would often meet at Russell's East Village apartment, or after gatherings at the Yeshe Nying Po center. Their conversations would often reflect upon and critique lamas, gurus, and other spiritual personages who passed through the city for lectures.

Russell was intensely critical of everything. He was quick to analyze and find faults, and equally quick to criticize and analyze himself with the same intense scrutiny. Nevertheless, during this time Russell met frequently with Kyabje Dudjom Rimpoche. Kyabje was a lama in the Nyingma school of Tibetan Vajrayana and would regularly visit the Tibet Center in New York City, ultimately choosing to live in New York during his last few years of life. Meetings with the Dudjom were like consultations with a priest and a friend. Jai Uttal was an old friend from Russell's days at the Ali Akbar Khan College. On Utall's website I found another person by the name of "Priya Das a.k.a. dumb bhikku," who recalled reconnecting with Russell years later in New York, where Russell brought him, and likely many others, to meet the Dudjom:

> Arthur brought me, with a little groundless trepidation on my part, to see Dudjom Rimpoche. Arthur had been sweeping the floors in the center unsolicited, and people thought that he was a homeless person doing it for money. They would make him take out the trash. As soon as we entered Dudjom's crowded chamber he gave us a look, subtle as only a master of Tantra and Terma could, slight turn of the head, sparkle in the eyes that could also be as dark and deep as to look right into the great void, he made

everyone sitting part for us to pass, and sat us down 4 inches in front of him and his table. I don't remember any questions, teaching, nara. Just pure presence (Uttal, 2009).

Hazarika recalls some more elaborate Vajrayana practices being performed during some of Russell's solo concerts in 1979. Though it is unusual to publicly perform prostration, Russell told Hazarika that one night he prostrated before the audience. Generally speaking, prostration is a ritualized physical gesture of submission and reverence—it may be encountered in numerous religious traditions. It is usually performed in private or before one's guru. Perhaps it was an especially horrible or wonderful crowd? Or perhaps Russell was seeking to transmit the dharma through "performing" Buddhist ritual itself? Hazarika was surprised and impressed when Russell told him of this concert prostration. "I'd never heard of anyone doing that before" he recalls. And his testimony of Russell having done this is the only one I've encountered. As with many aspects of Russell's music and life, we are left with mysterious fragments.

In regards to other aspects of ngondro, we have already noted Russell's use of mandala meditation, part four of ngondro practice. Russell was also focused on realizing bodhicitta (enlightened mind), the third part of ngondro practice. There are several instances in his notebooks where he acknowledges such realizations: "Thinking of my parents makes me think of bodhicitta," "fun present (be) (bodhicitta)," and elsewhere, "my old friend Cynthia (bodhicitta)... that buzzy feeling" (Russell, N). It was in like manner that Russell offered his music, as a sonic recognition, thanks, and prayer of loving kindness for all sentient beings. Certainly Russell could set aside the heft of spiritual discipline, as Steven Hall recalls the works they collaborated on were "basically a very dirty joke" (Hall, 2005). But as his once friend and business partner Will

Socolov recalled, Russell expressed equal concern with both musical playfulness as well as musical profundity. "Music can heal," Socolov recalls him saying. "Music isn't something that you just go dancing to, but that it can really heal you" (Wolf, 2009).

Music's role in esoteric spiritual practices has been noted and celebrated across the globe for centuries, and it plays no small part in Vajrayana Buddhism. The use of mantra, drone, repetition and trance, symbolic sounds, extra-musical imagery, and numerous other aspects of the "twilight language" would endlessly serve Russell's musical trajectory. But Russell never limited himself to Buddhism alone, he explored other esoteric traditions and practices, which he would incorporate into his "bubblegum music." Beyond Buddhist *bodhicitta*, it was the droning "buzzy feeling" of the sitar that roped Russell's ears into devotional North Indian music during his first years in California, while he would go on to explore other esoteric influences, including numerology and astrology throughout his time in New York during 1970's.

III.

OTHER ESOTERIC INFLUENCES

HINDUSTANI MUSIC:

A Sonic Theology

During his time at the commune, Russell, going by his birth name, enrolled at the Ali Akbar College of Music in 1970, where he would take courses over the next couple of years. He took courses directly with sarod master Ali Akbar Khan, often referred to as Khansahib, and Indian bamboo flute (*bansuri*) player G. S. Sachdev. Though the cello was yet to find its place in North Indian musical tradition, Russell persisted playing and as he recalled to David Toop, "cello is

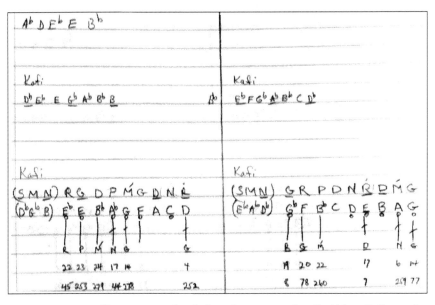

Image 11. Russell's music notebook from his time at the Ali Akbar College of Music. It is unclear what Russell's numerical notation refers to (Russell, BN).

Ali Akbar Khan's favorite instrument" (Lawrence, *Hold On* 27). Much of his study occurred off college grounds, with fellow students and local musicians, like flautist Jeff Whittier, Ellen Ziegler, Alan Abrams, and others, joining to explore different *ragas, talas,* and *bhajans.* Through North Indian music Russell found that the spiritual discipline he encountered at Warwick's ascetic commune could now be completely devoted to music itself. And while North Indian music can be taught and heard in exoteric fashion, its' Hindustani roots are to be found in the same sources that gave rise to Vajrayana Buddhism, that is, from the Vedas of ancient India. But in 1960's America, these esoteric devotional sounds were being imported and spread with increasing interest. Before going into Russell's more specific training, there are some general phenomena of Hindustani music that were of significant influence to Russell, such as the function of drone, the significance of the syllable, the role of ras or mood, and the importance given to disciplined practice, or *riaz.*

The spiritual discipline that Russell had been pursuing through Buddhist traditions easily transferred to devotional aspects of North Indian music. The musical expression of Hindu thought largely evolved out of the esoteric Bhakti movement, which combined Vedic-based mantra with classical ragas and talas. These devotional songs are known as bhajans, which we met in the previous chapter, where they were merged with the mantric chant of Buddhist sutras on Bay Area concert stages. An ancient Indian conception of sound, *nada brahma* ("Sound is God"), expresses how important music was within this spiritual tradition. As Vedic bija syllables were incorporated into Buddhist mantra, in India the voice, speech, and music were conceived through the esoteric concept of nada brahma, via *nada yoga* ("sonic yoga").

The adepts in Yoga perceive the communion of Sive [primordial ground; masculine] and Sakti [primordial cosmic energy; feminine] in every elemental sound (*nada*) and in every letter representing it. Siva is the common unchanged soul of all sounds and letters, and this is indicated by the bindu attached to every letter. Sakti assumes the diversified forms of sounds and letters (*nada* and *varna*). All forms of articulate speech, all forms of verbal expressions of mental ideas, all kinds of words and sentences uttered apparently by human tongues (and recorded in various written forms), are complex manifestations of original *nada* and *varna*. Yogis therefore perceive the self-manifestation of Siva and Sakti in all of them (Beck, 101).

It is through this conception that a spiritual practice of audition developed, in an extreme example, into a sonic meditation upon silence, or internal audition:

Let [the *yogi*] close the ears with his thumbs… This is my most beloved *yoga*. From practicing this gradually, the Yogi begins to hear mystic sounds (*nadas*). The first sound is like the hum of the honey-intoxicated bee, the next that of the flute, then of the harp; after this, by the gradual practice of Yoga, the destroyer of the darkness of the world, he hears the sounds of ringing bells; then sounds like roar of thunder. When one fixes his full attention on this sound, being free from fear, he gets absorption (*laya*)… when the mind of the Yogi is exceedingly engaged in this sound, he forgets all external things, and is absorbed in this sound (*nada*) (103).

The origins of traditional Hindustani music are rooted in this esoteric sonic theology. Russell's teachers at the Ali Akbar College were explicit about this spiritual lineage and its underlying intentionality in music. G. S. Sachdev, who had joined the college to teach in 1970, the same year Russell arrived, reflects in a more recent interview: "I feel that sound is God, *Nada Brahma* […] I am religious, for sure, but I think spirituality goes beyond [religion]. I feel that every human being is a spiritual person. Some have awakened that aspect of spirituality within themselves. Religion helps that to awaken. The rituals are a reminder […] We all have gifts. My music is God's gift" (Sachdev, 1989).

Just as the syllable was of fundamental importance in Vajrayana Buddhism, sharing a mutual Vedic source, the syllable is fundamentall in Hindustani music. George Ruckert, who co-wrote the textbook for the Ali Akbar College of Music, reflects on this syllabic primacy:

> We can watch this at work from the naming of the pitches, to the abstract patterns of drum and dance, to the disintegration of a song text in performance. The meaning of music is often abstracted beyond the syntactical meaning of words, and most musicians spend their artistic life in finding this point of balance between a syllable's verbal evocation and its utility in rhythmic combination and textural abstraction (Ruckert, 8).

This of course recalls us to the veneration of syllabic language we just met in Vajrayana Buddhist practices, as in the "A-Gate Meditation," or more general mantric practices which utilize the *bija*, or seed syllables, such as *om*. Stemming from the same Vedic sources as Buddhist mantra, the syllable in North Indian music manifests as a non-verbal solfege informed by detailed nuances concerning the musical relationship of the tones in a given raga. It is used similarly in regards to tala, in the form of an analogous rhythmic solfege. The texts associated with fixed compositions are often given over to spontaneous vocal abstraction. Furthermore, a single tone, by itself, may be inflected in numerous ways through vocal ornamentation and microtonal embellishment. One thing that defines Russell's vocal style is the use of microtonal inflection, which Indian music prioritizes by the name *shruti* (Sanskrit, "hearing, listening"), which is the smallest audible pitch interval: "I am still learning about the microtones," Ali Akbar Khan once noted, "[t]hey reach to your heart and help you feel the rags and the notes. In old theory, they say that there are twenty-two in number, but right now I feel that there are more like twenty-three and a half" (260). Despite the often indefinite theory that is put into practice, shrutis play a significant role in characterizing a raga as well as being resources for the refinement of a performers' expression of a given rag. While not systematized, as they are in Hindustani raga singing, Russell's vocals are filled with nuanced melismas, which clearly reflect his raga studies.

This emphasis on a single syllable would find its ultimate musical manifestation through the use of drone, which in N. Indian music is made by strumming the tanpura instrument. Dane Rudhyar would devote an entire book to the importance of "tone" in his *The Magic of Tone*. He channels Hindustani sonic theology to inform Varèse' phenomenological concept of sound [e.g. "Music is organized sound"] with his more holistic and extra-musical concept of "tone."

> [Music is "organized sound"…] Varèse used to say that of course, but […] rather than [saying] music is sound, I say music is tone. And I think there is a great difference between tone and sound. Now, sound is anything that makes sound, but tone is something which is quite a different thing. [Y]ou speak of the tone of a life, the tone of the body, the tone of the morale… of things like that. It is something which is related to a whole, to a living whole, to a living organism, it has tone. And sound is a tone when it is a living thing (Ertan, 171).

This focus on the phenomenological and extra-musical aspects of tone and the more holistic concept of drone were becoming key concepts and concerns in mid-20th century music, exemplified in the works by minimalists, such as Terry Riley, Steve Reich, Pauline Oliveros, La Monte Young, Phill Niblock, Tony Conrad, and numerous others, many of whom were students of Hindustani music.

Russell would use or imitate the tanpura in many of his own works—harmonica, Casio keyboard, strings, and numerous other instruments would supply the drone element. He would also incorporate the tabla or imitate its lithe but frenetic style of percussion on his cello. One of Russell's earliest folk recordings was the cover of Tex Ritter's "Goodbye, Old Paint." Russell begins the song with a 1-minute introduction of tanpura drone overlaid with composed atonal chamber instruments. Drone also had a strong presence in Russell's dance music, as on *24>24 Music, Let's Go Swimming,* and "In the Light of a Miracle." Many of Russell's collaborations with trombonist/composer Peter Zummo and the Singing Tractors band would focus on more drone-based experiments, often with explicit N. Indian references. While works like Zummo's "Song IV" (Arthur Russell, cello/voice; Peter Zummo, trombone; Bill Ruyle, tabla; Mustafa Ahmed, percussion) reinforced the importance of improvisation, mood, drone, endless melody, and echo all floating like smoke above the tactus of Ahmed's tabla.

Russell's approach to music was very contextual and holistic. He was attuned to the lunar calendar and the numerological meanings of his work titles. This extra-musical concern for social and environmental context was of great importance to Hindustani music. This is expressed by the conception of ras within North Indian musical tradition. A performer is always attempting to express the ras, or sentiment, of a raga. There are officially up to nine ras', collectively called navaras, or "the nine moods" (Khan, 275):

Karuna	sadness, pathos
Shringar	love, joy
Vira	heroism, valor
Hasya	laughter, comedy
Raudra	anger
Bhayanaka	fear
Vibhatsa	disgust
Adbhuta	surprise
Shanti	peace

The moods listed here were historically developed through their role in dramatic performance and theatre. Music was said to express all but anger, fear, disgust, and surprise, which are best expressed in dramatic performance. Over time a rich discourse and vocabulary developed to refine a musician's *bhavas*, which are more nuanced expressions of a given rasa. Many ragas and their associated ras' further divide these raga correspondences into eight hourly calendars, *prahars* which outline the raga correspondences in 3-hour increments over a 24-hour period. Before performing, the musician chooses a raga composition based on the time of day, the mood of the audience, and the feel of the performance space. This direct feedback and holistic concern then reinforces what is played and how it is expressed by the performer.

Though Russell attended the lunar calendar, he never referred explicitly to the concept of ras. However, in his notebooks he seemed to be trying to identify the moods of different works-in-progress. After asking "What is the interface of bliss + interesting?" he then lists several of his own song titles, from the *Calling Out of Context* era, with associated moods:

Deer in the Forest = bliss
I am a Saxophone = bliss
Hiding your present = fun
Platform on the Ocean = thought
Kissing = fun (Russell, SN)

As will be noted in subsequent chapters, Russell often accompanied his solo performances, as well as some ensemble works, with video or slide projections, typically of natural landscapes, children, or animals. In part this was a manner of establishing and reinforcing a kind of mood, often one of vulnerability, gentleness, playfulness, etc. Creating and sustaining a mood was of greater concern than the explication of any musical narrative or performative and compositional virtuosity. Through mood, one literally becomes saturated with the sound of a given disposition or feeling. Russell was very sensitive to this, and it is one reason why his works leaned towards minimalism, often being long in duration and lacking a specific beginning or end. Through the lens of Buddhism Russell often speaks of his music in aquatic terms, while the music itself has often been described by critics as "oceanic." As he makes known in his early works, Russell's music is vast and potentially endless. Like his audience, Russell could plug in and plug out as he desired, for he was tapping into an endless reservoir of sound and spirit.

Ultimately the virtuosity and mastery of Hindustani music, itself sourced to this endless reservoir, is found through disciplined practice. But the conception of "practice" in Hindustani music is informed by a more in depth spiritual intentionality than simply learning one's ragas and talas, or being able to play rapidly and accurately. As percussionist and friend Bill Ruyle noted upon first meeting Russell, "our first conversation had to do with Indian music, because I had just begun studying tabla—this was in the summer of 1974. And Arthur [after I told him]—his eyes lit up."

> **AR:** Oh, well I studied Indian music at Ali Akbar College of Music.
> **BR:** Well, of course I've heard of that.
> **AR:** So, you study tabla... Well, do you practice?
> **BR:** yeah
> **AR:** [emphatically] Everyday?! (Ruyle, 2012)

And amongst his closest musician friends at the time there was always discussion of the philosophical and spiritual aspects of Hindustani music in particular and music in general. One term frequently encountered in Hindustani music (and mentioned by Russell's collaborators from this period) is riaz. It's a significant term in approaching Russell's process. So let's briefly look to some helpful descriptions:

Riaz is the means by which the music student, having received instruction in both mechanical technique and musical definitions, "puts it all together." Having imparted the information, the teacher can only provide guidance and supervision of the student's individual journey towards internalizing and actualizing the music within him/herself. Riaz itself, then, turns into the ultimate lesson where the student interacts with the traditional structures on his/her own individual terms; indeed, Hindustani musicians often regard riaz as an art and an end in itself (Neuman, 36).

The Arabic word riaz came into North Indian languages via Persian. Above the meaning of "lucubration," "laborious study," the Persian usage of the word usually denotes "mortification," "rigour," "asceticism," meanings that are generally reserved for describing self-discipline toward a spiritual end (Simms, 9).

Russell clearly saw riaz "as an art and an end in itself." His friend Whittier recalls Russell being obsessed with riaz during his time in California: "Arthur would talk about the process being as important as the goal [...] I didn't entirely agree, because as a musician you are defined by how you play at a given time, and the product is the measure of the riaz. But Arthur would say that the process was more important than the end product" (Lawrence, *Hold On* 40). From his time at the Kailas Shugendo commune, Russell would have been likely to view riaz more in terms of this spiritual asceticism through extended physical striving—Shugendo ritual and cello playing. Whereas Warwick increasingly criticized Russell's obsession with music, Hindustani traditions provided him with complete musical abandon paired with rigorous spiritual discipline, a holy musical practice.

Just as Buddhism has various branches or schools of thought, the same is true for North Indian music, which is grouped according to various *gharanas*, or traditional schools of disciples lead by a *guru*, or "teacher." Russell's teacher, Ali Akbar Khan's practice was based in the Maihar gharana. Khan founded the Ali Akbar College of Music in Berkeley, CA in 1967. This latter recording was, for many American musicians, there first taste of North Indian music. A significant aspect of the Maihar gharana was its emphasis on tala, or rhythmic modes; and Maihar musicians are known for being skilled in various difficult talas and their complex manipulations of them. Russell was deeply influenced by this approach to rhythmic organization, with a majority of his compositions employing constantly changing rhythmic groupings. This virtuosic approach to the rhythms of tala, which was a defining feature of Maihar, was not unparalleled in the Maihar approach to melodic raga. In a contemporary digital curriculum pamphlet, the College defines raga as follows:

> It specifies rules for movements up and down the scale, which notes should figure more prominently, and which notes should be used more sparingly, which notes may be sung with various kinds of ornamentation, phrases to be used, phrases to be avoided, and so on. The result is a framework that can be used to compose or improvise melodies, allowing for endless variation within the set of notes (Khan, "Indian Music").

This approach to scored improvisation would remain a core element in Russell's creative process and in his unique conception of minimalism. And as Russell himself would synthesize numerous genres, it is appropriate to note that the more general musical aesthetic of Maihar practice was rooted in the synthesis of various popular, classical, and esoteric Indian styles that the gharana's originator, Ustad Allauddin Khan, famously fused together. However, the influence of the devotional aspects of dhrupad repertoire and the improvisational priorities of khyal repertoire were primary influences in the development of Maihar music. And the bhajan repertoire—including the forms of dhrupad, kirtan, and other devotional song forms—is the primary devotional repertoire of North Indian musical tradition in general.

In dhrupad, for example, a particular raga is drawn from a traditional corpus of fixed compositions based on Vedic scripture emphasizing divine love. These fixed compositions are usually formally preceded by an introductory section, called the *alap*. The alap—Sanskrit for "conversation"--is typically more free in form, de-emphasizing rhythm (tala), creating an abstract field of sound within which the notes of the raga are gradually revealed or introduced. Akbar Khan describes the alap as when "[…] you go someplace nice for a visit—like you go to France for a vacation. Then you come home and write a letter or tell your friend about where you were—where you stayed, what you did, what you saw, what you ate—like that the memory of the compositions come in the alap" (4). Khan compares the performance of dhrupad to "carrying a very full glass of water […] If you move quickly, you will spill the water, and like that you spoil the dhrupad" (290). Russell savored the atmosphere of the alap, its fuzzy memory and projective imagination leading to creative allusions and alternatives, and his intuitive drive was perfectly suited to the role of improvisation that the fixed songs are opened to during performance.

Khan was one of three significant Indian musicians to effectively introduce and teach the North Indian traditions to the people of America. Ali Akbar Khan was the first Indian classical musician to perform (sarod) on television, and the first to record a raga performance for album release (*Music of India: Morning and Evening Ragas*). The second critical musician was fellow maihar gharana student Ravi Shankar. In the 1960's through touring, teaching, and recording, Ravi Shankar would have an immediate impact on American popular music. He was friends with record-label owner Richard

Bock, at whose studios the Byrds were recording in 1965. The Byrds heard his music at the studio, fell in love with it, and shared it with the Beatles' George Harrison. Harrison would befriend Shankar, and it was their collaboration that helped expand awareness of Indian music worldwide. In the early 1970's Shankar would become Chair of the Department of Indian Music at the California Institute of the Arts. The third significant musician was Pandit Pran Nath. Pandit Pran Nath, of the Kirana gharana, moved to New York in 1970, founding the Kirana Center for Indian Classical Music there. While Pran Nath's presence in the media was significantly less than Shankar and Akbar Khan, he nevertheless had a significant influence on the emerging minimalist movement that was starting at the time, during which he would teach a majority of the artists within this scene. Regardless, through the travels, teaching, and popular influence of these three Indian artists and teachers, the raga tradition of North India would blossom and spread through America.

Pandit Pran Nath was instructed by his guru to take a wife and move to America for the specific purpose of spreading the *Kirana* style, which he did, effectively making the *Kirana* style the most influential gharana in New York. It was through Nath and his philosophy of musical practice that downtown minimalism found an aesthetic precedent. Pran Nath taught a majority of Manhattan's downtown musicians and artists, including Jon Hassell, LaMonte Young, Terry Riley, Charlemagne Palestine, Michael Harrison, Catherine Christer Hennix, and Russell's early mentor W.A. Mathieu. Many of Russell's contemporary friends were also studying with Pran Nath—like Rhys Chatham, Don Cherry, Jon Gibson, Elodie Lauten, and Henry Flynt. Pran Nath's influence, along with Harry Partch, in large part created the increasing interest in micro-tonal music that would have a strong presence in experimental American composition. And while Russell wasn't counting cents like Partch or LaMonte Young, microtonality has a rich presence in Russell's music both in his vocal style and in his use of drone textures. But Russell's affinity with Pran Nath lies above all in the latter's unique spiritual intentionality.

According to Terry Riley, Pran Nath "strongly believed that music should be an offering to God. In that sense it should have its purest intentions, always have the musician's deepest concentration, and that the musician should make this offering as beautiful and pure as he can. And in this way, he never thought of himself as singing for people. He used to say many times that, if a musician is saying to himself as he's singing, 'I am singing for other people,' then this would be a second rate kind of music. But if it's an offering for God, then it's done with the deepest emotional, mental, spiritual, and physical perfection" (Riley, 1996). Renowned musicologist, Bonnie C. Wade's describes Pran Nath's style as follows:

> Nath sings strikingly few *tans*; those that he does sing are very slow, with a loose vibrato that tends to hide the pitches. [His] espousal of slow speed and eschewance of fast speed are seen in the minimal acceleration pattern—practically none at all—that he follows in his performances, and also in the speed of his *chota khyals* [...] He clearly prefers slow, sustained singing, with primary attention given to the *raga* in *alap*, subtleties of intonation, and connections between pitches. He carries out his preferences with superb artistry (Wade, 224).

While the more exoteric devotion of Khan and Shankar were in Russell's formal education, the more esoteric musical philosophy of Pran Nath was thick in the air around him. And though Russell's formal study of Hindustani music would cease following his move to New York, he continued incorporating what he learned from the Ali Akbar College. He would appropriated a raga-like improvisation practice, a frequent use of drone (whether via Russell's cello, Casio keyboard, or orchestral composition), and the appropriation of

Indian instruments (tabla, sitar, etc). He placed a mutual emphasis on the primacy of the syllable and the abstraction of language. And he exercised a lifelong application of riaz. But beyond Buddhism and Hinduism, Russell was making use of any and all formal approaches to honing his intuition and the receptive spontaneity of first thoughts. From the 1970's into the 1980's Russell was drawn towards numerology, which aided his process of choosing song, band, and album titles.

NUMEROLOGY

Numbers and number-relations meant more to antiquity than they do to us, for we have lost the sense of mystery of number through our familiarity with price-lists, statistics, and balance sheets. The secret of the number 7 was well known; to conquer it was to become the master or the destroyer of the world. It is understandable that such a mystic and unfathomable number should have been looked upon as holy. And in the world of tone, too, we must acknowledge the holy circle to be inaccessible.

Paul Hindemith (Adamenko, 186)

[Arthur] looked to numerology to make sure he was choosing the best dates and song and album titles, in relation to proper number sequences and totals.

Tom Lee ("An Interview with Tom Lee")

Following practices found in the spiritual traditions of the Indian Vedas, Jewish Kabbalah, and other esoteric traditions, many composers would go on to be inspired by the practical and symbolic language of numbers to guide their creative process. During the Italian Renaissance, magician and philosopher Marsilio Ficino followed the numerology laid out in Jewish Kabbala while developing astrologically derived harmonies. J.S. Bach used letter-number correspondences to embed words in his instrumental works—many other composers would follow suit, including Claude Debussy, Arnold Schoenberg, William Grant Still, Alan Hovhaness, Karlheinz Stockhausen, John Cage, Morton Feldman, Alvin Lucier, et al.

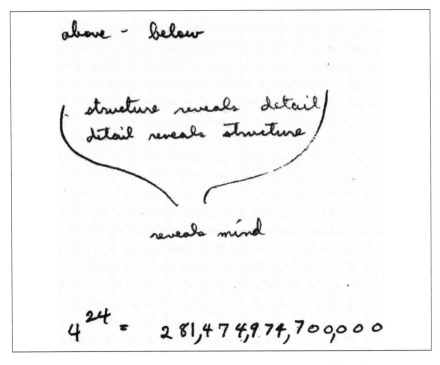

Image 12. Esoteric mathematical doodling (Russell, BN)

Arnold Schoenberg, father of the twelve-tone method, was a devout numerologist, particularly fearing the ill-fated number of his death year (76) and the number "3." John Cage, having explored formalist "rhythmic proportions" in his early years, would be rolling dice and consulting the *I-Ching* for the rest of his life.

Meanwhile one could meet numerological perspectives even in the realm of popular music. Bob Dylan, speaking of the revelatory triplet patterns in the music of Lonnie Johnson, would say: "I'm not a numerologist. I don't know why the number 3 is more metaphysically powerful than the number 2, but it is" (159). And inspired to embrace this technique in his own music, he described its' triadic nature as "an incantation code to infuse my vocals" (161). Suffice it to say that numerology and music have had a long history together, and Arthur Russell is part of that history.

Russell's initial exposure to numerology would likely have occurred through his involvement in the Kailas Shugen-do commune, if not sooner, and would have been based in the Hindu and Chinese traditions that were absorbed into Buddhism in combination with the numerological tradition (*gematria*) of Jewish Kabbalah. Buddhist philosophy, with many of its tenets being imbued by the significance of their number of aspects (e.g. "the four noble truths," "the seven jewels of royal power," "the twelve stages of dependent origination," etc), or by geometric design, as in mandala arrays and in temple architecture, would often incorporate numerology into its teachings. Numerological symbolism is of great importance, especially, in esoteric and tantric traditions.

Regardless, Russell's interest seemed to have been catalyzed through a semi-romantic relationship, during the mid 1970s, with filmmaker and photographer Kirk Winslow. Russell would part ways with Winslow before starting a domestic relationship with Tom Lee, but Winslow would continue numerological consultation with Russell up through 1980. Lee recalls, that "with the help of his friend, Kirk Winslow, [Russell] looked to numerology to make sure he was choosing the best dates and song and album titles, in relation to proper number sequences and totals" ("Q&A"). Steven Hall recalls more specifically, "Kirk approved the name of every group that Arthur and I played together in. Arthur would adjust or change titles of works according to Kirk's suggestions. A simple letter change in a word or group of words would make that title and by extrapolation the work itself more powerful and effective. This consultation was of key importance to him—as much as recording on the full moon and editing on

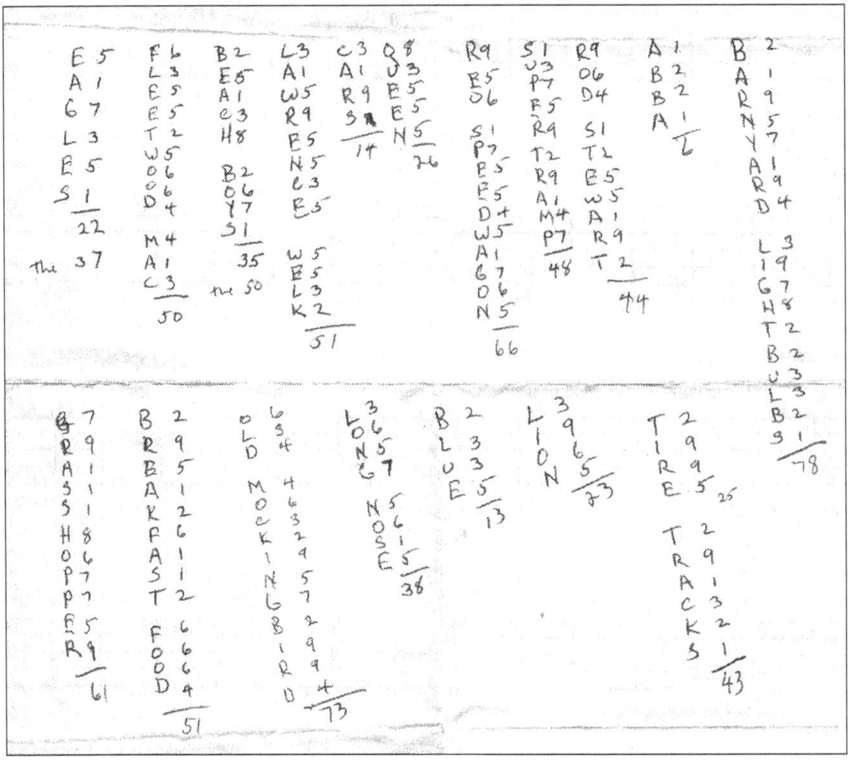

Image 13. Russell checks the numerological value of some of his favorite bands (Russell, SN)

the new moon" (Lawrence, *Hold On* 270). Russell's notebooks are filled with numerological additions. I found calculations for many future album and band titles: *Instrumentals*, Turbo Sporty, Dinosaur L, *World of Echo*, *Tower of Meaning*, Singing Tractors, and others. He even calculated the numerological value of existing popular bands like The Eagles, Fleetwood Mac, and The Beach Boys (image 13).

Unfortunately, while Russell practiced numerology for years, there is no way of knowing what he used to interpret those numbers. None of Russell's friends knew or could recall, while many that may have known, have since passed away. Before her recent passing, in 2014, I met with Elodie Lauten to talk about Russell. She said she shared his interest in numerology. I asked her what she used to interpret the numbers, and she handed me a popular numerology book, the kind one might find in a grocery store or novelty shop. Though used formally in certain cultural traditions, numerology is primarily a popular pastime. There is no credentialed, comprehensive, scholarly, or objective study of numerology's history and practice in current literature. In lieu of that I will offer my own general interpretations of Russell's numerology, based on Buddhist numerological associations and popular Western numerology literature, both of which likely informed Russell's personal interpretation to some degree.

Evidenced by his notebooks, Russell worked with a common numerological system that assigned a numerical value to each letter of the alphabet. He often wrote down the association table (below) for his own reference. In this table numbers, 1-9, are assigned to the 26 letters of the alphabet. After the 9th letter of the alphabet, "I," letters are assigned a larger successive number (e.g. 10-26). The individual digits of this double digit number are then added together to arrive at a corresponding single digit number, 1-9:

1	A, J (10)	S (19)
2	B, K (11)	T (20)
3	C, L (12)	U (21)
4	D, M (13)	V (22)
5	E, N (14)	W (23)
6	F, O (15)	X (24)
7	G, P (16)	Y (25)
8	H, Q (17)	Z (26)
9	I, R (18)	

We'll note numerological interpretations of specific works in later chapters, but let's take a quick look now at an example from Russell's notebooks. In finding the name for his album *World of Echo*, Russell had calculated several alternative titles, adjusting the number of letters in the group of words. He began with "crossover thru sound of echo" (2), which was shortened to "sound of echo" (8), and finally the numerologically preferred "world of echo" (7):

$$W - 23 \ (2+3=5)$$
$$O - 15 \ (1+5=6)$$
$$R - 18 \ (1+8=9)$$
$$L - 3$$
$$D - 4$$
$$O - 15 \ (1+5=6)$$
$$F - 6$$
$$E - 5$$
$$C - 3$$
$$H - 8$$
$$O - 15 \ (1+5=6)$$

$$\overline{61 = 6 + 1 = \boxed{7}}$$

When we add it all up, we meet the "holy" number, seven, which Hindemith glorified in the quote at the top of the chapter. Generally considered, the number seven seems to be tied to a grand task of spiritual evolution. From a Buddhist perspective the number 7 might represent the seven steps that Buddha walked upon first being born; or how Kukai practiced mantra seven years before finally mastering it. In one interpretation, via popular numerology, one author says that the number 7 is, "a symbol of humankind's attempt at achieving a higher state of development, expression, and a rarefied understanding of life and the universe. When you attempt to perfect any physical object, or to attain a humanitarian or spiritual ideal, you are feeling the influence of the number 7 in your life" (Decoz, 179). Above all, interpretations such as these would have reinforced the resolve that Russell sought to identify with. The mood or disposition of these interpretations would have "set the stage" for a project. As we'll see, the composition of *World of Echo* would indeed be under a "holy" septenary influence.

Perhaps this interest in numerology also attracted Russell to some of his notational preferences. In his scores, durations were never notated in traditional metric symbols, the standard grouping of rhythms common to Western European notation practice. Implying a constant, if sometimes slowed-down or inaudible 4-on-the-floor pulse, Russell would simply write the number of (quarter-note) pulses for a given bar of music, a single sound. It's unclear the extent to which numerology played into the numbers we find in his scores. He very well may have been exploring numerological additions in the composition of his meters.

Even in his earliest compositions Russell was applying mathematics to his compositional process. As in *Reach One* where he developed what he called a "numbers system," that was applied to the musicians' perceptions of their heartbeat. Still in other places, Russell's use of numbers remains indecipherable, at least to this author and Russell's collaborators. Peter Zummo, speaking for all of Russell's musical collaborators, once noted, "we all want to know what the numbers mean" (Zummo, 2012).

ASTROLOGY

Music, being identical with heaven, isn't a thing of momentary thrills, or even hourly ones. It's a condition of eternity.

Gustav Holst (Holmes, 62)

Perhaps no composer has ever been more associated with the planets and with astrology than Gustav Holst, whose *The Planets, Op. 32* (1916) remains the most popular musical portrait of the cosmos. Each piece of music corresponding to one of the seven planets and their corresponding emotional traits, this work has also become the culturally digested sound of cinematic moods, especially drama ("Mars") and mystery ("Neptune"), their harmonies and orchestrations being copied and imitated in film and video for decades now. Many centuries before Holst, Pythagoras had believed that affinities existed between the shared proportionality of musical pitches and intervals, planetary shapes and positions, and their associated numerology. And so the *musica universalis*, or "harmony of spheres" came into vogue in ancient Greece, enduring through the Middle Ages until the end of the Renaissance.

Inspired by this perspective and combining it with esoteric magical practices, Renaissance philosopher and astrologer, Marsilio Ficino, wrote therapeutic songs about the planets, each with its own associated musical harmony. He would typically supplement the music with talismans, images, and composed lighting. Ficino describes his astrological music as follows:

> Such species of songs, composed appropriately and according to the rule of the stars, full to the utmost with sense and meaning, pronounced opportunely with vehement affection (arising not only from the number and proportion of the phrases but also

from their resulting form) and with the impetus of the imagination, confer the greatest power on the enchanter and immediately transmit it to the thing enchanted, directing it and binding it wherever the emotions and words of the enchanter are aimed (Tomlinson, 64).

It wasn't until the 1960's, during the counter-culture revolution, that astrology and cosmic imagery would find artistic expression in America.. This was especially prevalent in experimental jazz circles, including artists such as Sun Ra, who claimed he was from the planet Saturn, Alice and John Coltrane, who used astrological charts and planetary imagery to guide their compositions, and Mary Lou Williams, who composed her *Zodiac Suite* in 1945. In the broader avant-guard we find similar astrological explorations in the work of Pauline Oliveros, Karlheinz Stockhausen, and John Cage. Interestingly, composer Dane Rudhyar, mentioned above, would go on to become one of the most influential figures in American astrology, which he redefined in the humanistic and personality-based system that we popularly know today. From a personality perspective, Rudhyar's understanding of the moon—a common theme in Russell's music—returns us to the mind and it's potential to be transformed:

[T]he moon, when full, can be gazed at—though even that was thought by some races to involve definite risks. In her cool disc, she reveals to us the attenuated light and form of the sun. She makes solar activity objective, clearly perceptible; she transforms it into a thing to be analyzed. Thus, the moon is also a symbol of the human intellect, for it is the intellect's function to objectivize and analyze the effulgent outpourings of the spirit in man (Rudhyar, 21).

As we've already seen, the moon is rich with symbolism in Shingon Buddhism, being the primary focus in *gachirinkan* meditation. Buddhist festivals are often held on the New and Full moons, believed to be times of strength, spiritual power, and divine intuition. Buddha's enlightenment was thought to have been achieved beneath a full moon (Cashford, 54). The full moon is generally associated with a potency of creative energy. Buddhist beliefs, borrowing from Chinese astrology, would enrich the moon's symbolism by adding the image of a white hare, representing the weak shadow *ying* principle of the number two (Beer, 81). At the same time, solar symbolism was of course a prime concern in Shugendo. Being associated with the purifying flame of fire, the sun was also worshipped through the deity known as Nitten. Traditional Shugendo practice richly incorporated—through deity worship, symbolism, and ritual—consultation with and reverence for the sun, moon, planets, stars, and the cosmos as an infinite whole.

Russell himself was born on May 21st, on the night of a full moon, situating him on the cusp of both Taurus and Gemini. Russell's astrological interests were practically oriented and lunar-centric—he seemed primarily interested in the moon's activity. He is known for preferring to record on the night of a full moon and edit music on the night of the new moon. This lunar preference has a history of multi-cultural significance. And Russell is not alone on valuing lunar effects on creativity. As Tom Lee recounts: "He faithfully purchased a small lunar calendar each year and scheduled his studio recording times, and moments when he would cut his hair, around the times of a full moon, which was thought to give you an extra boost of energy and spirit" ("Q&A").

Russell's conception of *Instrumentals vol. 2* and *World of Echo*, both of which blur the pulse of terrestrial rhythm, was rooted in the idea of taking music into outer space, where, Russell says, "you can't take your drums with you, but your mind." Cosmic themes would enter into other works as well: "Radishes Flying to Jupiter," "This is How We Walk On The

Moon," "Ballad of the Lights," *Fuzzbuster* (the name of a radio transmitter), "In the Light of a Miracle," "Big Moon," and "Go Bang." Sleeping Bag Records, Russell's joint effort with Will Sokolov used, for their logo, a spaceship hovering above a sleeping bag abandoned in the woods. Numerous songs, such as "Love Comes Back," make lyrical references to lunar imagery: "we're meeting in the moonlight, when you are there. Buzzing in the moonlight... Love comes back..." While, in his notebooks Russell mentions a piece that never seemed to come to fruition: a "circle of casios as sketch for phases of moon piece." And this cosmic perspective could also influence the way Russell related to overdubbing a recording, for example. On a sketch for "Tell You Today" Russell compares his "personal time" perception with the fixed time of the pre-recorded track, which he calls "astrological time" (Russell, SN).

In a sea of numbers and cosmic imagery, in the "buzzing" hum of Hindustani music and of Buddhist mantra and meditation, by the young age of 23 Russell's spiritual sensibility had found a vast repository of techniques, concepts, and imagery, as well as a disciplined philosophical underpinning. His move to New York, in June of 1973, would catalyze his personal and musical evolution in ways he could never have anticipated. It was just a few months before this move, that Russell presented his debut public concert.

IV.

EXPERIMENTS IN FIRST THOUGHT:
The Early Notebooks of Arthur Russell

The Early Works

[It] opened with a piano and cello duet before it moved into a jazz set and culminated with a surreal sound clash that consisted of insane, random drum rolls, nonsensical overlapping voices, demented laughter, and bursts of discordant cello. In between acts, an announcer read extracts from an essay about the spiritual qualities of Bugs Bunny, "the archetypal mystic," who was "devised to teach important esoteric lessons" (*Hold On* 40).

Tim Lawrence

This is biographer Tim Lawrence's description of the first public performance of Russell's own compositions, which took place in Berkeley, California, March 16-17, 1973. This concert underscored Russell's sense of humor, which can be found throughout his music. In notes for rehearsals of this event, for example, Russell's scores had the performers playing "a game of whiffle ball," "heartbeat juggling number exercises," and "blindfolded space tests" (Russell, BN). A decade later Russell would describe comedy as "the highest form of art" (Owen, 1987). In fact much of his experimentalism had a comedic aspect.

In one of Russell's early works, "Barefoot in New York," he would channel the whimsical mayhem of this Berkeley concert. Below is an excerpt of this piece, which is recited over a repeating pop rhythm, in which Russell reflects on attending Buddhist lectures, listening to the Rolling Stones, and the effects of repetitive music.

> On Broadway, one night, there was this fairly high-pitched loud tone that sounded like a siren. People were looking around to see where it came from: the food-store on the corner provided a lot of the light, because it was open. Pretty soon I realized that the sound was coming from the hood of this one car that was parked on the street nearby. It was empty and locked, and as you walked toward it, it became even louder.

> > I first noticed the sound when I walked past the store,
> > But now that I know what it is
> > It's even worse than before.

> I was listening to a tape of a lecture on Buddhism at which I was present. I heard myself asking a lot of stupid questions.

> > I was thick-headed at the lecture sitting there on the floor,
> > but to hear it now, it's even worse than before.

> The question is whether or not this kind of music is going to hypnotize you. Do you resent being made to listen to this monotonous music? Or having to listen to such boring sentences? Friends have said that by producing this kind of music, people are put to sleep. In fact, I've always thought this too; I've always disliked the Rolling Stones since I found out what they were up to. So when the prospect of doing this very hypnotic music came to my mind, I realized that I should at least discuss with you the problem of listening to this kind of rhythm, that its regularity may temporarily take your mind off the more important tasks we have. I had to decide if it was in our best interest to present this.

> > But now that I went ahead and did it
> > After asking what it was for,
> > Now, it's even worse than before.
> > After my friends attacked this idea,
> > It made me stall,
> > It didn't seem like such a far out joke after all

> > > (Russell, BN).

Russell was in an intellectually-driven and youthful phase

of rejecting popular music. But he couldn't help but include it in his "high art" avant-garde early works, even if only as a critique, while announcing his draw to a hypnotic kind of minimalism. And in the final words, above, Russell reveals the piece itself to be a kind of joke, if just a little "far out".

While he consistently brought humor into his work, the seriousness with which he approached music also weighed heavy in his offerings. This is evident in the analytical drive that we see guiding his emerging compositional process. Trungpa spoke to the need for this intellectual labor in relation to music and film [italics by author]:

> We probably feel that in listening to classical music or jazz, or some other kind of music, we are identifying with the sound, or going along with it or dancing with it; or when we watch a good movie, we might forget that we are sitting in a chair watching a movie. But in actual fact, we are fascinated rather than being one with the sound or the movie. So tuning into the energy, cosmic energy, is very difficult. It's not a matter of just swinging with it. *It needs a lot of techniques and manipulations, so to speak* (Lion's Roar 207-08).

First thought may be best thought, but Russell was tirelessly devising systems, imagery, concepts, and other extra-musical methods to develop his work. Such intellectual manipulations were used not so much to formalize and fix the musical content, but rather, as Trungpa encouraged, to discipline the mind and tune into cosmic energy, allowing the music to channel this intentionality into the audible realm. And whether he was playing traditional folk music ("Cumberland Gap"), avant-garde scores (Christian Wolff's "Exercises"), or chanting mantra (with the Shugendo Mantric Sun Band), Russell's primary concern was in developing and nurturing this spiritual consciousness through his musical practice. Many of these early scores were written by Russell between the ages of 18 and 22. Though they might be viewed as immature works, they are all the more compelling for the fact that Russell had almost fully formed an idiosyncratic aesthetic at such a young age and, more significantly, one that he would continue developing his entire life.

As he sought to study and develop his musical practice, his compositional process became increasingly focused on the subjective experience of performing. Because of this intense self-reflection and underlying extra-musical intentionality, Russell could rarely rest with the simple expression of a song. Instead he was obliged to study this pleasure, or open it up to the unexpected, by coming up with all manner of restraints, catapults, and translatory procedures to make his music—those "techniques and manipulations" that Trungpa mentions above. Much of this inclination was fortified in Russell by his Buddhist studies: the Shugendo *goma* and *hiwatari* fire rituals, *samatha* and *vipassana* meditation practices, *shugyo* and *sadhana*, mandala visualization, mantra, numerology, astrology... Russell carried all of these practices with him to New York City, where they would be channeled directly into his music.

For Russell such techniques were used primarily to move beyond any default habits in his creative practice, to keep his attention vigilant and focused, to hone his intuition, if not simply to open himself up to new and unknown musical territory. Russell's pre-New York works focused on fully notated pieces of a tuneful nature, experimental open form works, with a more direct Buddhist influence than he would subsequently use, and a series of text scores, strongly influenced by Fluxus and Cagean aesthetics. While he was still a member of Kailas Shugendo, Russell was also studying composition privately with W. A. Mathieu, a composer combining experimental, jazz, improvisation, and new age aesthetics in his own work. Mathieu recalls Russell as follows: "At our first meeting he spent a great deal of time explaining what he was doing and why he was doing it and who he was […] It was a very strange mix of intellectual process and pop influence […] Arthur's compositions increased in complexity […] He was fascinated by the complexity, but he couldn't figure out a way to use it" (Lawrence, *Hold On* 30). Russell would explore some of this tuneful complexity in Allaudin's master class, through pieces such as *Piece for Speakers*:

> [Russell asked] each musician to wear a set of headphones and sit back-to-back in two rows of chairs, after which he provided each with a script, which combined text and music, and a link into a long line of string—maybe a line from the *Diamond Sutra*, or a sequence of notes drawn from a sheet of music, or a *raga*—that related to the Indian or Western tone playing through the headphones at that particular moment, and as the collage of mantra, voice, and sound developed, Russell began playing cello (Lawrence, *Hold On* 38-39).

Russell's score for this piece is extensive, including music notations, visual and choreographic diagrams, and textual notes. While he was essentially composing a work based on Buddhist sutras and poems, he also shows a proclivity for a rational process that functions not unlike a Rube Goldberg machine, a complicated and imaginative means for arriving upon a simple realization. "Piece for two speakers, four singers and assorted instrumentalists" was just that. Aside from purely sonic or visual elements, Russell tied string from the hands and feet of the singers and speakers. Pulling on the string, the speakers were able to cue the singers, and the singers one another, as indicated in the score. Feet pertained to speakers ("mouth"), while hands pertained to singers ("larynx"). In addition, using headphones—something Russell did frequently in his early compositions—the singers listened to different pre-recorded drones, which allowed them to tune their voices to the drone.

Both speakers have as their text 8 sentences (written on another sheet) from the *Mahavairocana Sutra*. There is one sentence to a measure, spoken freely though simultaneously, the first word of each falling on the first beat. From the individual words in the sentences, the speakers know, from their written parts, where to give cues. All action is "instigated" by the speakers; the exceptions are written in red. In addition, the speakers' words are mouthed silently, unless otherwise indicated, when they are audible. The text for the singers is from a "poem" by Lama Anagarika Govinda (*Hymn to Maitreya*). The reasons for using this technique, while not delving into what they might be or become here, are not for a theatrical end and are best appreciated through live performance (Russell, EWF).

Another work based upon Buddhist sutras, is *Maka Hannya Haramita Shingyo,* a piece intended for trumpet, cellos, and "Buddhist chorus." *Maka Hannya* is the Japanese translation of the Sanskrit *Prajnaparamita (Heart) Sutra*, which Russell would perform numerous times throughout his life, often accompanying Allen Ginsberg's idiosyncratic incantation.

Throughout his notebooks from this period—which he described as "barriers of my own making—record of thoughts"—Russell was explicitly and analytically interested in the subjective experience of listening, how it effects what one is playing or composing in the moment, and vice versa. Again, the musical drive is directed towards the mind, towards consciousness. Focusing on one's consciousness of the musical moment, the same musical content could be understood or engaged in numerous ways. Following are a series of fragments from his notebooks, each one highlighting Russell's fascination with how an underlying mental intentionality affects musical performance.

How [does the] mental rhythmic orientation influence [the] contextual meaning of [the] composed phrase?

[...] The ability to change the intention of the music using the same musical materials—changing the perspective seen through the musical events from an eclectic shift to a basic shift using abstract (disconnected/connected through space) concrete events.

Conceive different mental modes of editing or deciding—consciously contrasting them.

While line is being conceived, time changes, perspective changes (similar to mixing) [concept could be allowed to change]. How does the change effect sensation of velocity (speed of interaction)? Implies use of procedural composition of monophonic lines...

Find analytical system which is most appropriate in terms of the situation as others see it, and use it as a means. Seeing analysis as freeze-frame of phenomena, investigate altering flows of thoughts (Russell, SN).

This investigation of "altering flows of thought" would saturate Russell's approach to every style and genre. From his earliest music making Russell would be increasingly involved in songwriting, which he would continue throughout his life. Though he went through a brief phase of dismissing popular music, he would never let go of its influence. His early influences included Bob Dylan, The Rolling Stones, the Velvet Underground, and Fleetwood Mac, as well as a host of lesser known American folk songs, such as those by Tex Ritter, E.C. and Orna Ball, or Michael Hurley. But as might be assumed by now, Russell was rarely satisfied simply playing through the changes of a song. He sought to nudge their familiar qualities into unfamiliar territory. **Image 14** shows Russell's sketch for the traditional Appalachian folk song "Cumberland Gap."

Here we begin to see Russell's formative experimental approach, as applied to song. Breaking aspects of his playing into numerical (or alphabetical) lists, chance operations with dice/number, and irregular formal organization, with all offering an array of actions and potential variations, which could be creatively engaged both performatively or compositionally.

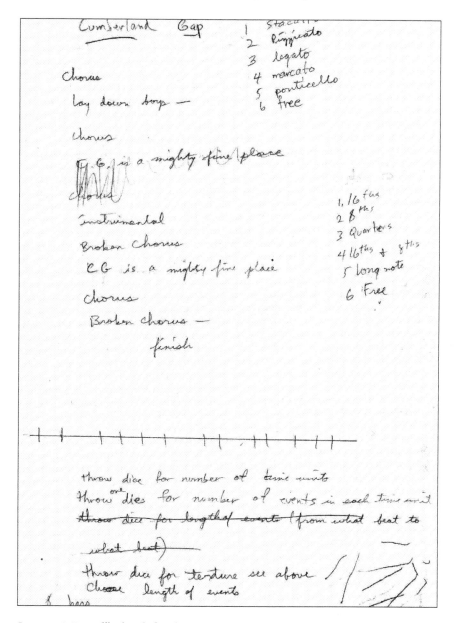

Image 14. Russell's sketch for the 19 century Appalachian folk song "Cumberland Gap" (Russell, BN)

Using the fixed structure of the song, Russell saw the interesting possibilities of subtly altering a familiar sounding tune by re-arranging its elements with a diligent kind of whimsy. Here, a throw of the dice accounted for the durations/ rhythms of sounds and for cello-playing techniques used in playing "Cumberland Gap." And often in Russell's notebook project musings, there is an explicit openness to including the opposite of what he first suggests. He constantly negates his original proposition, I presume, to remain open to alternate possibilities. Here's an example from his notebooks [italics by author],

> Composed solos or accompaniments which are executed over a long period for a short segment, designed to condense real time, but which also *are not* executed over a long period and *do not* condense real time (Russell, SN).

Meanwhile, in his own lyrics, Russell was exploring the intersections of the everyday and the transcendent. As we met in the previous chapter, this intersection was of prime concern for poets such as Ginsberg, Trungpa, Waldman, et al. Russell's notebooks are filled with musings, observations, found text, etc and often in non-linear lists or collages. He would then review his notebooks, extract his favorite observations, and re-write these into a new list. This new list would then serve as a reference for current and future works—a kind of "greatest hits" of his notebook fragments. On the next few pages we see two example pages from Russell's notebooks (**image 15** and **16**), and his self-made compilation of various notebook fragments (**image 17**):

While Russell may have continued to work on the "pop sound," his inherent experimentalism would drive him well beyond the realm of popular awareness or interest. Especially during his first few years in New York, Russell was steeped in avant-garde concerns. Going back to 1973, Russell attended

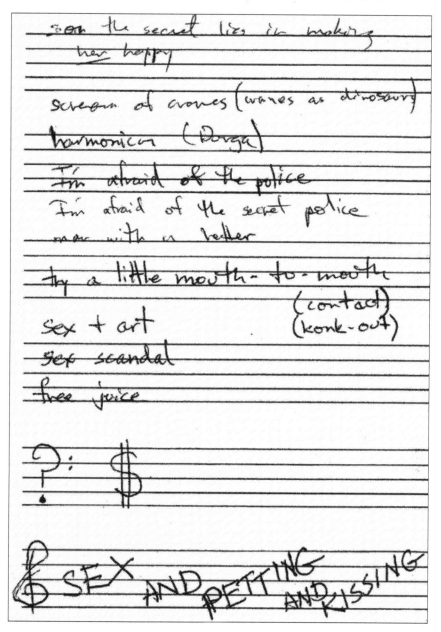

Image 15. A page from one of Russell's notebooks, date unknown (Russell, SN)

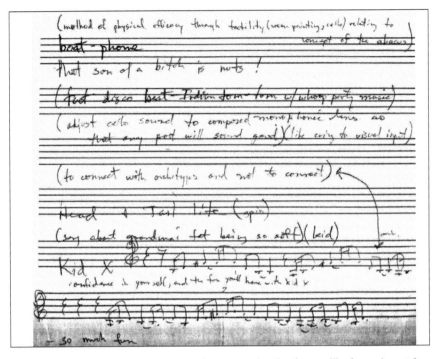

Image 16. Another page from a different notebook of Russell's, from the mid 1980s (Russell, SN)

the Manhattan School of Music, where he studied with Elias Tannenbaum, a sympathizer of his experimental oddities, and Charles Wuorinen, an unsympathetic composer of conservatively high-end serial music. Wuorinen wasn't fond of Russell's intuitive techniques nor their audible results.

Russell recalls of his *City Park* (1973) performance, for which Wuorinen was in attendance: "I said to him [Wuorinen] the thing that excited me about the piece was that you could pick up the needle anywhere and put it down and it always sounded the same. Not exactly the same, but you could plug into it for as long as you liked, then plug out and then plug back in again without losing anything essential unlike narrative music where your attention is required from beginning to end. He turned to me and said, 'That's the most

chords lying prone
vocals turn up unexpectedly
sound of a sailboat
playing with different time of light
colorful screen in front of music
guitar on some chords only
sudden trills in organ
all notes equal value
flying on controls
song about monster legend
opera singers w/ animals
"from now on"
sustained synth part like Elodie (ocean) in mix of Go Bang maybe in harmony
(modulate dorbulika speed via van or tape or both)
alternate between pure + distorted sound + sections
sudden silence in film sound effects
voice fading slowly
digitally recorded faint + medium beeps (bleeps)
extract beep-like strands for processing
hand held microphone dancing reproducing mono as reversing polarity
imagine that 1 you 2 van 3 both 4 anybody are DJs
which are examples of free will?
use short figures in 4 beat sections of "long section" for sampling
piece with cello-then gliss.
integrate setting changes (cassio + other) into structure (tremolo vibrato)

Image 17. A page from Russell's list of favorite notebook entries, unknown date
(Russell, SN)

117

Image 18. City Park, full score, page 1 of 2 (Russell, BN)

unattractive thing I've ever heard'" (Lawrence, *Hold On* 53). The score itself (**image 18**) was a modular set of textual directions and musical notations for the performers, who could read or perform the score, moving spontaneously from one numbered section to another.

Embedded in the score is Russell's "scratch pulse," which involved musicians listening to and responding to recorded animal sounds on vinyl, which Russell had "scratched" in order to create various rhythmized loops. Reminiscent of Cornelius Cardew's *Schooltime Composition*, and with a fluxus sense of humor, Russell's *City Park* is a grab bag of playful improvisatory directions:

> Close one eye. Look at the other players. At the sight of each play one of the following notes.
>
> Play like the clouds always.
>
> Think of 4 different notes to play and how to play them. Wait. Then play them.
>
> Give a signal to someone, another player, without explaining what it's for.
>
> Ask the drummer (when he's not playing) what section he's in, play something from that section.

Other compositions from this time were more elaborate and laborious. Andrew Franck, a musician and artist, who studied with Russell at the Manhattan School of Music (1973-4), recollects his collaborations with Russell during this time, and emphasizes the mosaic quality of Russell's artistic personality as well as his unrealistic demands for performance:

> Paramount in those days was Arthur's interest in process, which often entailed long, arcane number sequences. For some pieces, the performers would silently count, then... bang! Something might happen, like the thud of long wooden staffs clashing every several hundreds of pulses. These kinds of things could un-

nerve even some dyed-in-the-wool experimenters, some of whom would ask me about what had just happened. I, of course, would defer to Arthur, who might mention something about say, "San Francisco," leaving the questioner even more baffled.

At a live broadcast WBAI concert one Saturday evening Arthur had about a dozen musicians performing a full-length work. I was given the score and asked to play the Hammond organ facing away from the keyboard with my hands behind my back. Catching glimpses of the tone sequence out of the corners of my eye—between trying to adjust my arms and hands to feel the keys—I mentioned to Arthur that it'd be impossible to play in any coordinated tempo with the rest of the ensemble. "That's just fine," he beamed (Franck, 2010).

Many of the performances from his first years in New York were drawn from pieces which Russell had begun composing while living in California. They would often manifest as text scores, each an idea, a scenario, or a set of instructions, which Russell collected into what I call the "black book."

TEXT SCORES FROM "THE BLACK NOTEBOOK"

During his first year in New York (1973), Russell was composing constantly, and—as was en vogue at the time—he had been writing brief text scores with a Fluxus sense of conceptual, absurd, and mundane humor. I have found a total of 23 in his archives, half of which are dedicated to a known avant-guard figure or personal artistic friend. This collection of scores is a small treasury of experimental approaches and techniques for musical performance, including multimedia, choreography, visual props and tools, text and sound poetry, meditation, proprioceptive methods, sampling, and more. Below is a complete list of the text scores compiled by Russell in the black book:

Experimental Music for Ezra Pound
Music for 6 Flutes and As Many Pianists
Percussion Music for John Cage
Piece for Double Marching Band
Piece for Modified Voices
Piece Using Gravity
Piece Using John Giorno's Record
Reach One for Two Pianos
Who's Got the Power for A. Mathieu
Multiple Choice: A Short Quiz for 3 Tubas + 2 Conductors; 5 Tubas; 4
Tubas + 1 Conductor
New York Piece
Children's Piece for Beginners
Piece for Children Involving Shapes
Piece for Mr. Sachdev's Students Using Sa
Breathing Piece
Children's Pieces
Heat Piece
Linguist Piece
Lute and Cello
Piece for Breathers Thoughts
Piece for Mistakes (for J. Rosenberg)
Stray Cat for Stray Cat Band and Tape
Tape piece/Cello Piece

Reach One for two fender Rhodes is one of the few that were performed and documented (cf. *First Thought Best Thought*). The piece, recorded for the *Instrumentals* record, was performed by Beth Anderson-Harold and Dan Salmon at Phill Niblock's Experimental Intermedia on Dec, 1973. Anderson-Harold recalled the performance to me saying, "the music was very difficult, and we had very little rehearsal. Arthur loved the performance, he said. It seems to me the notation was completely traditional. I don't remember there being any improv sections. I don't remember being given any directions—just, here's the music and here's the keyboard and tonight's the concert" (Anderson-Harold, 2013). But in his score sketches, there was more than just a mere reading of music notation. Below is Russell's original description of the piece:

Reach for two pianos

Pianos at two arms out-stretched length
Keyboards facing
One or two players

~~Pianists are free to change tempo whenever they like~~

Tempo on heartbeat

Have index on each heartbeat on score of Piano I reproduced in different, or perhaps "macrocosmic" order on Piano II and vice versa, in the case of the former and likewise in the case of the latter. Assign certain time periods specifically to the Pianist I putting change marks on Pianist II and vice versa, perhaps using alphabet-numerical order, or numerical order back and forth, or some intuitive method—or colored numbers (Russell, BN).

It is from simple sketches like this that Russell would then be inclined to develop fairly complex compositional methods and scores. The ultimate score for *Reach One*, and it seems it is one that Anderson-Harold and Salmon had not seen, is shown in **image 19** [a section of the score for solo pianist B].

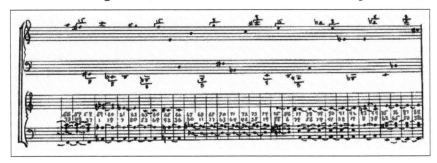

Image 19. A section from the sore for Reach One (Russell, EMF).

However, it seems *Reach One* was given a previous performance at NYU by Russell and his friend, and fellow esotericist, Andrew Franck. Franck recalls a different situation than Anderson-Harold, and notes the role of the heartbeat mentioned in the score:

> Arthur asked me to perform a work of his with him for two pianos. The work was conceived around counting one's heartbeats through a stethoscope strapped tightly onto the chest. Very few sounds, lots of silence, long, very long in duration. Well, the reception wasn't all that gracious for the piece to say the least. Afterwards, however, Elias Tannenbaum, who nursed in the school's fledgling electronic music program, came up to us and said, "You know, you two, you really wax mystical." Arthur and I were delighted (Franck, 2010).

The text accompanying the full score provides very specific instructions on how to carry out the work. Both pianists make use of a stethoscope, by which audible heartbeats are used to determine the durations of the notated pitches. Russell developed a somewhat complicated "number system," which is evident in the red ink notation seen in **image 19**. This system is drawn from the pianists' notations of their own heart rate. Russell further applies these cardiac notations to the process of the works performances, involving pianists exchanging pianos and heartbeat pulses. Russell's "numbers system" was apparently based on the formula below. Included with the full score and instructional texts was a single sheet of paper with the following indesciferable calculations along with pages of indecipherable mathematical equations (image 20).

Formula for determining number index:

$$\overset{b}{X} = (\text{index melody})(\text{chromatic rows}) + (\text{ext, notes})(\infty) = 12\,(b - 1) + a + 3$$

X = any or all given number relations

∞ = Here, the operation used to determine sequence of extra notes (A, Bb, B - lowest 3 notes and C - the highest note)

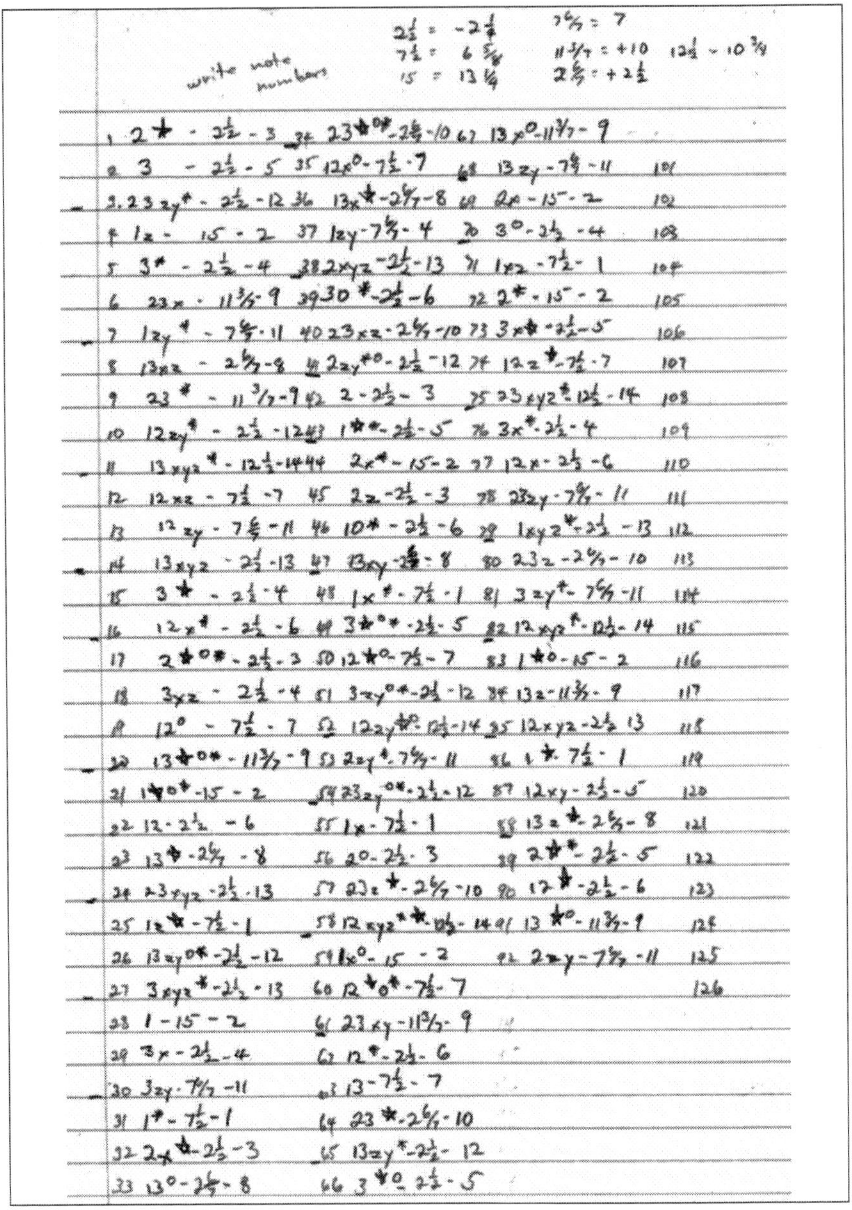

Image 20. Russell's calculations for Reach One (Russell, BN).

This quasi-scientific approach carries through much of Russell's music, and is itself a significant theme found in the black book scores. Throughout the 23 text scores there are recurrent themes and techniques, such as the physical use of the body in *Reach One*. Coinciding with Russell's study of linguistics, language figures prominently in several works (*Linguist Piece, Music for Ezra Pound, Tape Piece/Cello Piece*). *Music for Ezra Pound* derives its rhythmic and pitch material from phonemes in Pound's poetry. While *Piece for Modified Voices* seeks to combine an effects processor (audible via headphones) with an improvising poet to create a stuttering phonemic ocean of sound. Elsewhere, Russell muses "[Use] syntactical structures in which the meaning is delivered early in the word group and the words that follow are free to be whatever... polyphony of above, but not specified. How?" Many of the scores attempted to involve technology in some way (*Piece for Modified Voices, Piece for John Giorno, Piece for Performers' Breathing, Stray Cat Piece, Tape Piece/Cello Piece*).

Russell's approach is often to modify or remix another instrument in some way, but with an emphasis on doing this live, that is, someone causes or "performs" the modification. Another related technological aspect that Russell seemed drawn to was feedback processes, especially via headphone technology. In *Piece for Modified Voices* and *Piece for Performers' Breathing*, Russell asks musicians to interpret on their own musical instrument sounds that are heard, live-streaming, via headphones. Referring to either *City Park* or another similar work, the translation of animal sounds was again used in this live performance on WKCR-FM Columbia Radio: "Russell and Van Tieghem played cello and drums while listening through headphones to two separate vinyl L.P.'s of animal noises and sound effects that had been deliberately scratched—and adjusted their playing to the meter of the scratches" (Lawrence, *Hold On* 55). Elsewhere in his notebooks Russell had planned to use this headphone technique for an orchestral project: "New technique for orchestral arrangement (for me in studio): each player wears headphones, plays from individual stand; takes cues from sung lyrics heard in phones; each cued line written on separate staff."

Beyond the involvement of headphones, these feedback relationships would also be tethered to motion, weight, light, chemicals, etc in Russell's text pieces. *Heat Piece* has performers operating an on/off lighting mechanism triggered by scripted foot gestures. "The action one performs on the lights is revealed by what foot-nudge one receives, up or down by the foot it comes on." In *Lute & Cello Piece* the two instruments are conducted by an unidentified source of heat and its fluctuations of intensity. *Piece for Breathers* wanted to extend this use of "electrical cueing" to phosphorescent chemicals. In *Stray Cat* Russell has performers choreographed to move across a space, and, in the process, trigger a matrix of contact circuits on the floor, which in turn trigger lights at the control board, which in turn signal an alteration of volume, panning, etc. *Piece, using gravity, for performers* uses a scale, which weighs the performers movements across the scale, to operate musical devices, which in turn influence the performers' movements. This endless Rube Goldbergian feedback process figures prominently in all of Russell's work, culminating in his work with echo in the mid 1980's.

Game techniques were another common theme. *Piece for Mistakes* (**image 21**) is one such game-like piece. Using actions that ensure a degree of performative error, Russell sought to sonify these mistakes, allowing, humorously, for the "possibility of everything going right." *Percussion Piece for John Cage* is almost a *John Zorn-esque* game of a guerilla water-hosing of the audience; *Multiple Choice* hearkens back to high school quizzes; and *Who's Got the Power for A. Mathieu*, a dedication to his former composition teacher, uses a monopoly game board as its basis.

Along the lines of games and play, the presence of children is met in several works and was an important presence in all of Russell's music. Russell would often use the imagery of children in his sketches, imbuing the idea or the music with qualities of gentleness, playfulness, and innocence. Through the 1980's one of Russell's most prized critics was his sister Kate's 8-year-old son, Beau: "He didn't really want to play music with him or coach him. He wanted his input as a young person who might have his finger on the pulse of something"

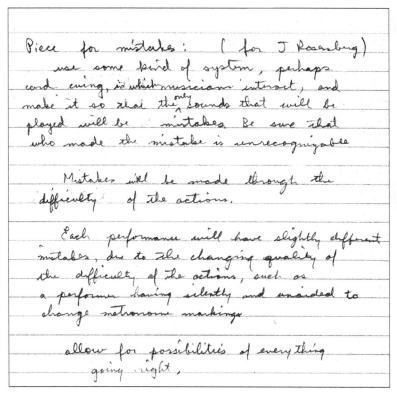

Image 21. Piece for Mistakes, text score (The Arthur Russell Estate)

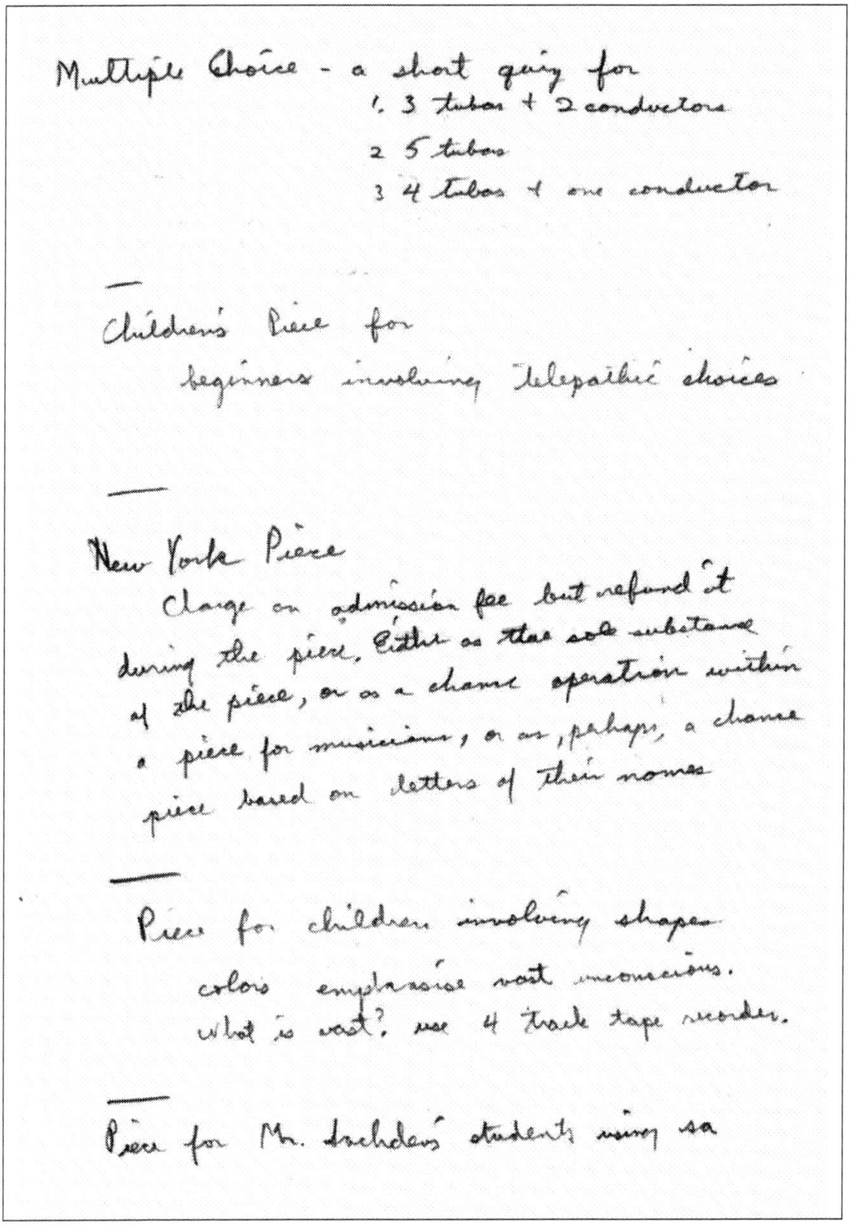

Multiple Choice - a short quiz for
1. 3 tubas + 2 conductors
2 5 tubas
3 4 tubas + one conductor

Children's Piece for
beginners involving telepathic choices

New York Piece
Charge an admission fee but refund it
during the piece. Either as the sole substance
of the piece, or as a chance operation within
a piece for musicians, or as, perhaps, a chance
piece based on letters of their names

Piece for children involving shapes
colors emphasize vast unconscious.
what is vast? use 4 track tape recorder.

Piece for Mr. Ichlder's students using sa

Image 22. Four of Russell's text scores from the Black Notebook (Russell, BN).

(Lawrence, *Hold On* 285). Within his text scores: *Piece for Ezra Pound* questions perhaps "adding children"; *Children's Piece* seeks to involve children and "telepathic devices"; while *Piece For Children* seeks to use shapes, colors, and a 4-track to unclear ends.

Alongside other writings, letters, and scores (including a "prelude for lute"), these scores were collected in a black binder by Russell himself. Essentially, this is Russell's hand collected summation of creative interests, techniques, scores, and sketches from an early but productive time period. While some are short and playful—"Children's piece for beginners involving telepathic choices"—others run two or more pages and show more practical organization. Pieces they are, flights of fancy, first thoughts, and youthful experimental probings. It's hard to say how many were actually performed during Russell's life—though we have a recording of *Reach One* confirming that this notebook was not merely a graveyard of ideas. Somewhere between a Rube Goldberg Machine and a child's uninhibited doodle, these scores show Russell at his most experimental, questioning the very meaning of music, while highlighting the playful humor and imagination that would permeate nearly all his work.

FINDING A SYSTEM

"Find an analytical system through which you can investigate altering flows of thought"—Russell's notebooks are filled with imperatives. As his mathematical musings show, Russell had an almost scientific approach to music composition. Not surprisingly, Trungpa described the knowledge required for the exercise of "crazy wisdom" as a "scientific knowledge" as the most accurate knowledge on how to react to situations (*Crazy Widsom*, 46). Russell's sketch for "Cumberland Gap" shows him devising techniques to complicate and reinvent the familiar changes of a traditional folk song, but he did so by analyzing the performative aspects of his instrument and devising a method to randomize those aspects. We see this same analytical approach at work in *Reach One* and numerous other early works. From these early and simpler efforts Russell would continue striving effortfully to devise a more elaborate system to guide his own science of the sounding spirit. In the following passages Russell speaks to much of the methodology that would come to be used in *Instrumentals* (1974) in what appears to be an early sketch of a more general approach. Here we see Russell's Rube Goldbergian methods being applied to music notation:

> Basic dialog is grouped into melodic brackets, as many different ways as there are sections in the piece. (This corresponds with the technique [of] differentiation in repetitions later on). The groupings need not be consecutive notes, but can be any set, one set for each performer. (This reflects the situation of maximum ambiguity) these sets are then used to build a framework for the total performance. The framework may be added to or taken away from by 1. repetitions 2. transformations 3. replacements (to and from). The framework may also be interfered with by special or more important processes.
>
> x relations determine pulse changes in framework, y relations determine what pulse is changed to.
>
> The above [x & y relation] is "a" degree. It forms the foundation for "b" degree, which is the foundation for "c" degree. Criterion for determining repetitions and other structure changes: if a passage shows too much cohesion in itself. [written vertically]: framework is filled in all at once, (not linearly)

Also of note is Russell's interest in single note arrays [he would frequently notate his works with a single whole note per measure], the construction of melodies through non-linear connections, and the use of open form techniques (modularity, transformation, substitution, repetition). Groupings of pitches are formed non-linearly with different sets of these given to players. The different sets of pitches given to the players risks unexpected pitch combinations, hence "maximum ambiguity." Here is the nascent state of Russell's emerging system. Underlying every compositional or conceptual effort however is an emphasis on the process of transformation. The smallest part could be expanded, the whole could be contracted, everything could be connected or substituted. Here we can start to see how an interest in transformational processes, which Russell was exploring in his text scores, begins to form the basis for his compositional practice.

Take small sections, transform to larger structure. Transform larger structure by:

1. relations of inner parts of dialog one—subjective qualities

2. autonomous source material intuitively determined

3. 'improvisatory pedal tone' durations

4. log-arithmic or exponential proportions (accelerando, decceleran-do)

5. inner relation of harmonic intersections

6. the principals of changing what has already been written (thereby accumulating a bank of unused material – echo on melodies) or

7. determining what will be written—will change structure automatically

y relations >> a. percussion as atonal/tonal
            b. cello as atonal/tonal

x relations >> metal (mallet) in perc—*col legno* in cello
            bow in cello—metal in perc

            pizz in cello—bow in cello
            nonmetal in perc—nonmetal in perc

b degree   identity of instrument—perc
          identity of technique—cello

c degree   identity of mallet, finger, etc—perc
          identity of dynamics—cello

From one page of the notebook to the next, logical identifiers of organization (alphabetical and numerical) will illogically change meaning or disappear. But their role is, as they were used in Russell's "Cumberland Gap," to create curated operations for randomized outcomes with room for personal intervention. However, it's not always clear how these distinctions might be applied. What becomes apparent is his interest in creating a formal interface to his creative process—using such a malleable structure in which one stage of creation could potentially give rise to another, and in which most aspects of the entire system can be transformed.

The ornamental or embellishing function which dynamics generally play in traditional musics were used by Russell to spontaneously extend and re-compose, for example, an entire melody. The subtle effects of his physical relationship with the instrument offered a path of improvising a mix of timbres and a polyphonic approach to a repeating melody on the solo cello. But then this was only one, number six, of his seven means, noted above, of structurally transforming an already existing work. But Russell was slowly fusing all of these methods into his own informal system of composition/performance.

Pulse changes are determined, bracketed sections are mapped out, new simultaneous occurrences are noted. those occurrences can be used in that section, to fill out spaces in time, and in their own section, of varying time length, these two sections just mentioned can overlap where pulses permit, and may be regrouped for different performances. "B degree" details form new frameworks, becoming only ordered sets without fixed numbers of beats between them, stripped of real time considerations, like time length of source segment. (These b degree details form "new relationships") c degree details are added.

Use the ordered sets set up to write new piece, determinate, improvisatory, indeterminate, four sections to total piece, any can be performed alone or in groups (Russell, BN).

This again makes explicit the *kind* of open-ness he was after, not just open interpretation of a score, but open composition, or infinite re-composition. Inherent in Russell's tantric training was the perceived elasticity and ephemerality of the material world and the identities we use to organize and control it. Recall that "[t]antric symbolism appears unsystematic and confused. Sets of symbols are rarely consistent from text to text, and may even vary within one text," such that new meaning did not supersede old meanings, but additively enriched their potential to signify (Bucknell; Stuart-Fox, 103).

Russell would note to himself that he "can't seem to understand music as product" (Russell, N). Through Russell's constant editing and re-mixing of works, he wasn't "not finishing them," he was listening to them, staying open to other meanings, and incorporating them into new works. Years later in his notebooks Russell offered a rare glimpse into a musical "theory" long at work in his thinking:

Chromatic attachments to a modal core

Transpositions super-imposed according to chromatic or modal relationship

That a music does not construct a theory for the future but constructs a future out of which comes several theories if necessary

One note—infinite theories

Chromatic composition (non-directional) in which each note is an instance of

1) modal cluster

2) imaginary chromatic melody (used to shape the structure of 'modal cluster')

Russell's music was deeply theorized, but it was never fixed by theory. It could be deeply systematized, but it was never fixed by any system. As we noted in the previous chapter, this focus on "one note," on single pitches, would guide all of Russell's music. But Russell's consistent conceptual probing was leading him to develop a system of composition. By 1975 Russell was converging his interests in popular and experimental practices more and more coherently. And it was during this time that his compositional system, a matrix of pitches and numbers, fully developed and gave rise to one of his largest and most enduring works, *Instrumentals*.

V.

INSTRUMENTALS, VOLUME 1 & 2:

The Matrix System

Before January [1975], and more and more since, I was awakened, or re-awakened, to the bright sound and magical qualities of the bubblegum and easy-listening currents in American popular music. I like it, and I recall Yuko Nonomura's comment about TV shows of the family variety. Combined with practice in Buddhist life-and-death matters (or even not combined), I get very excited. As has been said, "Life is short" or "Life is sweet" or something like that. And I guess this piece *Instrumentals* is an attempt to use some of that excitement (GA).

Arthur Russell

Instrumentals, Russell's largest and most ambitious work, was first development as he planned his move to New York. It all began in 1973 when Russell's Buddhist mentor, Yuko Nonomura, suggested that Russell compose some music about clouds, a propitious symbol within Shingon Buddhism. Russell embraced the idea, and by 1974 *Instrumentals* was an immersive audio-visual event lasting over 48 continuous hours. The visuals, slide-projected onto a screen, were to consist of Nonomura's nature photography—colorful images of clouds, flowers, and the general landscape surrounding Japan's Mount Koya, a mountain with symbolic importance to the Shingon religion.

The music was initially realized by a chamber pop ensemble improvising around melodic phrases and a series of chord changes. The first performance took place in Berkley, CA in January of 1975. *Instrumentals* would go on to have three other performances under Russell's guidance. The next would occur on April 27, 1975 at the Kitchen; then again on May 4, in 1977, at the Franklin Arts Center. Musicians in these pop ensembles included long-time collaborators like Bill Ruyle, David van Tiegham, Peter Gordon, Ernie Brooks (of The Modern Lovers), Larry Saltzman (who went on to tour with Paul Simon), Jon Gibson, Garret List (a member of the Julliard Ensemble and Musica Electronica Viva), among others. *Instrumentals* had its orchestral debut with Julius Eastman conducting the CETA orchestra at The Kitchen on May 10, 1978.

Russell explained the choice of the title as follows: "Since in most popular music a lyric is the focus of a song, and since in popular music a song without words, in order to be a commercial success, must have a special quality of its own, and since the music for the color slides was not structured on speech patterns, I ended up calling the piece *Instrumentals*" (Russell, N). Russell also noted the numerology of the title in his notebooks. The word "Instrumentals" has a numerological value of 50, which reduces to 5. In Shingon philosophy the number five is pervasively meaningful. From Kukai's five-part "body of wisdom"—directly connected to the five primary deities in Shingon mandalas—to the pentagonal network of these deities' five associated colors, mudras, bija, elements, spatial directions, and more. Meanwhile, numerous popular books on western numerology associate five with "visionary adventure and a constructive use of freedom" (Fanthorpe, 113).

Russell's use of Nonomura's photography was not merely a backdrop to the music. In fact, Russell claimed the ensemble performances served as "background music" to the projected images. He intended the images to subtly influence *how* the musicians played their instruments—"Be aware of it peripherally," Peter Gordon recalls Russell saying (Russell, IF). As the music flowed as continuously as possible, each image was projected for a brief period before moving onto another image. But Russell left these parameters open: "The composition and sequence of the slides can be revised for different performances." Elsewhere, in his notebooks, Russell expressed an interest in film as tantric visualization:

film as visualization
visualization of film through
fade ins
fade outs
stills
loops
insets
soundtrack

What is the dream state [...] how does it extend into waking?
How do you transform fearful thoughts into quiescent translucent diamonds? (Russell, N)

Another name for Esoteric Buddhism, Tantric Buddhism, or Vajrayana is the "Diamond Path." The vajra [Sanskrit, "thunderbolt, diamond"], a Buddhist ritual object, is a symbol of the diamond's indestructibility as well as of lightning's powerful force. Nonomura's photography (seen in **image 23**) was not merely an aesthetic offering, but a spiritual tool for meditation focused upon the natural symbolism specific to Shingon Vajrayana Buddhism. With direct links to the use of meditation in his early text scores, for Russell *Instrumentals* was nothing less than a multi-media meditation piece, both in terms of composition and performance.

The music of *Instrumentals* was ultimately grouped into two volumes of differing aesthetics. Volume One is catchy, rhythmic, and performed by a pop-rock ensemble with Nonomura's photography projected throughout. For Volume

Image 23. An image from Yuko Nonomura's nature photography used in Instrumentals, Volume One, performed live in concert under the direction of Peter Gordon, March 24, 2012. Photo by author

One's rhythm section Russell was looking to the raw economic drumming of the Velvet Underground as a model. And in a note to himself he writes of wanting a more diverse, and notably electro-acoustic, percussion array which was never realized: "Instrumentals: real tambourine, skin, mixed with Linn tambourine [...] percussion (handclap, clavé upbeat, with echo)" (Russell, N). The score for Volume One was reduced to a "lead sheet" or "fake book" score—a simple layout of a song's primary melody in relation to a fixed chord progression. Fittingly, the "lead sheet" had initially been designed for the amateur musician. By its simplicity, the lead sheet encourages creative interpretation and improvisation, major aspects of the composition and performances of Volume One.

Volume Two was arranged for orchestra. The music lacks any sense of fixed pulse, which was a staple of Volume One. While the latter was inspired by the popular radio of the past and present, Russell imagined Volume Two as "the popular radio of the future." In these compositions Russell savors lush chords sustained at length, brief melodic flares, slow progressions, pregnant pauses, and estranged harmonies. It feels very much how he described it to himself in his notebooks: "Chords lying prone [...]." Seeking a "stream of chords," Russell sought to "move through [the] chords like you're on a boat." The rhythmic structure of the pop form is thrown out in favor of losing "consciousness of duration" all together (Russell, SN).

In designing *Instrumentals* Russell conceived a vast compositional system and a series of methods to generate the music. Volume One of *Instrumentals* was based on what Russell called a "mother score," which was used to generate an endless variety of material for the project—Volume Two is based on a similar but different score. This "mother score" was itself derived from a matrix of 76 pitches compiled by Russell. After a series of intuitive procedures, which we'll go into soon, any single pitch from Russell's matrix could be combined with others and developed into an individual work, such as *Instrumentals*. With this system Russell was beginning to work with a set of procedures and concepts, but without any linear logic, without any fixed rules whatsoever. He focused solely on the matrix as a mantric syllabary for musical meditation and creation. Everything else was permutation and improvisation, playing with the matrix. He believed this process helped prevent habitual behaviors and lazy artistic choices. "The method of composition used for *Instrumentals*," he writes, "was derived to purify, discipline, and somewhat restrain/channel melodic or musical impulses towards a semi-improvisational performance situation" (Russell, GA).

Russell constantly emphasized the mutability of this work. "*Instrumentals* was conceived as a composition which is revised through time, with each revision standing as a completed statement on its own. Revisions take place using improvised techniques, but always within the framework or general locale of the mother score (a melodic structure), composed in 1974 [...] The arrangements, whether composed or improvised [...] and the mode of musical thought and practice change from concert to concert" (Russell, N). But the process underlying the composition of *Instrumentals* remained a consistent resource and would go on to generate a large body of work, including the score for Robert Wilson's *Medea* (a sampling of the music later released independently as *Tower of Meaning*), *24-24 Music*, and much of the ensemble music performed under the name "Singing Tractors."

The matrix systems that gave rise to *Instrumentals Vol. 1 & 2* show Russell at the height of his compositional powers: developing idiosyncratic notations, scoring for numerous ensembles— including orchestra and rock band—working with extended scale/duration, and synthesizing polar aesthetics (e.g. the popular radio sound and avant-guard minimalism). This was Russell laying a path for himself and defining himself as a composer, and he saw this path extending indefinitely into the future. "I spent most of my time," he would later recollect to David Toop, "working on that one piece [*Instrumentals*.] I had decided that I was going to do that for the rest of my life" (Toop, 35)—and, in many ways, he did just that.

The *Instrumentals* Matrix
and its Stages of Development

The original score is composed of passing harmonies, lines and timbres. Any part of the whole can be isolated as a "song." Truth seems to be totally subjective. The hierarchy of tonal music is negated (Russell, IR).

—Peter Gordon

Ultimately Russell developed an extremely laborious and nested series of processes to come up with the "mother score" for *Instrumentals*. As in many Buddhist techniques of meditation, the meticulousness and methodical ritual involved are largely in place to keep one's consciousness constantly in check, to ward off distraction, and to remove the crutches of habit—or, as Russell says, "to purify, discipline, and restrain impulses." This perspective also reflects a sentiment that Chögyam Trungpa affirmed in his view on the arts, which we noted earlier: "It's not a matter of just swinging with it. It needs a lot of techniques and manipulations, so to speak" (*Lion's Roar* 207-08).

As the last two chapters have shown, these techniques and manipulations were core aspects of Russell's approach to composition. There are mounds upon mounds of pre-compositional exercises found in Russell's archive. What started off as a curiosity on my part—peaked by Tim Lawrence's reference to "conceptual scores filled with staves and colored Cagean parabolas"—quickly became an effort of cryptology. So I was delighted to find in a submission letter to a grant organization, Russell's own voice so clearly describing his compositional process for *Instrumentals*. While Russell outlined four stages of the process in the grant application, I have extended this to six stages in order to make certain aspects of the actual process more clear. Below is a summary of the six stages of Russell's mother score.

STAGE ONE

First, Russell notated a large series of unrelated pitches, that were not intended to be read in any particular order. He stated that he used 76 pitches for the *Instrumentals* matrix. As this collection of 76 pitches was not found in the archive, I have used an excerpt (see, **image 24**) from another variation of this material, as a working example-- the pitches shown

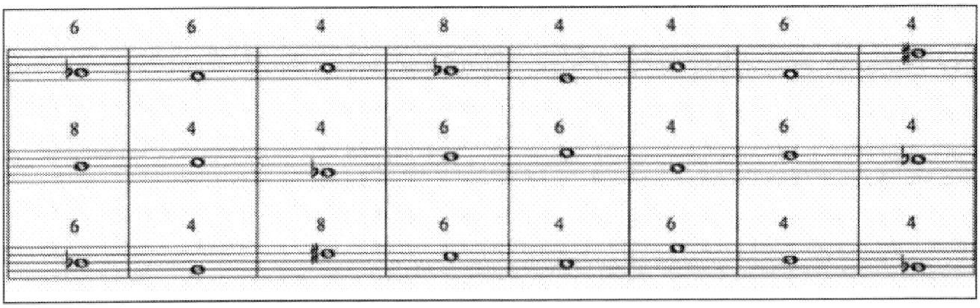

Image 24. Stage one of the Instrumentals matrix system. Russell draws out a series of whole note pitches. Numbers indicate the relative duration of a given pitch. Re-notated by author.

here were part of another 54-pitch matrix. It is unclear why or how Russell chose these pitches, but they form the conceptual basis for all that follows. Russell also used numbers to indicate the relative metric values of each bar—here working primarily with meters of 4, 6, and 8. One ongoing ambiguity in Russell's pre-compositional notations is the almost complete lack of clefs, which ambiguates the identity of pitches. Based on my research it seems that Russell used an "invisible" bass clef for all notations until he explicitly employs clefs in his final score, or "mother score." I have left the clefs off in the scores, here, where Russell had done the same, but the pitches are to be read in the bass clef, unless otherwise indicated (e.g. the top-left note in measure one of image 24 is a "Bb").

I call the score in stage one Russell's "matrix" score. While the term "matrix" has a more specific meaning in fields such as mathematics, its general definition is "something (such as a situation or a set of conditions) in which something else develops or forms" (Merriam-Webster, 766). In music, matrix composition involves an archive of ostensibly unrelated musical signs (graphic, notational, ideational). Encouraging personal or collective interpretation, these signs are then creatively interacted with, altered, combined, re-interpreted to give rise to any number of unified works.

This kind of matrical composition was common during Russell's time. For example, Terry Riley's "In C," which used modular notation for collective interpretation; the pitch matrices used by serialist composers, such as Russell's teacher Charles Wuorinen; the geometric pitch arrays used by John Coltrane and Yusef Lateef; the graphic scores of Morton Feldman; while Russell's compositional peers, Peter Zummo and Elodie Lauten, both used matrix interfaces in their own compositions—there are numerous examples. From the 1960's well into the 80s, the pervasiveness of minimalism reinforced an attraction towards grids and matrices amongst many in New York's Downtown arts community. Moreover, this matrical thinking is at the core of Buddhist mandala meditation, where meditation upon various aspects of the mandala's sacred geometry guide the meditator towards enlightenment. Russell's matrix was essentially a mantric syllabary (of pitches and durations) that he meditated upon, stretching, shrinking, combining, and re-combining them into original new works.

Though I found several similar looking matrices--perhaps used in *Instrumentals* or other works--I was unable to find the original matrix that matched with the *Instrumental* scores on the following pages. And so I re-composed the matrices in **images 24** and **25** by extracting the information from subsequent scores. The scores shown, following stage two, were found in Russell's "Instrumentals" folder and are the scores he used to compose *Instrumentals Vol 1*, as audible in Audika Records *First Thought, Best Thought*.

STAGE TWO

Next, Russell intuitively paired each note of the stage one

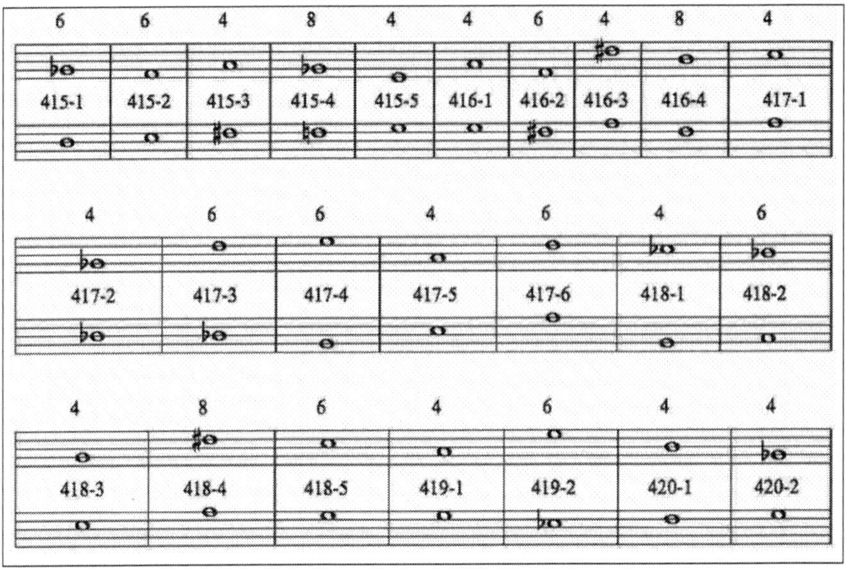

6	6	4	8	4	4	6	4	8	4
415-1	415-2	415-3	415-4	415-5	416-1	416-2	416-3	416-4	417-1

4	6	6	4	6	4	6
417-2	417-3	417-4	417-5	417-6	418-1	418-2

4	8	6	4	6	4	4
418-3	418-4	418-5	419-1	419-2	420-1	420-2

Image 25. Stage two of the Instrumentals matrix process, renotated by author. Russell adds a "companion tone" to each of the pitches listed in stage one. Numbers ("415-420") identify bars within the system.

matrix (**image 24**) with a set of pitches that he called "companion tones." The first pitch, Bb, is joined to D, and so on.

He did this 10 times for each pitch in the initial set, so that each note from the original matrix expands into 10 variable note pairings which are collectively shown in **image 26**. The numbers (e.g. 415-1, etc) shown between staves in **image 25** were used by Russell as identification for future use. These I.D.'s become primary references for the succeeding stages of composition as well as references to compositions in subsequent performances and projects. The numbers shown here, however, were taken out of context (they are not associated with this notation), but their inclusion helps us better understand Russell's process.

Considering the significance of these note pairings, I was reminded of the double-stops of the cello, or of how in Hindustani music, for example, the expression of a single pitch (*swara*) often implies its neighbor (*kan-swara*) by the reinforced tendency for one note to veer towards another. In fact, throughout the development of *Instrumentals* Russell would repeatedly return to his notebook to recall and preserve this poetic imagery, anthropomorphizing these paired tones:

> One note says "hi" to another, by sometimes lasting longer (duet)
> Spaces via composition
> two notes in love reflected in the whole world (orchestra)
> the notes can't decide if they're notes or instruments
> they tremble with love and fear (vibrato) (vocal)
> together they heal the whole world's problems (Russell, N)

And as the drone serves as the center of Indian music, Russell frequently uses these tone pairs as a drone in the works they give rise to. These two-note pairings are a strong character in much of Russell's music, most immediately audible in his cello playing, during which his voice supplies a third tone or harmony to the two-note drones of his cello. In many cases, however, Russell leaves out the triadic third in the compositional process. In doing so, he nullifies, as Peter Gordon noted, the conventional harmonic function that might otherwise incline the ears to a certain manner of narrative expectation.

Russell revels in drones, but not always static ones. With their two-note simplicity, his note pairs can move quite subtly, often forming melodies and chordal progressions in the process. The further overlaying of melody (Russell's "primary and secondary melodic material") upon these dyadic harmonies colors them with a seemingly familiar tonal sensibility, but in Russell's idiosyncratic musical language. Both in composition and in improvisation Russell is always playing with this between-space of the familiar and the otherwise.

STAGE THREE

Our analysis of stages one and two were based upon notational excerpts from unidentified and indirectly related scores. The analysis of stages three and onward are based on the original scores used to compose and perform *Instrumentals*. And from these documents we can trace a clear evolution of Russell's composition process through to the final recorded product. We have seen that Russell would give numerical I.D.'s to the individual bars of his matrix. However, these bars were often grouped in sub-sets, to unknown organizational ends. To these groupings Russell would add alphabetical I.D.'s—A, B, C, D, etc. The examples that follow are derived from the Section A materials in Russell's archive.

In stage three, Russell drafts a new notational interface (**image 26**). Now the original series of pitches from stage one are notated, vertically, along the left and right most stave columns in a mirror image of one another. Then, between each mirrored pitch of these two columns, Russell re-notates his companion tones—the 10 tones he paired with each single matrix pitch in stage two. The companion tones are notated in succession in the 10 bars between the outer columns of each mirrored pitch.

Next, Russell draws colored lines, note-to-note, in a non-linear fashion, giving rise to new melodies, or what he called "primary melodic material." We can see these "colored line" melodies in **image 27**. For example, let's look at the first line-drawn melody at the very top of the page. Starting with the first series of primary melodic material, Russell begins with the pitch "D" (the second note/measure in the top-left corner). He then draws a line to the neighboring pitch ("F"), then across staves to a "B", and finally leftward to an "A"—yeilding the melody "D-F-B-A. He makes these line-drawn melodies, again, 10 times, once for each set of companion tones.

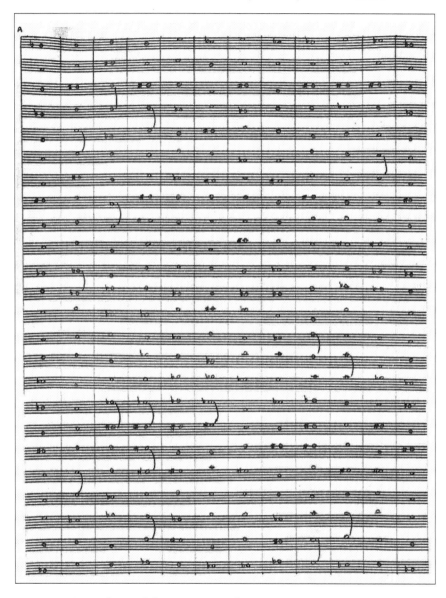

Image 26. Stage three of the Instrumentals matrix system. Here Russell's score shows "primary melodic material" in between two vertical rows of his original matrix pitches (Gordon, personal archives).

Thus, for the A-H groupings of his original pitch set, each set has 10 variations of colored line-drawn melodies. By now one can see how much material Russell was generating and how labor intensive this notational process would have been. Though I found no explicit reference in the archives, Russell's color palette—red, orange, green, blue, violet, black—generally, at least, refers us to the rainbow, one of the most auspicious symbols in Buddhist philosophy.

STAGE FOUR

In stage four Russell again changes the notational interface. **Image 28** shows Russell laying out the initial matrix pitches on the lowest stave. Russell then begins adding pitches from the line-drawn melodies, the "primary melodic material" or "companion tones," above these dyads. The secondary melodic material is treated as additional "harmonies" that are added above the dyads. The dyads serve as the ground for the composition. The numerical durations, associated with each pitch, that were explicit in stage one, now metrically align the emerging full score. Russell would then intuitively sift through the harmonies he derived in previous stages, and he would occasionally alter the meters of individual measures to his liking. From this material Russell would draft a score that would be used to derive a final score (**image 29**) in stage five.

STAGE FIVE

From all of this generated pitch material Russell then orchestrated a fully notated score "by ear." **Image 29** shows page 1 (of 11), which was found in the archives, of an ensemble score, fully notated for flute/saxophone, clarinet, trombone, percussion, and cello [chords at bottom]. In a sketch for his grant application Russell writes of the uselessness of a full score: "preparation of a full score for this application would be misleading, not to mention time consuming" (Russell, GA). Rhys Chatham explains, "It was so difficult [to per-

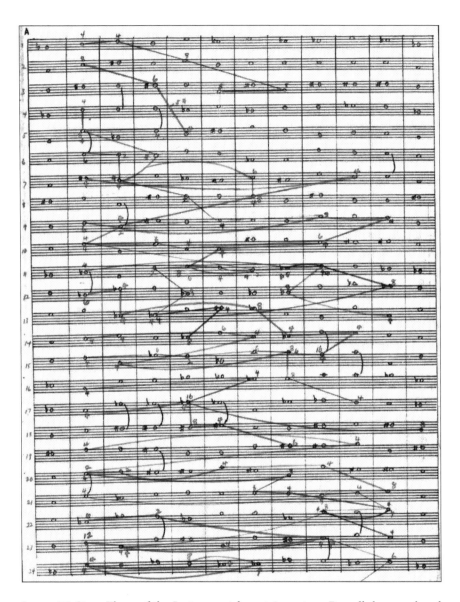

Image 27. Stage Three of the Instrumentals matrix system. Russell draws colored lines to form the "primary melodic material" for use in the forthcoming compositional stages (Gordon, personal archives).

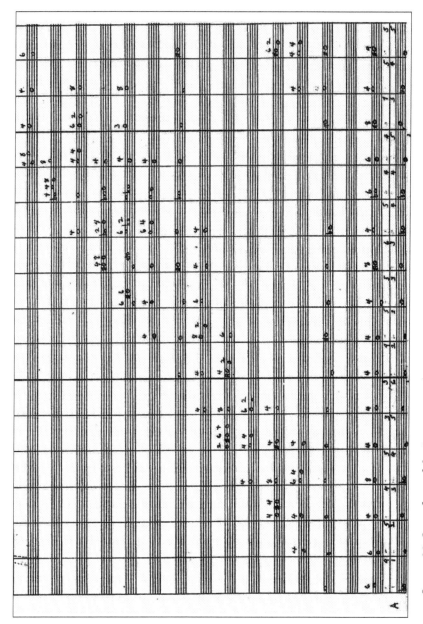

Image 28. Stage four of the Instrumentals matrix system. A page from Russell's harmonization of core me-lodic material (Russell, IF).

form] that one of the players asked Arthur why he didn't just write all the music out... But the whole point of the piece is to achieve a creative synthesis between the creative abilities of the performers and the direction which the composer gives them" (Russell, IF). So what we have below is not a full score in the sense that it was a fully realized piece. Rather, this is what Russell had referred to as the "mother score," which provided the elements for a potentially infinite number of realizations of *Instrumentals*.

In this "mother score" we can see several segments that would go on to be used in future performances of *Instrumentals*. We see Russell's unique mosaic approach to orchestration, which does not use individual instruments according to traditional groupings or linear lines. Rather, the individual voices are fragmented into brief appearances, again referencing the imagery of "jumping fishes," or "flashes of thought," and the instruments are woven together with constant variation. Often creating a kind of hocketing between voices or a Schoenbergian-like *klangfarben* effect, Russell weaves the instruments into a mosaic texture, through frequent exchanges of instruments over the course of a single note or along the trajectory of a melodic line. This is an orchestration style he would continue working with in his *Medea* score. It also relates to his solo approach on cello, voice, and effects in *World of Echo*—both works we'll be exploring in the coming chapters.

Beyond the excerpt of the "mother score" we see in **image 29**, the full score consists of 149 measures. Here, Russell articulates clear harmonies and melodic fragments, elements that will be retained in stage six. Incidentally, composer and reed player Peter Gordon's first paid job upon moving to New

York was to hand-write all the part scores from the full score--Gordon's hand is evident in image 30, which shows a single "mother score" part for guitar. Here we can see Russell maintaining the original bass line from the dyads in stage four, but altering them occasionally and/or changing their durations. Russell's "primary and secondary melodic material" have been narrowed down to select pitches, which are often harmonized with unisons or octaves.

STAGE SIX

Our final scores consisted of short numbered sections notated for the different instruments and with chords written above the staff to indicate a tonality on which one could improvise (Russell, IF).

Ernie Brooks

Russell describes the process of stage six rather succinctly in his grant application: "In the actual rehearsal, this series [the "mother score"] is played in its entirety into a tape recorder. When it's played back, whoever's interested listens and decides what short sections he or she would like to have abstracted from the whole series to be played as a repeated, short 'module'. The result of this is what you hear (in an edited version) on the tape of the concert at the Kitchen, April 28, 1975" (Russell, GA). Having gone through the preceding rigorous methodology, Russell was working largely with atonal, non-hierarchical musical building blocks. They are in effect randomly organized. He then injects a non-randomized, tonality-based minimalism by extracting a tiny portion of this atonal melting pot and then replicating this portion, intuitively developing it into an independent and substantial musical form. Many of these forms were inspired by Russell's

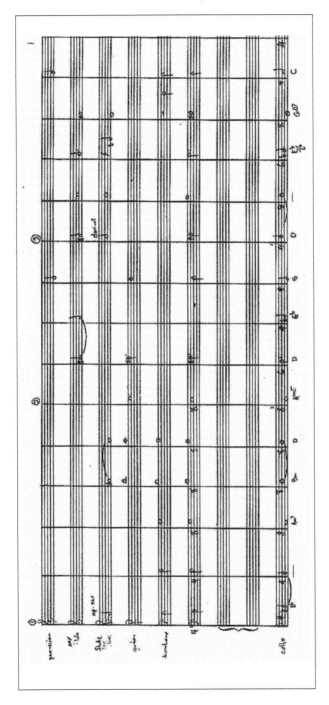

Image 29. Stage Five of the Instrumentals matrix system. Page one from the full score, or "mother score," of Instrumentals (Russell, IF).

Image 30. Stage six of the Instrumentals matrix system. Page one of the guitar part from the final score of Instrumentals, as notated by hand by Peter Gordon (Gordon, personal archives)

love of American popular music from the 30s and 40s, as well as contemporary "elevator music."

In stage six Russell further opens up the "mother score"

Image 31. A "lead sheet" score for Instrumentals, unspecified instrumentation (Brooks, personal archives)

to collective interpretation. Musicians can alter or influence not only their own musical part, through subjective interpretation and improvisation, but they can take on a compositional voice by choosing and re-developing aspects of the mother score democratically in the studio. In many cases these collectively collaged pieces—audible as "Instrumentals, Volume 1," on *First Thought, Best Thought*—were reduced to lead sheet notation in the final recorded performance. This vast composition system has then been reduced to one of the most basic forms of popular musical notation available.

The lead sheet shown in **image 31** is music that was featured in the second half of track 11 ("Instrumentals, 1974, Volume 2") from the *First Thought, Best Thought* album. I was unable to trace the source of this music to Russell's "mother score." As this track is attributed to Volume 2, it would likely have come from other matrix-derived scores. But this lead sheet remains a great example of the final scores that were

Image 32. Measures 23-25 from the "mother score" of Instrumentals (Russell, IF)

given to musicians after they had re-composed the "mother score" in the studio. Also of interest here is that Track 11 and Track 12 of this same disc use similar musical material. And so we are able to hear Russell rework the same or similar material, from Volume 2, with a floating arhythmic orchestra.

Certain passages from *First Thought, Best Thought* show a direct link to the "mother score." Following (see, **image 32**) is one example, among others, I was able to find through score analysis. Measure 23, 24, and 25 of the "mother score" were looped and used to form "track 7" of *Instrumentals 1974, Volume 1*—though it seems they added an extra beat (or measure) to the final arrangement. Many of the pieces in *Instrumentals* combine looped bars such as the one in **image 32** with other looped bars form the mother score. "Track 7" however uses these three measures for its entire duration (two minutes and 32 seconds on the Audika recording). With such simple compositional elements in this piece, the players offered improvisations and variations to their parts, and a build in energy lead by clarinetist and composer Jon Gibson.

Instrumentals shows Russell's efforts in composition at their most disciplined and idiosyncratic. Russell had made the most of his Buddhist mentor's suggestion, not only in the resulting music of the performances, but in how he composed the music as well. The score is worked through as a ritualized series of steps, all drawn from a matrix of pitches, to which were applied processes of connecting these elements, and of constant re-translation and replication. Collaborating with Nonomura's visuals, this music was explicitly formed within a Shingon Buddhist perspective. The rigorous steps of Russell's matrix, which evolve into the "mother score," are very much like the ritualistic steps of sadhanas and other meditation practices that Russell encountered within his Buddhist practice.

The nature of Russell's tendency to reproduce processes at varying scales, all mutually nested within one another, is found in numerous Shingon meditation practices. If we recall the *gachirinkan* or "moon disc" meditation, a physical semblance of the moon is used to initiate the meditation. Then one visualizes a moon disc in their mind, and then another moon disc in "the center of [the deity's] heart." A similar nested process is often at work in mandala meditation, as Yamasaki described the "spiral" process of mandala meditation, where the attributes of deities are interrelated and understood as various manifestations of the central deity. Russell's entire process rests on facilitating these nested, cross-referenced forms and methods, creating an infinite array of musical possibilities that he reflects and refracts, as in a hall of mirrors. Combining a disciplined compositional methodology with improvisation and performer input, *Instrumentals* seemed to capture all of Russell's interests in one net. It is safe to say, in this work, that Russell lives up to *Instrumentals'* numerological "5" persona: one who constructively uses freedom.

While highly idiosyncratic, Russell's matrix system shows significant parallels with other esoterically inclined composers—some we've already mentioned—such as John Cage and his application of the *I-Ching*, or Jerry Hunt and his application of John Dee's angelic tables to music composition. Composer Anthony Braxton's Tri-Axium system, involving his own symbolic graphic language and detailed personal philosophy, perhaps shares the most resonant intentionality and ingenuity: "In Tri-axium I tried to build a thinking system, a system of thought that does not tell anybody what to think, but rather it gives people different ways to look at things and then you find your own way" (Braxton). Russell's system was very much of this kind, a system of thought, open to interpretation, and empowering to the performer. All of these composers were using disciplined strategies and symbolic languages, not to control and dictate their work, but to open themselves and their listeners to a visceral, present audition and unpredictable creativity.

Russell worked on *Instrumentals* between 1974-78. During

this time, he continued to conceive of different manifestations of the project. *Instrumentals, Vol. 2* went on to be released, in 1984, by the Another Side label in Belgium. However, the pressing of the album was realized with numerous errors. Aside from mislabeled musician credits and recording dates, the B side of the record was mastered at half the original speed. It wasn't until 2006 that excerpts from Volume 1 were released for the first time and Volume 2 was corrected and re-released by Audika Records. Beginning with a show at The Kitchen in 2013, Peter Gordon continues to direct contemporary ensembles in new interpretations of Russell's "mother score." Gordon's direction fulfills, or at least initiates what collaborator, Ernie Brooks, anticipated in the liner notes of *First Thought Best Thought*:

> I understand now why Arthur showed a rare lack of ambivalence about *Instrumentals*, telling me more than once that it was one piece he had written that was somehow really "good." Maybe that was because of the way it bridged his formal modern training with his passion for what he saw as the transcendent and egalitarian possibilities of pop. Those very few times that *Instrumentals* was performed, just a small part of a voluminous score was touched upon, and this collection can only hint at the music some orchestra of the future will find there (Russell, FTBT).

VI.

TEMPLE OF SOUND, *TOWER OF MEANING*:
Other Matrix Works

DINOSAUR L: *24 > 24 MUSIC*

If the funky riff doubles as a modern music monolith,
It must have done so before it came into existence (SN).

Arthur Russell

Russell had said he thought he might work on *Instrumentals* "for the rest of his life," but when he "went to the disco one night—it made a big impression" on him (Toop, 35). Russell's life was fundamentally altered in 1976 when he went to The Gallery, a prominent dance club in SoHo, where he became entranced by the music (lead by D.J. Nicky Siano), the social communion, and the celebration of sound. Russell found himself within a strong musical and social culture, largely made-up of Manhattan's LGBTQ and multi-ethnic communities, who were peacefully and ecstatically creating what would come to be called "disco" music. Sonically, Russell was excited by the quality of the PA systems that would project the music, as well as the idea that music was being specifically designed for these systems, these venues, and the audience. Rhys Chatham recalled Russell encouraging him to check it out: "[These dance clubs] are like temples for sound, Rhys!" (Chatham, 2009). He spent more and more time immersed in the disco scene, going to The Loft, Paradise Garage, and other venues. He was exploring his own homosexuality, becoming more fascinated with studio production, and increasingly interested in crafting a "hit" record.

Though rarely mentioned, there was a spiritual intention underlying disco's origin, one which Russell could easily tap into. This was in part a response to the rock and folk music that came out of the 1960's counter-culture movement. Rock and folk placed the musical focus on the personal narrative of the singer—the focus was on the artist—or upon historical and political issues expressed through the lyrics. Telling its own stories, dance music used the repetition of the beat to anchor ecstatic communion and spontaneous expression. D.J. Frankie Knuckles reflects on his D.J. experience as being "[...] like church. Because, when you've got three thousand people in front of you, that's three thousand personalities. And when those three thousand personalities become one personality, it's the most amazing thing" (Sylvan, 120).

As D.J. Danny Krivit recalls, in regards to the nature of the NY dance scene—more was going on than might be at first apparent. The D.J. is "picking a record that's not just a hit record, but he's picking a record that's timely for these particular people; and he's also talking a message [...] There's a story being woven. With say, Nicky Siano at the Gallery, it would be a vocal story" (Brewster, 148). Steve D'Aquisto, another prominent D.J. who would collaborate with Russell, describes making his music as telling "mystical stories and political stories, stories about love and stories about freedom [...] Life was a trip, and I wanted everyone to be high on music" (Lawrence, *Love Saves* 56). Krivit continues, "With David [Mancuso, at The Loft] it was a mood story. David in general was always about love, and he'd always try to stay with that" (Brewster, 148). Founded in 1970, Mancuso's The Loft was the first underground disco club in New York. However, the venue didn't begin as a dance party, but rather with a few people taking psychedelic drugs and meditating on Mancuso's music mixes. The Loft took shape around this spiritual and social experience. The focus was on the music and the communion of people—who came by invitation only. Mancuso describes the early days:

> I would organize these gatherings where we would experiment with acid [...] There were never more than five of us when we did this. One person would take nothing, another would take half a tab, and the rest would take the whole tab. It was all very new, and we took it very seriously. We used *The Psychedelic Experience* as our guide [...] I built a yoga shrine, which I used for yoga and tripping. In the beginning it was three feet by five feet, and it eventually grew to fifteen feet by thirty feet. As you walked into the loft you were immediately drawn to this area. It was gorgeous.

> [Timothy] Leary played music at his lectures and parties, and I went in the same direction. I bought a Tandberg tape recorder so that I could play tapes. The Buddha was always positioned between my two speakers [...] I made these 'journey tapes' that would last for five hours. They drew on everything from classical music to the Moody Blues. They would start off very peacefully, and the reentry would be more about movement, more jazz-oriented. Somebody might get up and start dancing around the room at some point, although they weren't dance sessions [...] The sound was very intense. It was the best thing out there for dancing. My whole space was configured for the party [...] My tapes followed the same geography as before, but this time the trip was different. They started off slow but then progressed into something that was more dance-oriented than psychedelic. The purpose of the party was hardcore dancing (Lawrence, *Love Saves* 9-10).

The Loft was a place where local gays, of any ethnicity, who were being persecuted by cops and kicked out of other venues, could convene and celebrate in an atmosphere of acceptance and love. That Russell would connect with Mancuso's compassionate dance floor is no surprise. Mancuso stresses this stance in popular Buddhist terms:

> Om is the source of all sound—it's a Buddhist chant where voices gel together and vibrate—and I felt as though we had returned h-*om*-e. It was very childlike, very peaceful, very liberating. It seemed to be correct. It reflected what I thought the world was supposed to be about. Everybody was there and we were like a family. There didn't seem to be any conflicts. Music helped us reach that place. Music was the key to get back h-*om*-e (13).

Beyond the liberating and ecstatic spiritual context of disco's origins, Russell considered dance music a natural model for the kind of music he was inclined to create. "I think the kind of repetition that comes out of me and is in dance music is somewhat different to the repetition of minimalist works of the Sixties and Seventies. Dance music is more improvisatory. It uses an extendable structure which on the one hand is recognizable, and on the other, improvisatory. It's based on hearing what you do while you do it" (Lawrence, *Hold On* 164).

It was around 1978 that Russell began formulating a new musical project called "Dinosaur." That same year he composed and produced (with Nicky Siano) Sire Record's first single, "Kiss Me Again," and it was a hit in the New York dance scene. From the dance floor success of "Kiss Me Again," Russell became excited by the idea of re-contextualizing disco through a more focused lens of experimentalism. A shifting roster of musicians started forming around the Dinosaur moniker, including Rome Neal, Peter Zummo, Peter Gordon, Rik Albani, and others. Dinosaur music was played live in April of 1979 at the Kitchen as well as at various other venues over the next three years. But the musical identity of the "Dinosaur" project would culminate in *24>24 Music*, an album recorded at Blank Tape Studios in June of 1979, released in 1981, as the first full-length album on Sleeping Bag Records. As far as the name "Dinosaur L," Russell had toyed with various dinosaur-based names, such as "Triceratops M."

After poetic and numerological considerations, "Dinosaur" [a numerological value of "2"] became "El Dinosaur" ["1"] and, finally, "Dinosaur L" ["5"].

The album *24>24 Music* would take form as a collection of studio-collaged scored-improvisations, mixed and re-mixed into unorthodox disco tracks with a stellar array of musicians of diverse musical backgrounds, including the multi-talented Julius Eastman (voice/keyboards), the revered rhythm section of the Ingram Brothers (Butch, Timmy, John, and William), and Russell's more consistent cohorts (P. Gordon, P. Zummo, and J. Kroesen), among others. The aesthetic Russell offered here would come to represent the sub-genre of "mutant disco"; and the album stands as Russell's most experimental and compositional take on the genre of dance music. From the wistful harmonies of *Instrumentals Vol. 1*, *24>24 Music* takes on dissonance and disjunction with a frenzy, while the beat continues to pulse louder than in his previous compositions. DJ Steve D'Aquisto, who, following the explorations of Dinosaur L, would work with Russell as Loose Joints, and who would co-produced the material on *24>24*, spoke of the work as "a big disco jazz epic," "the white album of disco," and "a Beethoven symphony for the dance floor." In his journals Russell was explicit about his aesthetic aims for the album:

> Dinosaur L [was] originally a funky rock and roll rave-up band, organ groove, [that has been] remixed as part of Warner Bros disco program. [*24>24 Music*] attempts to bring white spiritual sound into dance music context [with a] fusion of hip-hop and continuous groove, modern music/minimalist performance. I hear a music where a funky riff doubles as modern music monolith, the former facilitating the latter's transformation through time, establishing a connection to improvisation and spontaneously conceived time sequences, the natural connection (via recording) between improvisation and composition. [And] while the actual content of a recorded riff does not change (except through deterioration), the understood meaning of it can change with repetition (Russell, N).

And while *24>24 Music* may stand out by its conceptual compositional process, Russell's friend and frequent collaborator, Steven Hall, recalls their shared love of dance music being rooted in playful sexuality and dirty jokes as much as any spiritual aspiration. For example, Hall and Russell got a kick out of the song "Is It All Over My Face?" becoming a club hit, as the lyrics referenced facial ejaculation (Lawrence, 169). While it is easy to romanticize one side over the other, it might be more accurate to say that both "heavenly" and "schoolboy" mentalities were equally present in Russell's music.

Imagery and symbolic objects played an ongoing role in helping Russell conceptualize this project. For *24>24 Music* he noted to himself to use "candlelight as integrating image" (Russell, N). Russell would note several images associated with *24>24 music,* such as "photo of a Dinosaur with one finger on mixing board on one leg." Russell's partner Tom Lee recalls: "When we would talk about record album designs he would ask me if my nephew, Kevin, who was around 5 or 6, could draw a "dinosaur disguised as a space ship," or was it a 'spaceship disguised as a dinosaur?" He was very interested in fresh ideas that were not influenced by things that were overly familiar or popular" ("Q&A"). Tom Lee ended up providing the design for the final album cover, featuring a dinosaur with a reptile in its mouth and hand-drawn red "24s" and arrows filling in the background space. Not uncommon for Russell, this symbolism extended to every aspect of the work.

The album title, *24>24 Music,* was chosen in part for the fact that the players were guided to alter what they were playing every 24 bars, but also because the final recorded work was composed in the studio by mixing and collaging the two 24-inch tape reels in post-production. Regardless, the number "24" was of great significance to Russell in developing this project. He writes elliptically about it in his notebook, where he seems to be visualizing a matrix of elements, or "points," here referring to a "position system."

> moving point among the 24 pages, lines, positions
> sense of location
> acknowledgement of static linearity of position system
> endlessness of beats vs finiteness of 24 positions
>
> positions more real than notes themselves
>   } true form
> positions more real than notes themselves
>
> missing point

But before we go into the scores and pre-compositional sketches for *24>24 Music*, I want to focus on one of its broader concepts, alluded to in the quote above. The music for this project was based on the idea of collaging multiple audio tracks into a patchwork of improvisations. As he writes to himself, "one of the preoccupations of the El Dinosaur project has been to find an interface or common thread between live performance (and the logic of its perceptions), and current multi-track recording studio techniques (and its logic of shifting time priorities)" (Russell, N). *24>24 Music* was above all an experiment in using the studio as instrument; Russell was composing for the studio as much as for the musicians, who were largely encouraged to improvise. Speaking on his own inspirations from dance music, composer and collaborator Peter Gordon reiterates this compositional approach to the music studio:

> The x-y axis wouldn't be, you know, treble, bass and the different instruments in an orchestral score, but would actually be frequency and time; and that's really how you could work. And you could make your own stage, thinking orchestrally, but represented by tracks on the tape recorder. So rather than a score for a 16-piece ensemble, you'd have a 16-track tape composition

and with tape what you could do was record intuitive impulses and either keep them or not keep them but then work with them selectively (Hallett, 2010).

Russell's use of the studio in *24>24 Music* is similar to the sixth stage of the matrix process from *Instrumentals*. He saw editing as another level of transformation, and sought "a process where through recording medium the sequence of original real time performances is altered through editing with new conclusions reached through the results" (Russell, N). In the studio, after having made ensemble recordings and solo overdubs, by himself, Russell layered recordings, cut-and-pasted pieces, overdubbed new parts, altered tempos, and added effects. For several years Russell seemed to be specifically interested in "shifting time priorities," altering and overlapping tempos, making notes to himself like: "speeding up clock-like places," "let melody speed up past beat in parts." This is audible, via effects pedals, in several of his recorded works, clearest and most concise of all at the beginning of one of the dance versions of "Let's Go Swimming" ("See my brother, he's jumping out"), in which there is a swift single acceleration of tempo as the music comes in [this can also be heard in Zummo's Song IV]. Russell would create similar kinds of elastic temporal effects through multi-tracking different rhythm tracks or, for example, adding delay to the bass, vocals, and trombone in "Clean on your bean #1."

For Russell the walkman would play a large role in his relationship with analog tape. walking or jogging around Manhattan, riding the Staten Island Ferry, and switching from Side A to Side B of a cassette recording, comparing different mixes of the same work. This back and forth between cassette reels would be expanded to the studio reel-to-reel in *24>24 Music*. Russell would take the tapes from the recording sessions and make 24-track copies of those. Overdubs were added to these and placed back on the reels. He was working from a concept that these two 24-track reels would be overdubbed onto another, *without* synchronization, to arrive at haphazard shifts in tempo, something that was rather non-traditional at the time. Familiar with experimental studio procedures and inspired by the looped drums of the Bee Gees "Stayin Alive," Blank and Russell experimented with loops in the studio, which meant literally turning the 2-inch tape into a loop, as Blank held the lengthy strip of tape up to the side of the machine with a pencil. From his experience in jingle production, Blank would help in overdubbing vocals and instruments, which required recording the vocals on a 2-track (or 4-track), while playing pre-recorded vocals on a multi-track. According to Blank, "What I brought Arthur was efficiency. When you got into the studio everything was set up. We were like a jingle studio in that way. Everything was preset and ready to go as soon as you walked in the door" (Blank, 2011).

Russell was certainly aware of dub music, the Beatles' *Sgt. Peppers*, *musique concrete*, and other experimental tape procedures arising in the 60s and 70s, but he made a personal note of Richard Maxfield, whose assistant had once been the influential minimalist composer, LaMonte Young. In one of his re-copied notes, Russell writes: *tape as time length (Maxfield) (measured, agreed upon in advance, u.m. [unmeasured] improvised)*. This points towards Russell's treatment of both the music and analog tape itself, always oscillating between rational foresight and spontaneous intervention. Young's writing on Maxfield expresses a similar approach:

> Much of Maxfield's tape music was created through a technique which included pre-recording and electronically manipulating sound sources of various duration, then cutting lengths of tape containing these sounds and putting them in large glass mixing bowls. He would randomly draw pieces of tape from the bowls and splice them together placing blank tape of various durations between each of the pre-recorded sounds. What was interesting

was that although this was theoretically a Cagean aleatorical approach, Maxfield reserved the right to put back any sounds he did not like and continue to draw new sounds until he found the piece sounding in a way that inspired him. Sometimes several of these reels of spliced together sounds and silences, called inter-masters, were played simultaneously on separate tape decks in concert or mixed together to form a new stereo or mono original master (Dawes, 1989).

Bob Blank emphasized another unique aspect of the *24>24 Music* studio process, that "[t]hey would just press record and jam. You have to remember, at the time, outside of the Grateful Dead, nobody would just come into a studio and jam" (Blank, 2011). Though others had been doing this, it was not the more common approach—in part because of the cost of studio time and the more standard approach to utilizing that time and money. But this wasn't the typical group that entered a recording studio; it was a thoughtfully curated mix of highly skilled musicians from different backgrounds, who had never met. A large part of the process was just letting things happen, seeing what these kinds of combinations, both social and musical, generated in the moment via Russell's score. And while Russell's music is often remembered in a glowing state of collectivism, very often the musicians did not know what piece they were playing. For an overdub, Russell would bring in a friend, who might never know what Russell went on to do with the recording. Peter Zummo reflects on his experience in *24>24 Music*:

> Arthur might have had a sense of what the finished product would be, but I saw it as a process. He'd put some music in front of me and I'd say, "Where do you want me to play from?" He'd say, "Just play." I never understood how the score guided the process. It was a very open sound field (Lawrence, *Hold On* 161).

During the recording of the work, Russell was working with the aforementioned Bob Blank (producer of Donna

Summer, Talking Heads, Sting, Sun Ra, et al), first working at Blank's studio in Connecticut and finally settling into his home studio in Manhattan. He was consciously seeking to pair musicians from diverse backgrounds. "I found that band members functioned best when the talents contrasted and one takes up where the other takes off, this frequently means that personalities contrast sometimes and occasionally conflict" (Russell, N). Regardless, from this contrast and conflict Russell found a vital creative energy. For *24>24 Music* Russell had brought in the Ingram brothers, highly regarded musicians in the funk world, to lay down the rhythm and bass section. He combined their skilled chops with the guitar playing of Larry Saltzman (who now tours with Paul Simon), the saxophone of Peter Gordon (a composer who was also exploring experimental takes on dance music with his Love of Life Orchestra), and a variety of guest vocalists, notably among them the intoxicated no-wave singer Jill Kroesen and conductor/dancer/singer/composer Julius Eastman. So, a strange brew from the start. As Peter Zummo has said, Russell chose the musicians for his pieces as much for their person as for which musical instrument they played (Wolf, 2009).

Russell's concept and process were largely personal and unclear to the musicians. Peter Gordon reflects, "Arthur didn't say, 'I've got a song called 'Go Bang!' Let's record it.'" It was more like discovering the song in the raw material" (Lawrence, *Hold On* 218). But that raw material was rigorously arrived upon by Russell. In an interview Russell emphasizes the improvisational freedom, minimizing though still referencing formal restraints: "I tried to do this long composition called *24>24 Music* that was based on something that I could do and other people could play along with me, and... basically do anything [...] within a very wide area of restriction..." (Russell, "Beats in Space"). Even with the amount of raw intuition and improvisation audibly involved at every step of the creative process, Russell's approach to *24>24 Music* was still rooted in an esoteric and systematic methodology. He may have, at times, derived melodic passages via improvising over a two-note drone, as he was accustomed to doing with his matrix system in *Instrumentals* and *Tower of Meaning*. He had conceived *24>24 Music* in part as an extension of *Instrumentals*. With *Instrumentals* as well as the *Tower of Meaning* works in mind Russell imagines a potential *24>24 Music* which realizes itself "at regular intervals (24>24 possibly) two or more notes (swirling around one) 'valence' of notes. Location transmuted from around one to differing locations (each time) also; quivering-pulse articulation/bowing bow (temple music)."

However, having looked closely at Russell's *24>24 Music* notations, it became clear to me that Russell had devised a pre-compositional matrix system for *24>24 Music* that was significantly different than the one he was using previously. It is possible that the pitches in **image 33**, were derived from a previous matrix of pitches, much like that used in *Instrumentals*, though that cannot be confirmed, so the reason for his choosing these pitches remains unclear. **Image 33** shows a page from the *24>24 Music* matrix that Russell kept in his archives.

In **image 33** Russell horizontally lays out seven series of pitches, with each series having different pitches and a different quantity of pitches. While I have been unable to decipher the extensive and likely varied use of all the numbers applied in this matrix, I speculate Russell was working in the following manner, as he had described a few years prior for an unidentified work in the early 1970's.

Put sequences of notes, un-notated as to time, after specified places in each part; the players are to keep track of the number of beats it takes them to play this sequence musically, in other

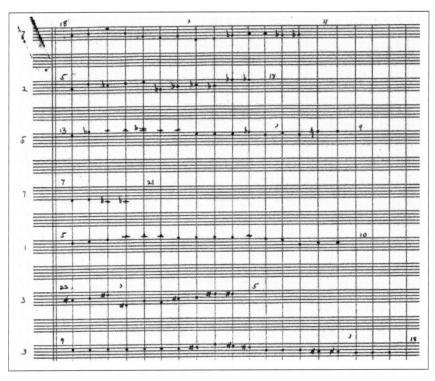

Image 33. Pre-compositional matrix for 24>24 Music, (Russell, 24F)

words improvised. When he is finished he then notates a break *according to number system*. Two or three such places. Let the number correspond to the sequence of notes and vice versa (N).

It is likely Russell was working with this matrix of pitches in a similar way, improvising through each of the pitch collections, perhaps over a backing rhythm or drone track, marking "breaks" and notating the varying rhythms and pitch durations that he liked from these improvisations. The score of **image 33** was paper-clipped to a group of seven duplicate copies; and each page displays different pitches, markings, and numbers. It is my assumption that each page, may have been used to generate a given section of this work. Peter Gordon, who was heavily involved in the making of *24>24 Music*, does not recall seeing this chart. So, I am assuming this is something Russell, pre-compositionally, worked with on his own, just as he did with his *Instrumentals* matrix. In a similar way, Russell's own relationship with this matrix would develop into the more nuanced notated passages, which we'll go into shortly.

The pieces then developed out of a continuous jam session, responding to Russell's modular notations. "Arthur," producer Bob Blank recalls, "would bring in stacks of music paper" (Blank, 2011). Russell grouped these scores into three kinds: 1) a series of "drone" sections, 2) a series of "between drone" sections, and 3) chord charts and notated melodies. Some of the drone sections included melodic notations, while others were simply labeled "Free," with no musical notation at all. However, I have confirmed that all the melodic material presented in at least one "Between Drone" section was derived from the original matrix in **image 33**. For example, looking at the beginning of "Between Drone 4 & 5" (**image 34**), we can see that the melodic material was taken directly from the tone grouping, labeled "2" (the second row from the top) in the matrix of **image 33**. This score part then evolved, through performance and recording, into some of the melodic material used in "#2 No, Thank You":

To this restless melody, Russell would add the belligerently polite speech of Julius Eastman's voice ("No, thank you! I said 'No, thank you, pleeeeeeze!"), lending the piece to a surreal parody of mundane miscommunication on the street; while two organs deliver the shifting harmonies just mentioned: one more insistent, the other more ornamental. Notated melodic passages, like the one for "No Thank You," would have been given in snippets, re-arranged or re-notated during the recording process and then altered again via editing and collaging the analog tapes in the studio. Russell's

173

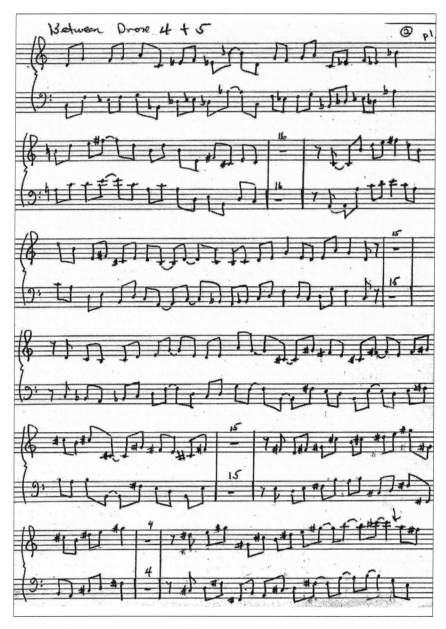

Image 34. "Between Drone 4 & 5" from 24-24 Music scores, (Russell, 24F).

notated melodies however only occur in three of the main tracks on the album ("#2 No Thank You," "#3 Corn Belt," and "#6 Get Set"). So, it seems much of Russell's notations, derived from his matrix, might have been left on the cutting room floor. Meanwhile, tracks which had either consistent riffs ("Clean on Your Bean") or a semi-fixed song form ("Go Bang," "Corn Belt"), would supplement the "drone"/"between-drone" format Russell was using to generate other instrumental material.

"Clean on Your Bean" largely revolves around this saxophone riff (**image 35**), loosely anchored over undulating percussion and a repeating bass line. The organ churns out a repeated and strange chord progression, which we'll go deeper into shortly. Some local rappers, recruited by Peter Gordon, brought their voices into the session. However, their rapping is abstracted by the array of effects (reverb, echo) that were layered upon the vocal track. Russell, as he does so many times throughout his life, abstracts the language to savor its purely sonic and multivalent meaningfulness. In 1983 Russell would experiment again with abstracted rap on his remix of "Chill Pill (Underwater Mix)," in which he nearly drowns, in echo, the rapping of high school students from JHS 126 in Brooklyn.

On the other hand, "Go Bang" has lyrics and a more song-based chord structure, making it the most tuneful work on the album, and incidentally the most catchy, especially after

Image 35. "#1 (You're Gonna Be Clean On Your Bean)," saxophone riff, as transcribed by the author.

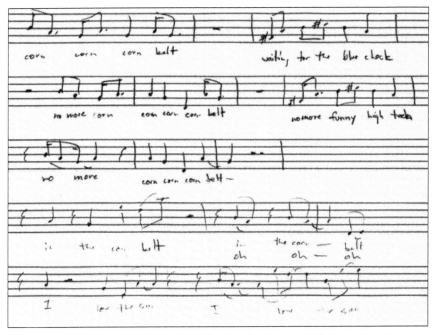

Image 36. A notebook sketch of "#3 (In the Corn Belt)" (Russell, 24F)

being remixed by renowned DJ Fraçois Kervorkian. But even that handle of familiarity is complicated by the fact that Jill Kroesen, the singer, is audibly intoxicated. Russell's lyrics fuse themes of social, sexual, and cosmic union. This recalls us to the meditation practice of Tibetan *mahamudra*, which breaks through materiality and delusion through meditative questioning.

[line 1] Thank you for asking the question.

[line 2] You showed us the face of delusion

[line 3] to uproot the cause of confusion.

[line 4] I wanna see all my friends at once.

[line 5] I need an armchair to put myself in your shoes.

[line 6] I'm in the mood to ask the question."

In "#3 (In the Corn belt)" Julius Eastman's wildly operatic voice viscerally invokes the corn belt. Like "Go Bang" this track had its origins as variable song sketches that Russell would perform as a soloist. But with *24>24 Music* Russell was de-emphasizing the song form in favor of dance minimalism and sonic abstraction.

Interestingly, aside from the chords in the song-based works and "jam sessions," there is one harmonic progression that can be heard repeated or varied in all but one track on the entire album. Often used as a harmonic texture more than a "progression," **image 37** shows what I call the "dinosaur" progression, with the chords likely derived from one of Russell's matrix dyads:

The "dinosaur" progression is essentially a series of ninth chords [as Russell labeled them in his notebook: F9—Ab9—E9—Db9—Eb9—D9—F9], the kind of which are more commonly found in jazz or gospel music styles. Russell's voicing of the chords is more unorthodox, emphasizing dissonant intervals and large intervallic leaps. "Go Bang" (begins with the same progression at a lower volume, audible again after the first minute of music), "Get Set" (at 1:30 and then again at 3:30), at the tail ending of "#3 (In the Corn Belt)," several times in both "Clean on your bean #1" and "#1 (You're gonna be clean on your bean)." This progression would seem to be the unifying element throughout the *24>24 Music*'s composition, serving almost like the glue Russell used to stick the pieces together. It's also worth noting that when

Image 37. The "Dinosaur" Progression. Re-notated by author from Russell's original notation (24F)

adding the metrical divisions of this progression together (4+2+2+2+6+6+2), they add up to 24. The progression would crop up in some of Russell's live experiments with the work as well, notably in his documented duet performance, "Radishes Flying To Jupiter," performed in March of 1980 with Russell on spoken voice and "wah-wah" effected cello and Rome Neal on percussion and organ. In this performance, at Niblock's EI loft, the "dinosaur" progression—played by Neal on the organ—provided a backbone for Russell's loosely rhythmic 17 minute *pizzicato* cello improvisation. Steeped in a variant of Russell's matrix composition process, *24>24 Music* proved to be one of his most bizarre musical projects, effectively facilitating a creative situation where he and his accomplices could "basically do anything."

With *24>24 Music* Russell's experimental approach was a bit intense for the popular reception he was hoping for. Francois Kevorkian reinforces this sentiment: "There are people who think the original version is a work of genius, which I'm not going to disclaim, because Arthur had his own vision of things, which was very peculiar and very much genius-like. But sometimes genius works are harder to play at parties" (Lawrence, *Hold On* 220). Two tracks from the *24>24 Music* project went on to be released as dance singles. "#5 Go Bang" was remixed by Larry Levan, and the B-side "Go Bang" and "Clearn on Your Bean" were both remixed by Francois Kevorkian for a 12" single released in 1982. "Go Bang" was a unanimous success in New York, and is still today widely regarded as an "underground classic" of the period.

Following the recording of *24>24 Music* Russell would perform works from the album at various venues. One featured live vocals by Lola Blank and Wendell Morrison, while often Russell would be joined by his Singing Tractor crew (Lauten, Zummo, Ahmed, et al.). It was by bringing them into his experimental dance realm that the song "Living in the Light" came to evolve. Lauten recalls, "He had his experimental side, which is the kind of music Peter and I would get into, and then he had his pop side. He wanted to write Buddhist pop music, because he felt it would be karmically better to reach out to as many people as possible. I think he was hoping to make some money with it too" (Lawrence, *Hold On* 226). Russell would continue to work on composing more dance works, some leaning to the experimental side ("In the Light of a Miracle" and "Tiger Stripes"), while others leaned toward a cleaner, more commercial, pop sensibility ("Tell You (Today)"). Though even with this pop gloss D.J. Steve D'Aquisto recognized the spiritual underpinning that Russell was working with:

> It's really Zen—it's Buddhism you see. It was all about symbolism in the higher sense. [Tell You Today] is one of the most beautiful songs I've ever heard. You could sing it over and over 1000 times and it'll never bore you and that was Arthur Russell. It was all these little tuneful messages that can be sung in any different number of ways but the meaning was always deep. Arthur Russell was Cole Porter and Bob Dylan and one of the great singers and writers of all times. The songs, if you listen to them now, they're as bright and as fresh as they were 20 years ago and that's what makes them so different. It's a depth of emotion, a feeling of love and warmth it's all these things ("Arthur Russell").

During this time Russell was working a lot with D.J. Steve D'Aquisto. At Blank Studios, they brought in the Ingram Brothers and other musicians, as well as singer/dance-goers from the Loft to add actual party sounds and feelings into the mix. As was often Russell's custom, they recorded on the nights of the full moon. Guiding Russell and D'Aquisto's work together were Trungpa's concepts of "crazy wisdom" and "first thought, best thought." D'Aquisto recalls that his primary roll in the studio "was to encourage people to go with the first idea. The first idea is always the best because it's always the absolute freshest. Ninety-nine out of a hundred times, the first take is the best take, because it's not studied [...] We were living in a stream of consciousness existence. We went with the flow" (Lawrence, *Hold On* 151). D'Aqusito recalls the awkwardness of bringing in musicians from different backgrounds:

Arthur's music is really avant-garde—and here is a very traditional Philadelphia/R&B family which he had to cajole into doing this stuff. He told me that Butch (Ingram) would look at him like "you're out of your fucking mind!" But the younger ones—Timmy and Johnny Ingram—would really get into it, just grooving with Arthur ("Arthur Russell").

D'Aquisto recalls the making of "Pop Your Funk," a track recorded at the time, as follows:

There was a 32 bar section of the beat that was just superb! Arthur says "We need another 24 track machine." So we started copying the 32 bars, then 2 bar, "4 bar, 8 bar," etc... pieces, and then we intercut them. It was almost like we threw the tape up in the air, then when it landed we picked up pieces and then put them together because it was just a beat. Then we overlaid percussion and vocal tracks; we were just experimenting. There was this big gong in the studio, which is that big ambient noise you hear throughout the whole thing. We kept hitting it over and over again. We had a microphone out the window so it's mixed with traffic noise! We were just seizing every moment. There was no forethought about what we were going to do. About 12 seconds of rehearsal and we just went right into recording. We spent every penny on recording and made all these records and then Mel didn't want to release them ("Arthur Russell").

As Russell had Blank do during the recording of 24>24

Music, he and D'Aquisto would just let the tapes run. From this Trungpa-influenced flow of spontaneity they produced several significant tracks, including "Is it all over my face?" "Pop Your Funk," "Tell You (Today)," and others, many unfinished and unreleased. Bob Blank recalls being impressed by Russell's process: "Arthur showed me that anything is possible, that music is a continuous flow or process. Music can evolve out of things. It's not a form that you fit things into" (Lawrence, *Hold On* 151).

Around the same time that Russell had begun diving head-first into the dance world, he was approached by Robert Wilson, renowned New York dramaturge, to compose the music for his new production, an experimental take on the ancient Greek play, *Medea*.

MEDEA / TOWER OF MEANING

Russell would expand the musical aesthetic and compositional stylings of *Instrumentals Vol. 2* into his next, and final, large-scale orchestral project, which was an orchestral scoring of Robert Wilson's Greek myth adaptation, *Medea*. It was through the encouragement of Philip Glass that Robert Wilson commissioned Russell to compose orchestral music for his latest theatrical production, *Medea* (1980). Though Russell was ultimately fired due to personality differences with Wilson and an inability to compose or revise his composition in a timely fashion, the music was performed and documented during a few full dress rehearsals and remains one of Russell's most concerted efforts in ensemble composition. The only existing recording of Russell's music was made during one of these rehearsal periods on February of 1981. It

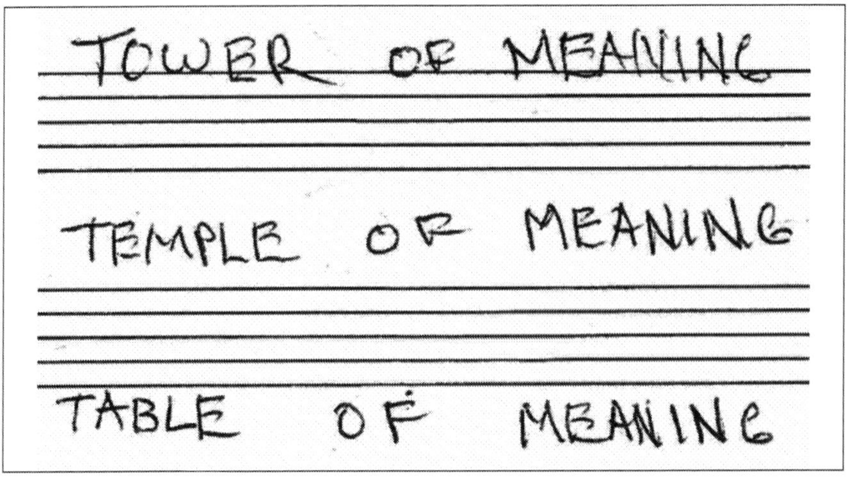

Image 38. Tower of Meaning, alternates titles listed in notebook (Russell, N)

was performed by the CETA New York Orchestra, a branch from the Brooklyn Philharmonia [CETA = Changing Education Through the Arts] and conducted by Russell's friend and collaborator Julius Eastman. The full instrumentation was: Brass (Trumpet, Horn, Trombone, Tuba), Strings (Violin, Viola, Cello, Bass), Woodwinds (Flute, Oboe, Bassoon, Clarinet), Harp, Percussion [including chime, doumbek], Chorus (arranged by Wilson and Gene Paul Rickard with Arthur Russell).

The collaboration between Wilson and Russell began enthusiastically and with mutual admiration. "I really really like the last tape I got. I have played it over many times here in Texas and I think it is perfect for the new play" wrote Wilson to Russell in December of 1980 (Russell, L). Wilson opted to perform the play in the original Greek, reveling in its rhythms and abstracted sound, and presented primarily through lengthy monologous speeches. The setting was sparse and stoic: the outline of a dwelling and two columns all shrouded in dim lighting and dark shadows. The choreography reflected this atmosphere, featuring movements based on statuesque poses, with lead vocalists often standing still during their singing and spoken monologues. Russell's music reflected this general mood of austerity and ominousness. The majority of the music was instrumental in nature, while the remaining portions were "musical" settings of the Greek text, which Russell divided into varieties of "speech" and "song."

But Russell had his own vision of what the music should be for *Medea*, a vision which was, more and more, at odds with Wilson's perspective. Their collaborative relationship began to feel strained. In Russell's musical vision he sought more openness, or the possibility of change throughout the creative process. He described the music, in general, as "a wide receptacle for an infinite variety of input." He also fix-ated on more conceptual applications of the music, which he "de-signed for walking." Russell's vision and his confidence in it could be felt in his letters to Wilson:

> Although I find the prolonged speeches of many of the principals to be, in their simplicity, an inspiring visual object of meditation and offering the possibility of ecstatic exploration (i.e. Nurses' opening speech)... I think the best way to consolidate the sequence is to run the long speeches simultaneously; that is, to let the chorus sing and Medea (for example) to deliver her long speech over the music. As I said before, the music was designed for formalized movement, like walking. And while the music is static; it does not "develop" but rather goes backwards in concept; it is yet I believe a wide receptacle for an infinite variety of space and time input, etc. Events could even be doubled up if necessary (Russell, MF).

With *Medea*, as with every other project, Russell was striving to create or tap into that "wide receptacle for an infinite variety of input" (Russell, N). He spoke of *Instrumentals* in this manner; he spoke of *World of Echo* in this manner. Perhaps this loose, though disciplined, approach proved too indefinite for a major production like Wilson's *Medea*. Regardless, over time, their equitable efforts to control the project by their individual visions became mutually frustrating and combative. As well, Russell was struggling to provide revisions in a timely manner.

Russell received his indemnity papers from Wilson's company, Byrd Hoffman, in November of 1982. Meanwhile, the production had been continued with British composer Gavin Bryars taking Russell's place, in 1981. *Medea* would never become a prized work of Wilson's. However, Russell's music for *Medea* would live on. Russell decided to release the instrumental portions of the orchestral recordings and handed them over to Philip Glass. Russell had used the music, renamed as "Temple of Meaning," with dancer Daniel McIntosh. More time passed. The recordings were altered—Russell intentionally slowed the speed of the recording and overdubbed other sounds—extensively mixed with Eric Liljestrand, and were released under the new name *Tower of Meaning* by Chatham Square Productions in 1983.

Again, it seems Russell went through several numerological derivations for the name of this re-mixed project. From "Temple of Meaning" (a numerological value of 2), Russell went to "Table of Meaning" (7, the same numerological value as "World of Echo"), ultimately opting for "Tower of Meaning" (3). From a Shingon Buddhist perspective, one might be recalled to the three vajras, a.k.a the "three jewels," or the "three mysteries": Body, speech, and mind. These are philosophical projections that speak to the enlightened state of the Buddha. This state of being is one without qualification; it is an expression of emptiness. With this in mind *Medea* was shaping up to be an intensely meditative project. The stark minimalism of Wilson and Russell's initial sketches present the stage as the mind, the human body as sculpture, dialogue as abstract expression, and scenes as meditations.

In reviewing several popular numerology publications, those with a "3" mentality are portrayed as enthusiastically creative, magnetic and inspiring, but intensely sensitive to criticism or negative feedback—child-like was a common descriptor (e.g. Lagerquist, 65). Russell took to *Medea* with overflowing excitement. He was ambitious, filled with ideas, and he took it all very seriously. But when Wilson disagreed with the composer or demanded sudden changes, Russell would argue, fall behind, and recoil—he was quick to show the "negative" aspects of this project's tertiary nature.

As with all of his works, the music made for *Medea* was often re-fitted to be used in solo performance and other contexts. We can even hear Russell, chanting over his distorted cello, performing a solo version of *Tower of Meaning* material on his album *World of Echo* (1985) (c.f. "Tower Of Meaning/ Rabbit's Ear/Home Away From Home"). Here, again we see the versatility of Russell's matrix scores. The same work can be realized through the intimacy of solo performance as well as the dramatic scale of an orchestra. The number of possible musics, realizations, and transformations was limitless.

Like Russell's other matrix works, the score for *Medea/ Tower of Meaning* involved a massive series of pre-compositional steps. He was working from pitch matrices for both the instrumental and vocal portions of the work. He would compile various elements of the pitch matrices and then orchestrate them into a full orchestral score. Russell describes the music himself, and alludes to its derivation from the matrix system, to Wilson:

"Instrumental music" means: that music made up of the basic substance of the composition, not including the prologue or Scene III-A, which is stated directly. It is played ideally by harps, with a lower voice (pizzicato or plucked cello) pacing the regularity of the rhythmic intervals which comprise this instrumental music structure's only element of variation. While this basic scheme remains intact, the texture, dynamics, and even tempo must be manipulated to inhabit the natural environment of different spatial moments (Russell, MF).

Below is the score, again based on a series of dyads, which was used to compose one of the tracks from *Tower of Meaning* [Disc 2, Track 6, *First Thought, Best Thought*]. We'll look at some of Russell's orchestrations shortly, but the passage below, looped four times here, continues looping to form the entirety of track six on the album.

A first listen to *Tower of Meaning*, gives the listener endless waves of changing chords. They move along, slowly, measured, with pregnant pauses. They seem to repeat, but never feel the same. It turns out, that this was no mere accident, but that Russell had, yet a gain, a strategy guiding the process. In the *Instrumentals* music, a pattern or melody is repeated and improvised over, and mutated through the matrix process. Here, Russell's matrix process is simplified. A pattern from the matrix is chosen. As in *Instrumentals* it is repeated, and often the repetitions of one passage are conjoined to those of another in a continuous flow. But Russell's strategy with *Tower of Meaning* was perhaps even more methodical in its method of composition.

Russell took a passage of tones (10 measures long) from his matrix and then applied alternating meters (4, 6, 7, 8, 10, 12 beats to the measure). We can see the repeated passage's first exposition in measures 1-10 of **image 39**. There are three more repetitions of this passage, on the same page, starting at measures 11, 21, and 31. What Russell does with

Image 39. The author's reductive notation of a passage from Tower of Meaning (Disc 2, Track 6, First Thought, Best Thought). The first bar of each repeat is numbered

these repetitions, with each iteration, is alter their metrical flow. So, while the pitches remain the same in each repetition, their durations are constantly altered, essentially in a random manner. For example, let's compare the meters of the first 4 measures from each repetition above.

Passage 1 (ms. 1-4):	4/4	8/4	6/4	4/4
Passage 2 (ms. 11-14):	6/4	4/4	8/4	4/4
Passage 3 (ms. 21-24):	4/4	6/4	4/4	4/4
Passage 4 (ms. 31-34):	4/4	8/4	12/4	4/4

Here we can see the constant shifting of meters. And while certain meters reappear for a given measure, the context of their return is nevertheless altered by the meter changes in neighboring measures. Interestingly Russell tends to keep the forth and fifth measure of each repetition the same tones *and* the same meter (4/4), providing a mnemonic anchor of consistency as the piece endlessly morphs. This method of repetition/alternation is much like the compositional style of Morton Feldman, who worked with shifting meters to similar effect in his own music.

Always drawn towards aquatic metaphors, Russell described this music as a desire to "move through chords like you're on a boat." And like the waves of the sea, there is a rhythmic flow, but it is constantly varied, an elastic respiration. This gives us an idea of how Russell was strategically, through harmonic repetition and metric variation, attempting to "lose consciousness of duration" (Russell, N). To compose this music Russell was working off of a matrix of pitch pairings, to which he pencils in minimal harmonies, adding a second voice to the top staff at times. For the final orchestral score, Russell would add additional harmonies, orchestrated for the full orchestra.

The final scores for *Medea* are incompletely preserved. I was able to find one excerpt of a full score (the first few bars are shown in **image 40**). Here we see Russell has continued with his notational style of using only whole notes, with single numbers indicating the duration of a given whole note or measure. Characteristic is the use of drone, or sustained tones, and Russell's mosaic orchestration. By mosaic orchestration I mean to emphasize the fact that Russell's music, while extremely melodic, does not give a linear melodic line to any one voice, rather the instruments exchange and substitute one another within a more broadly-formed sonic image, like tiles of different colored glass reflecting the same light source. This mosaic style is also exemplified in the way he alternates meters, dynamics, and many other parameters.

As in *Instrumentals Vol.* 2 the chords transform very slowly, often through a permutation of pitch material, expressing the same pitches in different registers and instruments—again, this "mosaic" orchestration. Above the matrix dyads, the bottom two staves, Russell adds another staff where he includes a kind of *cantus firmus*, or as he might have called it, "primary melodic material." Above this melodic staff are penciled-in pairings of instruments, which, after a survey of the score, seem to indicate the orchestration of unisons or pitch sets, largely randomized measure-to-measure. Again, Russell's predilection for unisons, inspired by those he heard on All India radio broadcasts, significantly define the sound. This is evident not only in Russell's orchestration, but even in the original dyads of his matrix, in which tones from one measure to another are sustained, creating a drone, or ostinato, when played consecutively.

Image 41 shows a piano reduction of the orchestral score shown in **image 40**. Again, here we can notice how Russell's orchestral music often reduces down to a single pitch, interval, or triad, connecting the orchestration directly to the 2-3 note chords that Russell was exploring with his matrix and

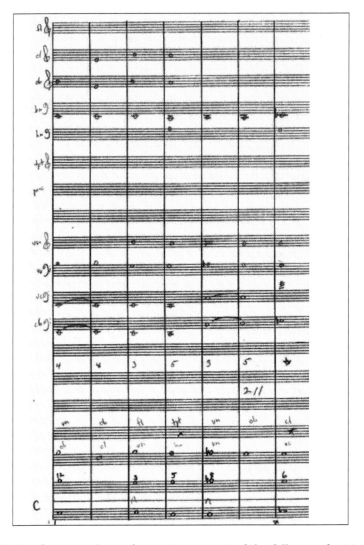

Image 40. The first seven bars of page 1, section C of the full score for Medea (Russell, MF).

which he could play and sing in performance with his cello. The first three measures, for example, only employ three pitches (E, G, and B).

Much less familiar—only the video is publicly available

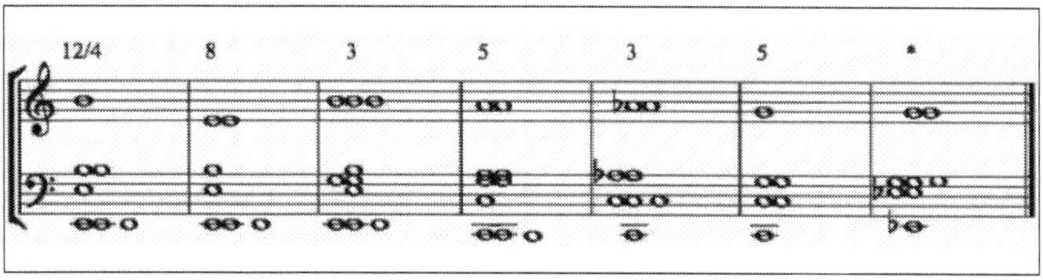

Image 41. Author's piano reduction of Medea full score, section C, page 1, first 7 bars. Numbers indicate the duration. The "*" has an unclear meaning. Duplicates of the same pitch indicate Russell's unison orchestrations.

at the NY Public Library—is the vocal content of Russell's *Medea* score. Probably out of a desire to separate his music from Wilson's production, Russell left the vocal portions of the work off of the *Tower of Meaning* album. But even his composition for voices was rooted in the matrix format, as he describes here "music for choral sections composed w/chord changes on each note defined by pairs of notes moving like a slow wheel/gear" (Russell, SN). Russell's text-setting scores (**image 42**) show him assigning matrix pitches/durations to each syllable of the original Greek text of the play, I could not find subsequent scores for the text-setting, but I imagine Russell notated a through composed orchestration to give to the performers. And, here, it should be easy to recall the primary importance given to the syllable in both Vajrayana Buddhism as well as in Hindustani music. 10 years after living at the Kailas Shugendo commune, Russell is still pursuing the same spiritually-based abstraction of the voice.

Whereas the chords of *Medea* might be placid lakes, Russell's continuous melodic settings of the text come off as a babbling brook. The melodies themselves were generally modal, but would more often veer into unexpected melodic territory. Such alterations are found both in the melodic line as well as the harmonies occasionally added to it. The phrases, if not continuous (e.g. without pause/silence), are almost always separated by a rest (a single quarter note in the first

Image 42. Notational sketches of Greek syllables from Medea (Russell, MF)

example, and elsewhere 1-3 beats of silence), the irregular repetition of which lends the whole to a sense of continuity rather than of formal grouping. It seems very much as if Russell were trying to use conversational speech (perhaps informed by Greek linguistics) to compose the text-based portions of the music.

Many of the instrumental sections were clearly derived from these speech-based compositions. And as in the rhythmic regularity of the speech-based portions, this piece as a whole works off of a silent four-on-the-floor pulse onto which Russell has grafted a series of constantly changing meters. The beginning of track 5 from *Tower of Meaning* (*First Thought, Best Thought*, CD 2, LP 3) is a great example of this. We hear a series of pulsed chordal phrases, each separated, except at the end of the "intro," by a single quarter note pause. These fluid speech-like rhythms are audible in many sections of the work, the whole of which could be understood as a matrix-derived music directly influenced by the rhythmic flow and intonational quality of human speech.

With the encouragement of Philip Glass, Russell turned his rejected music for Wilson's production into an album length collage of the music from the rehearsal recordings, what we now know as *Tower of Meaning*. For this recording excerpts were taken from the original *Medea* recordings, and in some cases these recordings were intentionally slowed down by Russell himself. He also overdubbed other recordings (for example Elodie Lauten on Casio keyboard).

SINGING TRACTORS

The music itself was very experimental and mostly improvised although there were usually a couple of lines written out but no strict arrangement for them. We would explore harmonically and melodically reacting to one another's sounds and occasionally reading a part but always expanding from there. We were merging influences from post-Cagean randomness to free jazz to rock and pop music to classical elements to African beat and dance music (2009).

Elodie Lauten

Amidst the above activities, as well as performing and recording pop and folk songs and other more ephemeral experimental works, Russell was forming an ongoing music project/ensemble under the name "Singing Tractors," the name referring to his Iowan farm roots. Having met Elodie Lauten when Russell first moved to New York, it wasn't until 1977 that the two began to play more regularly. Living proximally, they began meeting at sunset to play music, with Lauten on Casio keyboard and Russell on cello. Peter Zummo would join in with Casio and trombone; Ernie Brooks would play on bass. Ken Goshorn, guitar, and Ron Kuivila, electronics, would join occasionally, but the full ensemble peaked as a quartet of Russell, Lauten, Zummo, Brooks, and percussionist Mustafa Ahmed. Through 1982 the quartet was playing regularly. At Experimental Media with Ned Sublette, at Wesleyan University with Kuivila, at the Tibetan Institute, at CBGB's with Sublette and Arnold Dreyblatt, and at numerous other venues and with numerous other guests. The one currently available recording made by the quartet was "In the Light of the Miracle" (1982, Battery Sound), a dance-driven, Buddhist infused, improvisational work. While Singing Tractors embraced styles of dance and popular music, as in "In the Light," they would more often focus on subtler works of an experimental nature, both scored, by any member of the ensemble, or freely improvised.

Into the 90s the Singing Tractors remained an ongoing forum in which Russell and like-eared friends could work in a more open and intuitive way, each bringing their works and ideas into the creative mix. Casio keyboards were a consistent part of the Tractors' music, providing a drone element (being either sustained or tremeloed), which, as Zummo noted, had ties to the drone function of the sitar in Indian music (personal interview). Recalling the rehearsals for the Singing Tractors Zummo says, "We would rehearse, get a set list out of Arthur, go on stage, and have no idea what was happening... There was no way to tell whether we were playing the songs in the order they were indicated on the set list or not. He would just start going and you would have to make a decision, but it would be a difficult time to make a decision. That happened *all* the time" (Lawrence, *Hold On* 213). Zummo shared a deep interest in incorporating improvisation—as well as the languages of pop, rock, jazz, and world musics—into serious composed music.

An ensemble of like-minded friends offered the perfect forum for Russell to continue exploring his matrix system in an improvisatory way. The scores left to us show he was notating melodies over two-note drones in exactly the same manner as we have seen in *Instrumentals* and *24>24 Music*. According to Zummo, he and Russell were consciously working with what he calls a "multi-modal" compositional process. Zummo had been exploring this more deliberately for quite some time in his own work. He emphasizes the term "multi-modal" to differentiate it from "poly-modal," in that two modes are not over-laid upon each other, but evolve, melodically or linearly, one from the other. In this way the melody can create harmonic colors while not referring to harmonic logic, giving the music an air of familiarity with a mist of strangeness. This would make Russell's emphasis on two-note drones harmonically significant—avoiding a defining triad de-stabilizes harmonic function (typically guided by complete triads). A similar multi-modal aesthetic can be heard in much of Russell's work, especially in those we just reviewed in this chapter.

And as in stage four of *Instrumentals*, Russell would write out numerous melodies over short changes, with the Tractors' material, he was combining these changes, creating slightly larger pieces. Individual pieces would be developed by repeating a single stave of notation and then connecting multiple staves for a continuous performance, looping the notation as long as they desired. More recently Russell's work with the Singing Tractors has been made publicly available through the recorded work of Arthur's Landing and the Ne(x)tworks ensemble. Dating from the late 1980s, **image 43** is the first page of the score for an unidentified Singing Tractors work.

Through a process of looping and infinite alteration, the piece is capable of evolving and expanding radically during performance, well beyond the duration notated on the page. While improvising, the melody would be altered or sometimes completely abandoned by individual performers, rhythms would form and dissolve into drone textures, only one of the dyad tones would be played, or dyads would be embellished with neighboring tones (further opening up the harmonic field), Casio keyboards would add tremeloed drone textures, while other instruments and noisemakers might join in the mix. N.B. the matrix dyads are here notated in the treble clef (though Russell leaves out the clef).

Looking back at the *Instrumentals* system, we notice a very

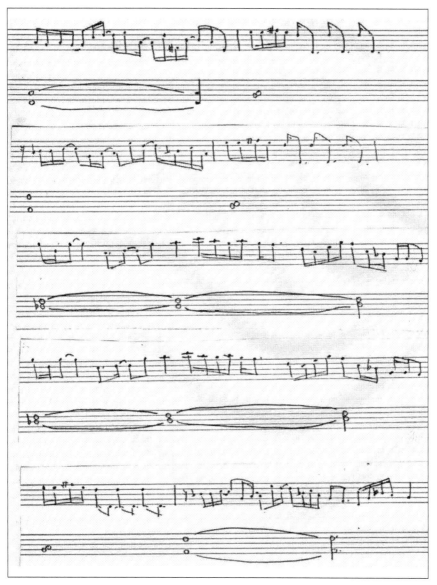

Image 43. Page one from an unidentified score for the Singing Tractors (Zummo, personal archives)

similar approach in stage three of the process. Again, fairly continuous melodic phrases of varying time-lengths with corresponding two-note drones are collaged one to another. Though engaging in drone and noise textures, the Tractors' music was often rhythmically oriented (even without percussion), with an underlying if softly spoken pulse along which the various instrumentalists could wrap their tones around. As in Christian Wolff's *Exercises*, the Tractors would loop a passage, with individuals oscillating between playing all or part of a written melody or drone, or improvising with the others. The effect, again similar to Russell's orchestration tendencies, is to create a kind of mosaic aesthetic, which, in brief unsuspecting moments, will suddenly have everyone converging upon the same small phrase. The melodic lines themselves tend to be very active. As was typical for Russell, the rhythms move along a 16th note tactus, constantly though subtly displacing the downbeat—like a fly outwitting a giant with its quick tiny moves. I was able to find in an unidentified score matrix (**image 44**) the primary dyads from which Russell derived the final score for the Singing Tractors composition (**image 43**).

Russell and Zummo would often go to Wesleyan University in Middletown, CT to use the recording studio. There they befriended Ron Kuivila who began joining in their performances, often playing a Casio keyboard and other media. Russell's interaction with Kuivila seemed to inspire him a great deal. As he regularly did, Russell would jot down memorable moments and suggestions for future performances. In his own five page compilation of notebook entries, Russell references Kuivila multiple times. There are numerous entries pertaining to Kuivila:

period of cello drone where ron takes off

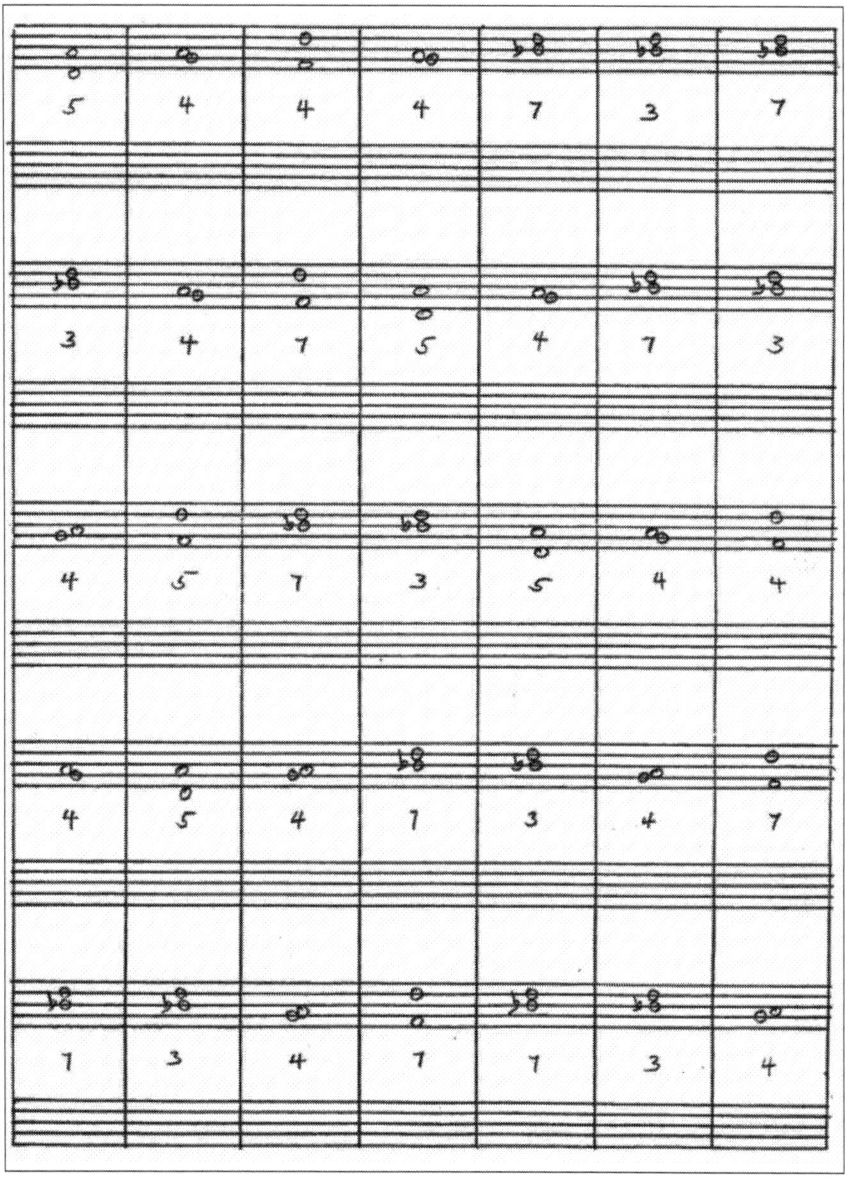

Image 44. Pre-compositional dyads used to create Singing Tractors score in image 43 (Russell, N).

gliss. for ron tbn + cello (using shorter 16 phrases)

modulate *darbuka* [a Middle Eastern hand drum] speed via ron or tape or both

imagine that 1) you 2) ron 3) both 4) anybody are DJ's

visualize ron's sample as *amrita* [a ritual nectar, from the Rigveda, said to give one immortality]

3-bar structure for ron's noise-over (one on, two off) (into 1st, 2nd beat of two)

Regarding his "amrita sample" Kuivila recalled making the sample "using a homemade delay line where the output tapes could run at completely different rates from the inputs (Kuivila). This could be like a harmonizer or, by doubling speed, a funny sped up playing where if you stayed in sync with the delay you could play live with articulations at double your performed rate." Expanding upon his memories of Russell, Kuivila offered one of the most concise and probing descriptions of Russell's process that I have encountered.

> I would describe his approach as largely the standard pop model where you bring someone in for their "sound" and they have considerable autonomy within some set of parameters. But there was also a sense of what I would describe as "experimentalist passive aggression," where you don't want to unduly influence the other, but rather let them proceed from their own center allowing the piece to sound completely different from what you thought, as long as it follows the basic premise set up.

> I think a lot of the difficulties around his legacy (and difficulties he had with collaborators) have to do with his constant slippage between these two models. They share a lot of characteristics but are fundamentally different. Collaborators who didn't understand him might feel either exploited or over-directed and people hearing the work could feel it was uncooked. At the time I heard several people comment that he was capable of doing an extraordinarily beautiful concert one week and something horrifying the next (Kuivila, 2011).

Russell's constant straddling of the line between a systemic score-based approach and an intuitive improvisatory one is, as we have emphasized, a defining aspect of his work. It is part of what has made his reception into both the experimental and popular music scenes so gradual and polarizing. And, while mastering their native languages, he was never willing to rest in either camp alone for too long. The 1980's would show Russell absorbing more popular music genres (Bright & Early, Corn/Calling Out of Context), founding and being fired from a disco record label he co-founded, recording and releasing several dance singles, and honing his compositional system into a solo format for himself on voice, cello, and effects. This solo format would manifest into a performance practice that Russell would continue until his death, and which would be distilled into one of his most notable body of works, *World of Echo*.

VII.

WORLD OF ECHO

P-Idea: while the contradiction between popular and serious (art) music may still be a live issue, the arena for its disclosure [it's form] has changed: it has, I feel, receded into the inaudible and the invisible.

WOE: the universe where nothing is ever repeated

WOE: not being able to know/hear what one does while one is doing it (SN)

Arthur Russell

The essence of mind is like space. Therefore, there is nothing which it does not encompass [...] Let your speech become an echo (*Myth* 200).

Chögyam Trungpa

With Russell's 1985 album, *World of Echo* ("WOE" in shorthand), his interests in popular song, dance music, experimental composition, north Indian music, and Buddhism were all mixed, re-mixed, and sieved through the bare one-man-band of his voice, cello, and effects pedals. No other work of his so perfectly fuses the "common denominators" of such disparate influences or the rigorous discipline and gentle whimsy of his day-to-day performances and personal practice. While *Instrumentals*, *Tower of Meaning*, and *24>24 Music* were composed through intricate compositional systems, by the time of *World of Echo* Russell seemed to have digested his matrix system. Though still drawing on numerology and the lunar cycle, WOE was made through an even more esoteric process, involving mantric approaches to the voice, and idiosyncratic concepts such as Russell's "parenthetical ideas" and the "equilateral backdrop," which informed the project.

Russell had performed solo throughout his time in New York, but he had begun a concerted focus on a solo practice with cello and electronic effects in the early 1980's. WOE performances began as early as 1983 (at the New York Theatre), and around the same time Russell began recording solo sketches at Battery Sound Studio. Composer (and self-proclaimed "protegé" of Philip Glass), John Moran recalled that the first thing Glass proposed Moran do as his protégé was to accompany Glass to a concert of Russell's in Soho. This was around the time of WOE (1984-85). Moran claimed the experience was "life-changing":

> Arthur was on stage playing solo, and behind him a film of a baby chick and a kitten playing together. Arthur's music changed my life that night. I had never heard "pop" rhythms blended with melodies so intangibly before. As a composer, I was fascinated with the "endless melody" which I'd previously thought of as belonging to some classical figure or another... and that "pop" melodies were to be thought of as "simple." Coinciding, someone had handed me a tape titled, *Indonesian Whorehouse Music*—which, again, featured the "endless melody." I studied and studied this cassette tape and its exotic qualities, until I came to realize something about these structures. They were not "endless," they were simply very "long" phrases. So long, that as a listener, it was easy to get lost a little in them from time to time. Then, I realized that Arthur's melodies also had such a quality. "Open phrases": this was a key to Arthur's ability to leave one feeling that a question had been asked of them. The statements don't "close" like a rock band...they linger and ponder once again, "endlessly" in feeling (Moran, 2013).

By March of 1984 Russell was advertising his performances (at The Kitchen and other venues) with the title *World of Echo*. And in June of the same year he played a piece entitled *Sketch for World of Echo* at Experimental Intermedia Foundation (or, EI). EI is an experimental music venue founded in the Soho neighborhood by Phill Niblock in 1973. A good friend of Niblock, Russell had played at EI since he first moved to New York. It was in the Summer of 1984 that Russell and Niblock began to toy with the idea of a collaboration.

Niblock would film Russell, playing against the backdrop of a lighting system. "Arthur had this strange lighting setup with a bunch of cheap lamps and filters and a dimmer board that Steven Hall was manipulating. The lighting changed dramatically from moment to moment, so it was all quite interesting" (Lawrence, *Hold On* 213). Niblock's video moves slowly around Russell as he sings and plays cello, with intimate close-ups of his hands and acne-scarred face and an abstraction of flickering light and muscular motion. After listening back to the audio tracks of Niblock's videos—featuring songs like "Soon-to-be innocent fun," "Unfamiliar place," "Answers me," and "Let's See"—Russell decided to record an album based on this material. The only remaining documents of their video collaboration are the two videos that Niblock has since contributed and made public as *Terrace of Unintelligibility*, via Audika Records. Niblock remembers the collaboration as follows:

> I liked the weirdness of what he was doing in the concert, and we decided to shoot this video. I think he did two or three altogether over the years before he died. After the concert, I proposed to him that we do this collaboration where I would shoot video and we would set up about the same set up as the concert and so we did [...] The music from *World of Echo* came mostly from that session. I liked that music. We made separate recordings on PCM digital in the old days when you were recording digital music on videotape. Arthur had stereo tapes from the PCM digital and he made the record out of that material (Khider, 2005).

Russell describes their collaboration in his own conceptual language in a grant application:

World of Echo is the name of a project generally intended to explore the ramifications of signal reproduction or mimicry by organisms through the performance of, as well as contemplation of, deliberate signal generation (music) and breathing (video). Signal reproduction refers in this case [to] digital recording devices (delays). Signal generation has up to now referred to me playing the cello and singing the music from the scores grouped as *World of Echo*. While the composition employs the developing technology, I feel the essential elements of the music are conveyed directly in live performance. *World of Echo* specifically concerns the movements [that] the music and dance take in the process of being recorded, how they are altered and not altered (Russell, N).

In the meantime, Russell continued taking advantage of the recording studio Battery Sound, located at 90 West Street, working with producer Mark Freedman and engineering assistant Eric Liljestrand. There he was also assisted by volunteer Eric Muiderman, a student of Peter Zummo. Between Battery Sound and EI, Russell had a new freedom of recording that allowed him to work late into the moonlight, his preferred time of experimenting. But beyond the confines of the studio, Russell was imagining something broader.

Sketch for World of Echo

With this record, *World of Echo*, my ambition is to play the songs again and again… make them happen twice, as it were ("Beats in Space").

Why have I made a record with just vocals and cello? Well, it's like you want to go to outer space but you're not allowed to take your drums with you. It's like some huge soundtrack to some pornographic science-fiction movie, absolutely drenched in irony, of course (Lawrence, *Hold On* 372).

Arthur Russell

In the process of creating *World of Echo*, Russell ended up devising a unique kind of brainstorming. Fragmented thoughts, littering his notebook, tend to refer to *World of Echo*

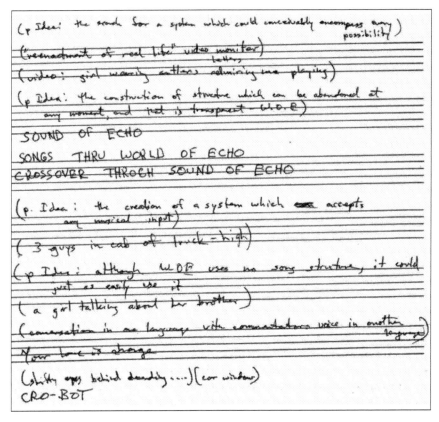

Image 45. P-Ideas from Russell's notebooks (Russell, SN)

when they are preceded by the term "P-Idea" and/or in passages that are placed in parentheses. The "P" in "P-Idea" I presume to stand for "parentheses," as I found it written in Russell's notes. This solo format was a linguistic and visual means of isolating Russell's various "first thoughts," allowing them to exist independent of others, but also allowing them to be endlessly and variably re-combined with one another. Every aspect of the development of WOE was based on a similar parenthetical modularity.

> **P-Idea:** (Develop dynamic relationship of material in and out of parentheses)
> (Use above as model for unaccompanied cello piece)

(Two takes from different days of same song juxtaposed sequentially)

(Layer of echoes added over above) (can they be juxtaposed any other way?)

(Relation of juxtaposition of songs with juxtaposition of *parenthetical ideas*) (none)

Here Russell makes an explicit connection between the parentheses of his notebooks and the parenthetical nature of the compositional process of WOE, which prioritized the collaging of fragments taken from different times and experiences. Another notebook excerpt reads, "W.O.E. working alone–collaboration like parenthetical juxtaposition." Russell was using these structural juxtapositions as *the* structure of WOE, not unlike how he had conceived the structural composition of *24>24 Music*, in which the input of other musicians influenced the final composition, WOE has Russell "collaborating" with himself in a hyper-reflective process.

This parenthetical concept guided Russell's lyrical writing, which was one of varied repetition and abstraction, the formal relationships of the songs, whose choruses, verses, and refrains are endlessly recombined, as well as his application of echo, reverb, and other effects. Every aspect of a given song was opened to parenthetical isolation and recombination. Below are some of the more significant "P-Ideas," I compiled from several of Russell's spiral-bound notebooks:

P-Idea: (incidents of occult perspective, regardless of whatever they are—geometrical or accidental or other—involve a spontaneous pre-cognitive moment, improvised or other wise, in their creation of perception.)

P-Idea: (the construction of structure which can be abandoned at any moment, and that is transparent--WOE)

P-Idea: (the creation of a system which accepts any musical input)

P-Idea: (although WOE uses no song structure, it could just as easily use it)

P-Idea: (the live segment was included also to demonstrate the acoustic or psycho-acoustic change apparent from recording situation to recording situation)

P-Idea: (it's clear that any style can be heard in the recording, yet critics continue to put a "price" on the trappings of form, really in the imagination, sometimes very cleverly)

P-Idea: (the search for a system which could conceivably encompass every possibility)

P-Idea: my training was not to combine musical genres, but to ignore them

P-Idea: World of Echo attempts to acknowledge (that composers tend to compose the same song again and again in order to accomplish a change)

P-Idea: an approach which extends the idea that "chance" is not only synthesized through various means but completely integrated into the process of working, and always has been

P-Idea: improvisation which is based on time and space limitations and composition which is not properly concerned with limitations, including long list of impossible things, and the integration of the two.

As in the many text scores we encountered in Russell's early "black notebook," these ideas could be silly, practical, visionary, observational, poetic, or seemingly non-sensible. Looking through as many P-Ideas as I could, clear themes took shape. Above all there is the general reiteration of fusing structure and complete freedom or chance in the music itself; of an approach to repetition such that repetition is constantly altered; of the ephemerality of formal musical structure; and of the importance of the live moment in composing and recording—Russell wanted to incorporate these moments (and the different feelings/ideas that inhered to them) into the creative process.

Essentially Russell is freely combining a set of predetermined elements which he fastidiously collected and archived. The primary focus is given to repetition, the repetition of chords, lyrics, melodies. But this repetition is then given over to a complex dynamism, through Russell's compositional strategy and P.A. System. And he makes it his aim to create a definitive music whose every aspect can be made indefinitely mutable, ephemerally re-combinatory, and absolutely infinite in its manner of manifestation. In one of many confusing comments that repeat this sentiment, he writes: "Instead of fashioning open-associated sequence (of notes) to archetypal accompaniment, find archetypical sequence, find archetypical accompaniment, then find open-associated accompaniment, then find accompaniment for open associated sequence free of the foregoing." Russell's strategies are often stated clearly in some sense to himself, but they immediately contradict and recoil upon themselves (e.g. "do this, but also don't do it"). In this manner at every step of composition, there is a proposition or a question asked, a contradiction presented, a choice to be made. Combining his P-Ideas and making these choices, Russell's songs for WOE began to form.

Going into the 1980s Russell's matrix system is still in play, being used in live improvisations, and perhaps being used to develop some of the WOE songs. But for the most part that system had been digested by this point—though he would continue to use it more explicitly in the scores for Singing Tractors. What remains strongest from Russell's mother score aesthetic and thought process is his working with the dyads of the cello and his ever evolving form-as-process. Working within the mother score, individual dyads could transform into melodies, foreground melodies could transform into background or textural harmonies, while performance techniques (dynamics, bowing techniques, etc) could further transform a repetitive element. With WOE this

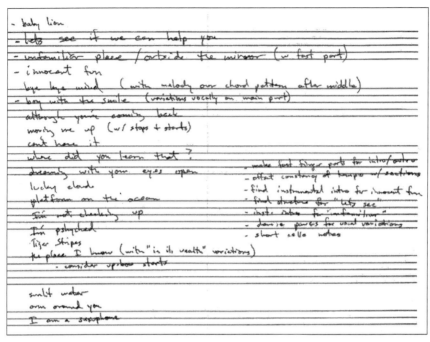

Image 46. List of WOE-era songs from Russell's notebook (Russell, SN)

approach focuses more intentionally upon the elements of melodic phrasing and expression, on the mutable formal relationships between verse/chorus/refrain, and on the relationships between the songs themselves.

In an unpublished sketch for what would become WOE's liner notes Russell saw WOE as "offering the possibilities of expanding/extending, say, part of a verse into a longer instrumental sequence, or, on the other hand, ultimately condensing an epic sense of proportion into a short vocal phrase, as in radio hits, but doing so all in the same musical breath" (SN). Russell's work in general, and especially in WOE, show an ongoing obsession with the idea, or experience, of mutability. This was at the foundation of Russell's *Instrumentals* matrix system, in which a few single tones are transmuted into an orchestral score. His notebook commentary on *Springfield—*

one of Russell's final recorded works—is insightfully applicable to a post-WOE work in this regard.

> This is a basic principle: that all materials, once perceivable, "enter" the realm of the equilateral backdrop. This enables the stylistic function of the music, once perceived in its cultural environment only, to alter any moment without losing its basic identity or usability, so that styles of music can be learned or understood within the context of other styles, of those introduced, as much as feasible, providing the limitations of energy and ability. These functions can go while a neutral plateau or revolving field of perception is cultivated. Musical input then becomes a fixed element which the mind uses and adds to (Russell, SN).

I understand the "equilateral backdrop" as a non-linear framework or matrix. A series of elements to use, combine, or develop. Mutability and interchangeability were applied to every aspect of Russell's creative process. As Russell mentioned above—in regards to song form—a verse could be expanded into a long instrumental passage, or a long passage into a short phrase.

Applying this to a broader perspective, the asymmetrical could be transformed into the symmetrical: "Symmetricality is, in this case, a function of repetition—any asymmetrical sequence becomes symmetrical when repeated, or when auditioned repeatedly (rewind)." Russell was also interested in the collaging of different takes of the same song that were made at different times, inducing a mutability of time, memory, feelings from different performances into a single song. The same interchangeability was applied to the track order of WOE: "I took a lot of time to try and find a good order to put the songs in, but finally I decided that any order would work; even so, I'm not sorry for spending the time—it informed the process and influenced the result in ways beyond awareness" (Russell, N).

Being solo, Russell plugged himself direct into the mixing board and recorded himself in the control room, where the engineer generally sits, rather than the sound room. "Then," describes Lawrence, "when he was done with singing or playing, he would cut, re-equalize, and manipulate the recordings, weaving them together as if he were a time-traveling tapestry artist" (Lawrence, *Hold On* 274). Again, reflecting on *Springfield* (and WOE), Russell writes with more detail about his concept of the "equilateral backdrop" and the nature of his "time-travel" editing.

> How is it possible to combine a view of musical content with no sign posts, as to style structure, with a view that holds a decidedly deterministic attitude to content? By dividing the process into equal sections: living portions made up of the actual life of the performer on the one hand, and deliberate choices arising out of thought and construct on the other. Inter-facing factors could be the number of sections of the former, identical in the latter only named and assigned to architectural and numeric functions, generally and entirely dedicated to the purpose of the vows. In the former the "equilateral" sections, abstract positions, partake of all available energies of the subject, in this case myself, improvisations, generic talents, knowledges, energies in the purer definition, that of dynamic union of space [silence] and movement [deliberate music], refresh the presence of the performance, the notion of identity, as well as the concept of architectonics joined within the continuity of the structural presentation actually perceived as the composition (Russell, SN).

"Living portions"—this is what Russell composed WOE with--slices of tape, ephemeral moments. Again, we are recalled to the single tones of Russell's matrix system, the lone syllable of Buddhist mantra and Hindustani drone. Using the studio as his notational field, these ephemeral slices of tape become like elements in a new matrix that Russell drew from to create WOE. As in previous projects, Russell cherished and determined these vivid elements; then he would weave them together in the studio by intuition and/or by conceptual deign. It is through this enduring method of analytical intuition that Russell is capable of fusing so many disparate elements into a sense of unity. And it is through this constant respiration of analysis and intuition that Russell's own aesthetic emerges. "Seeing analysis as freeze frame of phenomena," Russell writes of *Springfield*, "investigate altering flows of thought" (Russell, SN).

In the *Springfield* notes above Russell briefly refers to the Buddhist backbone underlying his music, when he writes of assigning the formal musical elements of *Springfield* to "architectural and numeric functions, generally and entirely dedicated to the purpose of the vows." There are many such "vows" in Buddhist teaching. I speculate that Russell is referring to the bodhisattva vows, which guide the bodhisattva along his spiritual path toward liberating all beings from suffering and the cycle of birth and death. As Nagarjuna described in *Precious Garland*, a central Buddhist text:

> If you and the world want to attain
> Unsurpassable enlightenment,
> Its roots are the altruistic intention,
> As stable as the king of mountains,
> Compassion that reaches every quarter
> And wisdom that does not rely on duality (Rinchen, 9).

For years, numerology and the matrix or mantric syllabary he had devised would provide Russell with the "architectural and numeric functions" and the discipline that he required to remain, as Trungpa described, "tuned into cosmic energy." Russell's concepts of parenthetical ideas, repetition and asymmetry, interchangeability, stylistic fusion—all broke away from perspectives of duality, identity, attachment. Russell used these musical techniques and methods as a spiritual discipline, to hone his awareness and harness his intuition—to assist himself in keeping his Buddhist vows.

World of Echo grew out of a long and thoughtful conception of music for solo performance. The "score" becomes less used because Russell is left to his own whims and working through the medium of the recording studio. To realize his conception Russell developed a rigorous solo performance practice that could incorporate his P-Ideas and the compositional strategies and effects he had achieved through his past work with live ensembles. "Working solo—it can change a lot, from moment to moment, because I'm not accountable to anyone else, in terms of what the continuity is. It's amazing how little it changes, considering that" (Radio Interview). And Russell continued to conceive of the *World of Echo* material as existing within or manifesting itself as a space. As he noted in his liner notes, the use of echo reinforces a literal acoustic sense of space, but Russell was also tapping into his lifelong practice of visualization meditation. Imagining this "world," Russell's aim, as he put it, was to "use technology to put the musician or listener in the same intuitive 'room'" (Russell, SN).

The "World of Echo P.A. System"

[...] It was my hope, through the various possibilities of a *World of Echo* PA system, to redefine "songs" from the point of view of instrumental music, in the hopes of liquefying a raw material where concert music and popular song can crisscross (WOE).

I got into having this solo configuration so I could somehow make a "live" drum machine, or something like that... Just kind of starting off as a challenge, and gradually working into almost a full time commitment, which is what it's become now (MME).

Arthur Russell

Russell's use of technological effects would increase and come to define the sound of his music in *World of Echo* and subsequent recordings. Reverb, chorus, phase, distortion, and especially echo all uniquely applied to his voice and cello. These technologies and effects came together as Russell sought a "World of Echo P.A. System." Running through it all is Russell's cello. His own style of playing the cello was both highly percussive and softly bowed, with extreme nuances to his articulations. His use of light, fleeting harmonics and frequent *sul ponticello* (bowing the cello near the bridge, yielding high-frequency harmonics) mix rapidly and easily with the dance-able pulse of his *pizzicato* (plucking the string with the finger) and the lapping upsurges of the P.A.'s feedback and distortion. His *pizzicatos* or *col legno battuto*'s (hitting the string with the wooden part of the bow), or simply slapping the fingers of his left hand onto the fret board, often provided a percussive bass line, novel in the classical history of the cello, softly driving his dance-based work. This is audible in numerous places throughout the final album, but notably in "Answers Me," "Lucky Cloud," and "She's The Star/I Take This Time."

Having been actively studying and playing the cello for a few years, it was in 1972 in San Francisco that Arthur first amplified his cello. This was in part an experimental gesture, a practical means of hearing himself in noisy or large ensemble performances, and aesthetically an inspiration from heavy metal music. He was well aware of the novelty and potential of its sound: "I don't think anyone plays this instrument this way, amplified with such a clear sound" (Lawrence, *Hold On* 27). But to this clear sound, Russell readily added effects. Nowhere is Russell's use of distortion more apparent in WOE than in the tracks "Being It" and "I Take This Time," whose raw power chords ground their lyrical tunes in firm rock ground. Two other tracks—"Tower of Meaning" and "Let's Go Swimming"—start off with solo atonal cello, thick and distorted interpretations of progressions likely drawn from his matrix dyads. This richly distorted sound continues to be part of Russell's music after WOE, including numerous pieces on *Calling Out of Context* and the posthumously released *Springfield* E.P. (e.g. "Corn #3"). Distortion became but another way that Russell could obscure the familiar, create a thick flux of sound in which to musically swim, or manifest that "buzzing feeling" of the Hindustani tanpura timbre.

Aside from constant technological add-ons and variations over the years (Russell was always buying or borrowing new technologies), the core of the WOE PA system was the MXR Graphic Equalizer, Mutron Bi-phase Box, and a Delta Lab 2 Delay Box. The Mutron Bi-phase pedal—advertised as "A quick way back to 1975 or ahead to 2050!"—allowed Russell to manually adjust 1 of 2 phasors and 2 sweep generators. Within these phasors Russell could also play with distortion, depth, sweep syncing, etc. Other effects, such as backwards delay, would give a unique character to tracks like "Wax the Van." The bi-phase stands out on WOE especially, being the source of those abstract whooshes and tabla-like yelps, which Russell would also run through his delay pedal, as in "Hiding Your Present From You," or the high chirps in "Tone Bone Kone." He would explicitly describe such sounds in his notebooks, seeking, for example, an "extended beep mood," which might include any of the following: "digitally recorded faint and medium beeps (bleeps)," "extract[ed] beep-like strands for processing," or more specifically "two altered beeps, Bb—G, in slightly higher frequency than the original 'silent' source.'" Russell also focused, as he had been for a few years, on manipulating the tempo, in this case the rate of the delay: "Systematize relationships between clocks by testing with feedback knob" (Russell, N).

But of course the title of the album points to the effect most foregrounded in the music. In his notebooks Russell reflected on the role of echo and reverberation in WOE in many of his P-Ideas:

P-Idea: (W.O.E.): various structural devices are heard through varying kinds and degrees of reverberation, both as an internal element and an added "texture")

(Reverberation subjected to additional reverberation)

(When the change of echo is an active element in the composition)

(**P-Idea:** different kinds of echo co-existing, like plants growing within plants) (like delay and reverb)

(**P-Idea:** since every sound is a complex combination of echoes and after sound, S.O.E. ["Sound Over Echo"] accepts virtually any possible combination of echoes and delays without further processing. The actual musical configurations are limited by more personal considerations)

P-Idea: (for the record the use of echo is more subtle, than in live performances... the drama of no echo)

Though quickly becoming Russell's signature sound, the use of echo in music is certainly not novel to his world alone. Its' earliest popular use was in rockabilly music, where echo was derived to emulate the "slap-back" architecturally-based echo sound that would accompany recordings originally made in the old ballroom at Decca recording studios—an early example being Bill Haley and His Comets' "Rock Around the Clock." Later, dub, an offshoot of Reggae music, took the reggae style and electro-acoustically altered, collaged, and soaked it in more ambient realms drenched in reverberation, echo, and cut-up techniques. Early dub pioneers such as Lee "Scratch" Perry and Osbourne Ruddock (a.k.a. "King Tubby") became prominent DJ's and were relishing in the bath of sound as they discovered the role of the studio as an artistic instrument. But Russell was looking for something beyond these aesthetics. As Steven Hall recalled:

[W]hereas most dub producers sought out murkiness, Arthur hoped to create an echo that was scintillating rather than muted. "I like the bright sound, I like compression," Arthur wrote in a letter to the mastering engineer of the tapes. "Please make it as

217

loud as possible." Arthur asked friends if they thought he was using too much reverb, and Ernie Brooks, who placed a high value on hearing the words of a song, told him that he was. Persevering, Arthur created a chorus of voices that combined in a flickering, spectral harmony (Lawrence, *Hold On* 278).

Russell himself described his interest in echo as follows, using terms and concepts that will have recurred throughout this chapter:

As I considered echo in various meanings, as acoustic reverberation or electronically as a single delay, it seemed that in it, concepts of time and space were expressed sonically, and the latter case projected dynamically into a theoretical "world," with a more practical application using currently available echo/delay guitar boxes to provide an independently generated world of time to move through, like a PA system that can process any input, introducing a concept of interchangeability of material (Russell, WOE).

In Russell's p-Ideas he used evocative metaphors to describe what he was after, such as "different kinds of echo co-existing, like plants growing within plants" (Russell, SN). Steven Hall noted that Russell loved "constant, random modulation," such that the activity and quality of a given effect was constantly being altered. Hall related this to a Cagean aesthetic of indeterminacy, which had always inspired Russell. Russell had numerous notes to himself emphasizing an inclusion of randomness and change applied to all aspects of his recorded performances with the WOE P.A. System:

[...] Suddenly turning on vocal track in mix, and off.

Changing echo settings on solo voice

Abrupt changes in lighting

P-Idea: System which would momentarily disconnect amplification in a concert (cello/vocal)

Layering of vocal unisons—thoughts on different days (multi-track)

Alternate between pure and distorted sounds and sections

We noted this phenomenon in the transformative refraction at work in Russell's early sketch of "Cumberland Gap" and in the mosaic orchestration that would be channeled through his matrix system. Again, here, in the songs of WOE the same aesthetic is in operation through the WOE P.A. System. The effect can sound both richly organic or erratically accidental, with Russell, often audibly, ceasing to play and/or adjusting or cueing effects switches as he's playing.

This use of the P.A. system is perhaps most effective and most audible in "Hiding Your Present From You," where Russell is constantly switching the echo on and off, altering the rate of echo, and adding or subtracting reverb and chorus. The sound of his cello is constantly changing throughout the song, which rests unhurried on a sustained G or C chord and occasional drone textures supplied by harmonica, the latter recalling but destabilizing the sonic image of the "folk singer," a la Dylan. Through a re-combinatory application of echo and reverb effects as well as playing techniques, Russell, as was his aim, "mystifies" the familiarity of the popular song as much as he "de-mystifies" it. And Russell spoke of it in these terms.

For example, in consideration of the material face of the artist and the album, he writes of "the use of WOE to demystify the process of presentations, packaging, and glamour of the music at the same time as mystifying it" (Russell, N).

Russell literally creates the sense of several different acoustic spaces co-existing in WOE. His conception of echo, as he makes clear in WOE's liner notes, was as a synthesis of numerous perspectives. For example, in considering echo in its spatial sense, Russell was seeking more than just an electronic simulacrum of the natural phenomena. In fact, he was ultimately hoping the project would move outdoors:

> *World Of Echo* isn't a complete version of echo, it's a sketch version of echo. I want to do the full version which will have brass bands and orchestras playing outdoors in parks with those bandstands that project echo. I also want to have Casio keyboards on sailboats. Have you ever been on a sailboat? It's so quiet, all you hear is wind and sea (Lawrence, *Hold On* 287).

But, again, the meaning of Russell's use of echo went beyond purely sonic attractions. It continued his endless creative drive to work within nested experiences of the thought process itself. Interestingly Chögyam Trungpa wrote about the significance of echo in a 1979 seminar entitled "The Warrior Tradition: Conquering Fear":

> The second guide on the warrior's path is represented by the analogy of an echo, which is connected with meditative awareness, or samadhi. When you try to take time off from being a warrior, when you want to let go of your discipline or indulge mindlessly in some activity, your action produces an echo. It's like a sound echoing in a canyon, bouncing back on itself, producing more echoes that bounce off of one another. Those echoes or reflections happen all the time, and if we pay attention to them, they provide constant reminders to be awake. At first, the reminder might be fairly timid, but then the second, third and fourth time you hear it, it's a much louder echo. These echoes remind you to be on the spot, on the dot [...] However, you can't just wait for an echo to wake you up. You have to put your awareness out into the situation. You have to put effort into being aware (*Smile at Fear* 65).

Russell's use of echo, as with his matrix system of composition, was in part a discipline of the mind, a confusion of sound used as a "reminder to be awake." From a similar perspective, Samir Nath, in his *Encyclopedic Dictionary of Buddhism*, uses the concept of echo in his definition of the Buddhist concept of human destiny (karma and reincarnation):

> If one shouts from the precipice of a deep ravine one soon hears the echoes of one's own voice. Notice now how one echo, in

ceasing to be, gives rise to the next echo. Nothing is left of the first echo. Similarly, the second echo, in giving rise to the third, ceases to be, and yet in the very act of ceasing to be gives rise to the next echoes. Our various lives, therefore may be compared profitably, from the point of Buddhist philosophy, to a series of echoes down the corridor of time (Nath, 333-34).

Both Trungpa and Nath use the echo essentially to describe the Buddhist concept of *karma*. Trungpa would define karma with greater nuance however. According to his conception there is a "greater" and a "lesser" karma. The lesser karma is the more common understanding of karma as a causal chain-reaction. If one does X, then it will directly impact Y and Z. One often tries to stop this endless cycle, especially concerning bad karmic actions, while reinforcing the cycling of good karmic actions. However, in the greater karma, there is no good or bad karma and the chain-reaction has been dissolved or broken through. Greater karma, he says, "is applied to action in the moment, on the spot" (*Complete Works Vol. 7* xxix). In this sense, "karma" is action that is appropriate to a given situation, rather than imposed upon it from beyond situational immediacy or by pre-meditated logic.

Though doubtful Russell knew these particular musings of Trungpa (and, less likely, Nath), I have no doubt such musings would resonate with his own interest in echo. Russell even spoke of karma in musical terms: "Buoyed by Karma (the cause of one sound leading to another) sounds or ideas come with rubber bands" (Russell, NB). Every sound (a single note, a chord, a beat, etc) was for Russell a karmic act, and only through the accumulation of these karmic acts would a musical work emerge from a place of true compassion and openness. That they "come with rubber bands" simply means that they are flexible, can be stretched, changed, re-arranged or re-mixed. This was also true of Russell's lyrics, which are steeped in mantric thought.

Language in Twilight

> After listening to tapes of World of Echo as well as foreign language singing, I've enjoyed the musical effect of words as sounds, but where the meaning is not totally withdrawn. As the intention is not determined by genre, nor meaning by dialect, thresholds of musical understanding can occupy any threshold defined within a style and musical structure, or outside it. Breakthroughs can occur at any point in the chain (Russell, WOE).

> Words can be many things at once, like a mantra […] Also, people can understand a phrase on a visceral level, and it would mean the same thing that they understand on a spiritual level (Lawrence, *Hold On* 111).

Throughout *World of Echo* the listener can hear Russell's application of chant, mantra, and the raga singing practices he had studied early on. Though he may have hoped otherwise, this was not a music destined for the mass market. And after seeing the initial poor sales of the record, Russell wanted to place on the cover of the album a football-shaped sticker, which would have read: "Unintelligible." But this unintelligibility, especially in regards to Russell's voice and lyrics is a core aspect of WOE (Lawrence, *Hold On* 281).

Inspired by listening to the pure sound of foreign language tapes, Russell's approach to the language of WOE was one of deep abstraction, one aligned with the history of sound poetry and entranced glossolalia as much as with Bob Dylan's lyrics or Allen Ginsberg's poetry. Befriending and living next to Ginsberg meant Russell got lots of feedback on his lyrics. "He'd come downstairs to give me lyrics—or samples of lyrics—and asked my opinion as a poet. And we had a constant

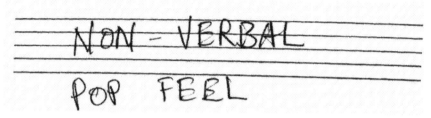

Image 47. Notebook entry by Russell on WOE (Russell, SN)

fight over whether he was being too general, too abstract, too allusive" [Wild Combination]. Many of the songs on WOE appear as lyrical meditations upon a friend or stranger. The first track, "Tone Bone Kone"—before shifting into the mantric recitation of its elliptical title—begins with a melodically catchy verse, which is never returned to. The lyrics seem drawn from the conversation of two strangers meeting for the first time in a concert audience:

> I'm so happy that I met you and came to find a seat near you.
> You gave me good advice—and, more than that...

There were other verses in Russell's archive. But he deliberately chose to edit out this one recorded verse, and attach it to the abstraction that follows. Through the haze of echo and reverb, the words are hard to make out. When Russell starts singing the words "tone, bone kone," with each repetition he alters the effects on his voice, e.g. changing the frequency of the echo effect. Lasting only a minute, you couldn't ask for a more honest introduction or promo for the album.

As Ginsberg noted, Russell was consciously between the realms of generality and abstraction, though perhaps with stronger instinct towards abstract esotericism. He met this abstraction of language, in the work of other artists, such as John Cage and Jackson MacLow. Both of whom abstracted language into raw quasi-musical elements. Relevant to his own use of language in his musical works, Cage describes the approach to his book *Empty Words*:

> It's a transition from language to music certainly. It's bewildering at first, but it's extremely pleasurable as time goes on. And that's what I'm up to. "Empty Words" begins by omitting sentences, has only phrases, words, syllables and letters. The second part omits the phrases, has only words, syllables and letters. The third part omits the words, has only syllables and letters. And the last part...has nothing but letters and sounds (Cage, 64-65).

Like Cage before him, Russell was explicit in pursuing lyrical content that emphasized what Russell called its "non-verbal" and "neutral" character. Sonically, with the microphone in mind, he preferred a "close vocal sound, to get 'high energy—event horizon'" (Russell, N). Despite this emphasis on the abstract or visceral sound of language and the voice, lyric writing and sensibility are not totally lost in these songs. Themes of love, personal relationships, childhood, transcendentalism, sexuality, animals and nature remain, but their contexts and referrals are more vague than they had been in Russell's earlier songs. Songs like WOE's "See Through"— which was subsequently remixed into a dance single, "C-Thru," by Walter Gibbons—speak to more ethereal realms.

> See-through me, see-through.
> See-through me, see...
> See-through me, see...
> If you appear what's airy sends a friend to my imagination.

Nevertheless, Russell's recitation of the lyrics is extremely abstracted, often completely obscuring the sensibility of the text. Beyond the obscurations of studio effects, this is achieved by Russell restraining the physiology of his articulations while compacting the vowel energy in various parts of his mouth: in the top cavity of the throat, in the side pocket of his cheeks, with the teeth closed, etc. He would have been conscious of this physiology through the vocal lessons he'd taken with Joan La Barbara a few years back. But the unique delivery of Russell's voice is in its' close-mic'ed and gentle delivery, often so soft as to be unintelligible. Russell speaks to this in his notebooks, "P-Idea: considering the responsibility of language to communicate, I can see where unintelligibility could be not outside that process" (Russell, N). Through notebook musings, Russell would continue noting the intentionality underlying his use of language, and its abstraction, in WOE:

> **P-Idea:** In order to accept a variety of language forms into sense/ melody... unintelligible
>
> **P-Idea:** the use of "neutral" language exposes the areas of [its'] usage.
>
> **P-Idea:** echo on delay: structure on structure: ("what you're trying to say" linguistic argument and interface of local growth of details of language and change of language structure)

Russell had toyed with many poetic techniques of ambiguity in his previous work: puns, innuendo, metaphor, homophony, malapropism, metonymy, antanaclassis. Most of us are familiar with puns and innuendos, most commonly found in blues and dance music, e.g. Robert Johnson's "Squeeze my lemon till the juice runs down my leg" (from "Traveling Riverside Blues"). Russell naturally appropriated that technique (e.g. "I wanna go bang," "wax the van," etc), but he would meditate on these linguistic techniques more than most folk/ pop singers. "Mix double entendre and direct reference," Russell reflects, "in such a way as to objectify both." Antanaclassis, another linguistic device, is the repetition of a word (often a phrase for Russell), the repetitions of which are each used to imbue that word with a different meaning. Using erasure and elision in his vocal delivery, Russell's "Hiding Your Present" is a good example of this mutability of meaning:

Where you see where it is, but don't know where it is...
Where you see where it is...
Where you see where...

Now I'm hiding your present from you.
Now I'm hiding...
Now I'm hiding...

Where you see where it is, but don't know where it is...

Recalling his early text scores, one of the most explicit manifestations of Russell's adherence to "first thought, best thought" on WOE is his "The Name of the Next Song," a live performance in which Russell alternates processed cello improvisations and a sung refrain—"California, here I come!"— with transitional unaccompanied "introductions" to each improvisation. In one notebook sketch Russell expressed an interest in developing "singing title announcements for instrumental bits" with his typical list of thoughts/observations serving for the titles, which are audible on "The Name of the Next Song" (cf. Russell, WOE): "I'm sorry (but) this is how I learn," "A new man will come in to do... [that]," "blinkorama," "take a gander (at that)," "painted box," and "dodo."

"First thought, best thought" is literally performed here as a kind of looping tune with spaces where any spontaneous thought, or scribble from Russell's notebooks, might arise and be sung, providing a thematic-like role for the subsequent instrumental improvisations. More commonly, Russell's performances would realize the lyrics of a song, via sight-reading a score, as a kind of "choose your own adventure" method. On the following page we can see the lead sheet, in Russell's handwriting, for "Soon-to-be Innocent Fun"—the longest track on the album. Lyrically, we can see how his mind thinks up-or-down as much as left-to-right, with some words being vertically stacked upon each other. Reading linearly through the lines, and then repeating them again and again, Russell improvises with melodic and rhythmic ones, as in **image 48**: innocent love... the light... in a sense fun.

The role of spontaneous sight-reading is even more evident in this notational image (**image 48**). At one point Russell says, "Oh, good!" between verses. I'd assumed he was responding to a sonic effect that he or the engineer had done in the moment. But in fact, the words "oh, good" were scribbled, off to the side, on the sheet Russell was sight-reading the song from. He simply included that scribble in his performance. Interestingly, Russell had done something similarly during a rehearsal for Peter Zummo's *Experimenting With Household Chemicals* (circa, 1989). Percussionist Bill Ruyle recalls one

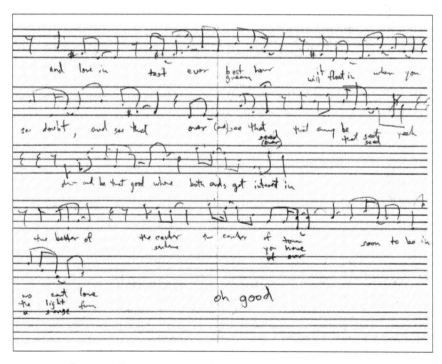

Image 48. "Soon-to-be Innocent Fun," notebook sketch and performance score (Russell, SN)

thing in particular that struck him during the performance, "as we were playing, Arthur started reading aloud some of the notation. He did it completely seriously, as though it were a vocal part, as though this were a totally sensible way of interpreting the piece. And it was" (Zummo, 1995).

Many of Russell's lyrics, as Tom Lee has noted, while often seeming esoteric or unintelligible, are in fact drawn from simple or mundane experiences, e.g. making a phone call. Lee recalls Russell's lyrical process as being "loose and free, and just saying simple things coming from conversation— they're very experiential [...] like "Make 1,2" [from *Calling Out of Context*] is about making a phone call. He's just taking a phrase and repeating it, making it into a song, but the experience is very simple: "I want to call you." That's what I really like about his songs, that they are speaking about a particular feeling, a moment in time" (Lee, "Q+A"). At the same time, not unlike the album *World of Echo* itself, many songs would elevate such mundane reflections through a more meditated concept or philosophy. For example, as Russell describes the song "Treehouse":

> "Treehouse" is my idea of where commercial music could be going. My idea of a treehouse is a platform—or a house with fewer walls. Yet ideas or concepts close or identified with ourselves seem to manifest tangible form only on the other side of a partition from an immediate vision. Echo delays the onset of a sound in air long enough to engender perceptibility, however short a time (Russell, N).

Russell describes the music (and his use of echo) as if he were constructing a kind of audible consciousness within the song. A similar sense was also expressed in a short song lyric tucked into Russell's "Some Imaginary Far Away Type Things, a.k.a. Lost in the Meshes.: "It's an unfamiliar sight [or "site"]... in an unfamiliar place... outside the mirror." Russell was consciously thinking of and aspiring to a music that was at once an expression of daily life, as well as a space for meditation and a spiritual form of communication. He even doodled a graphic depiction of this when sketching ideas for the mental conception of songs like "Treehouse." In **image 49** Russell depicts a cloud-like form ("idea/music"), on the left, dynamically connected to a figure ("thinker/listener"), on the right. Overcoming a divisive wall, the listener receives the idea through song, whose sound waves easily overcome the wall. While one could imagine a mundane site of arboreal adolescent play, Russell was also trying to communicate a liberation of mind.

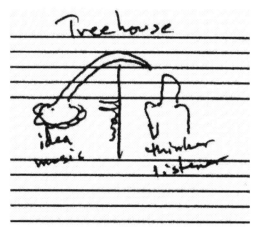

Image 49. "Treehouse" drawing by Russell (SN)

While the WOE version is more lyrically stripped down, emphasizing an innocent youthful perspective, other versions, such as "School Bell/Treehouse (Version)" [4th & Broadway, 1985] equate adolescent education with sexual and spiritual experience:

> School Bell, Treehouse
> Treehouse, Downtown
>
> Let me in, let me learn;
> Let me have a longer warm-up.

I'm 100, and I still am going to school...
I'm 1,000, and I still am going to school...

Like "See-through," "Wax the Van," and "Let's Go Swimming," "Schoolbell Treehouse" was one of the many songs that Russell's envisioned as having a beat driven dance alter-ego after the release of WOE, and which he would realize as such, often in collaboration with New York's most celebrated D.J.'s. In 1985 "School Bell/Treehouse" was mixed by Walter Gibbons and released as a single on 4th and Broadway Records. The 12" record had a plain sleeve with a sticker that playfully read, "Arthur Russell's Scat Dance Extravaganza."

This idea of a transmission of consciousness via music underlies much of Russell's work, as we noted in Chapter two, concerning his depiction of metaphysical spaces and his oracular reading of the environment. In a note to himself he reflects on the nature of this communication and the "theoretical world" of his music:

> Building up a world or genre [sic. "game"?] using a musical "language" may not in fact be that world it is thought to be, or say what it is thought to say once it is considered in the light freed from the determining logic of the situation. Conscious effort in the direction of a specific idea will fulfill a potential for communication after it has been grasped what the idea is, but in order for the idea, process, and outcome to coincide, the idea has to live its' own life and can't be revealed until fulfillment approaches or even is consummated (Russell, N).

In order for the idea to ever be received or understood, "the idea has to live its' own life," it must be absolutely truthful to itself. With this "world," composed of ephemerally honest gestures, Russell was in part attempting to emulate the nature of consciousness, of mind, through music. It is nothing less than meditation. Through his dynamic, multivalent approach to musical composition, both musical and lyrical, Russell worked somewhat similarly to composers such as Morton Feldman and Jerry Hunt, or film directors such as David Lynch and Alan Resnais—all of whom used techniques of esoteric spirituality and/or illusionism to compose their dream-like work. Through the use of reflection, erasure, and varied repetition, in his *Last Year at Marienbad* (1961) Resnais, for example, creates his own multivalent echo-chamber of ideas, images, sounds, and moods, or as he states: "For me this film is an attempt, still very crude and very primitive, to approach the complexity of thought, of its processes" (Benayoun, 104).

With *World Of Echo* Russell's formal compositional system, the matrix methodology we met in *Instrumentals*, was digested and broadened into a more conceptual philosophy and intuitive practice. For WOE Russell then developed his parenthetical ideas, or P-Ideas, themselves an archive of ideas and observations that he could draw from and recombine into lyrical and musical forms. He developed the WOE P.A. system into which he "plugged in" the expressions of his parenthetical elements, and through which he could spontaneously interact with these inputs, while composing sonic space with echo. And as we just noted, he further experimented with his lyric writing, which was effortfully pushed toward greater degrees of abstraction and mantracization.

If you'll recall, Allen Ginsberg once encouraged Bob Dylan to take for his model the Tibetan yogi and poet, Milarepa, who would improvise spontaneous hymns of Buddhist poetry. With *World Of Echo* it seems Arthur Russell instinctively took that advice for himself. Nowhere, despite his constant parenthetical brainstorming, was his creative process more transparent and fluid. And nowhere was the fusion of his Buddhist and musical practices more synthesized. Perhaps now that WOE has had 30 years "to live its own life" in relative obscurity, its "idea, process, and outcome" may coincide—and its message be received.

VIII.

GONE, GONE BEYOND

GATE, GATE, PARAGATE, PARASAMGATE, BODHI, SVAHA!

"Gone, gone, gone to the other shore, landed at the other shore!"
The Heart Sutra (Suzuki, 25).

Russell was diagnosed with H.I.V. in 1986, during the height of the disease's impact upon New York's gay community. Upon receiving the news, Lee and Russell consoled one another and cried while listening to recordings of Mississippi bluesman Robert Johnson. And though his health faltered from that point on, Russell continued to voraciously perform and create music. He would continue to heavily theorize his projects—we saw this in the previous chapter in reference to Russell's commentary on *Springfield* (1987), one of his final recorded compositions. In the latter part of the 1980s Russell would release several dance singles: "Let's Go Swimming" (1986), as well as "Wax the Van" (1987) and "I Need More" (1988) with Lola Blank. Russell also recorded several new projects that were posthumously released on various compilation albums: *Another Thought, Corn, Calling Out of Context.* With a subtle reference to the newspaper hat Russell wears on the cover of his posthumous *Another Thought* album, Peter Gordon recalls working with Russell on a track, "That Hat," featured on Gordon's 1986 Love of Life Orchestra album, *Innocent.* Russell penned the lyrics and co-wrote the track, which focused upon someone/anyone wearing a hat, worn with shamanic and erotic connotations:

From what Arthur told me, it's a hat you put on, it has a pointed top, and all the powers and energy of the universe would go through your head through the point of your pointed hat. He also explained that it could be a reference to a condom (Dayal, "Recalling Experimental Music").

Following his diagnosis, Russell's process and style continued unabated, though inhibited by the onset of the disease and its symptoms. Russell's Buddhist practice began to shift focus upon death and reincarnation, for which the *Tibetan Book of the Dead* would become Russell's primary guide.

From 1985 onward, Russell—amidst a slew of other projects—was increasingly active in providing musical accompaniment to numerous dancers, such as Alison Salzinger, Diane Madden, Ishmael Houston-Jones, Stephanie Woodard, and others. Russell worked the most with Salzinger who was pursuing a "deliberately clumsy, funky, anti-dance" aesthetic. Salzinger recalls that Russell "always seemed to reside simultaneously in some mystical and erudite musical plane and down on the ground among the teenagers, MTV, and drum machines" (Lawrence, *Hold On* 334). "He was mesmerized by abstract dance," recalls Peter Zummo (271). After his death Tom Lee received a memorial certificate honoring Russell for his "outstanding creative achievement during the 1992-1993 season." The certificate, from Dance Theatre Workshop, where Russell performed regularly, offers a heartfelt reflection upon Russell's practice and persona:

For a brave, cross-pollinated adventure in music-making, an eloquent voice and swashbuckling bow and cello, an articulate intelligence scanning the musical skies for signs of answering life, as tellingly revealed in the retrospective produced at the World Financial Center [n.b. a tribute to Russell was performed there in 1993]; for a life as remarkable for its generosity towards its artistic peers as for its own discoveries; for a life cut unbearably short, lived deep in the unfolding secrets of the art (Russell, DF).

Though endlessly productive, Russell was somewhat jaded during these final years of his life and career. And the exhaustion that accompanied his disease only exacerbated such a perspective. He had been struggling for decades now to gain the attention and success he believed his music warranted. In his 40's, he was still reliant on his partner and more successful musical allies for money and support to continue his musical pursuits. He had also developed a paranoia that others were deceptively stealing or imitating his work in their own name.

After the mid 80's Russell becomes more explicitly self-evaluative, at least in his notebooks. As he notes, self-consolingly, in one of his P-ideas during the time of WOE: "Although not as successful as I would like to be, I have not been entirely without success" (Russell, SN). In a later notebook entry Russell shows some disparagement: "I thought I would get smarter, but I'm not smart enough to get a job. I guess that will never change. It becomes apparent I was not in the psychiatrist's office, but in the principal's office. What I could attain as a singer I could perhaps never attain as a composer, though the composer sings audibly" (Russell, SN).

Bardo Thodol

while the artistic Buddhist composer
On the sixth floor
Lay spaced out feet swollen with water
Dying slowly of AIDS over a year (Lawrence, *Hold On* 337)

Excerpt from *The Charnel Ground*, by **Allen Ginsberg**

When respiration has completely stopped, one should firmly press the arteries of sleep and remind him with these words, if he was a guru or spiritual friend higher than oneself: "Sir, now the basic luminosity is shining before you; recognize it, and rest in the practice (Fremantle, 55).

The Tibetan Book of the Dead

Russell's last year was largely confined to bed and hospital care. He frequently received visitors. Allen Ginsberg would stop by regularly, often bringing friends to meet Russell or give him their fond farewell. Believing that a direct confrontation of death and physical suffering educated one in humility and the ephemerality of life, Ginsberg would bring many visitors to see Russell's bodily scars, Kaposi's sarcoma, and other physical degradation. One day Ginsberg brought Gehlek Rimpoche, who had once lived with a young Chögyam Trungpa, to visit Russell in his final months.

> Arthur came downstairs a few times and talked with Gehlek, and the main subject of the talks within this twelve-month period was, "What do you do with your mind at the moment of death? Where do you place your mind, and how do you relate to it?" [...] The suggestion was to cultivate a sense of sympathy or compassion toward all sentient beings in the universe at that moment, some sense of openness or emptiness, and to revert to whatever meditation practice you are most familiar with... because it's too late by that time to rearrange your bookshelf or to complete ordering your tapes (Lawrence, *Hold On* 328).

Kyabje Gelek Rimpoche, from the Gelugpa school of Tibetan Vajrayana, was recognized as the reincarnation of the Gyuto Tantric College abbot, Tashi Namgyal. After leaving monastic life, Gelek founded Jewel Heart, an organization, based in Ann Arbor, MI, that has sought to preserve and educate the public on Tibetan Buddhism. Rimpoche was introduced to Allen Ginsberg by Philip Glass and the latter two have been strong supporters of Gelek's mission in America. Much of the Rimpoche's consultation with Russell was a reinforcement of the teachings passed down through the *Tibetan Book of the Dead* (*Bardo Thodol*), a book that Russell had kept near him since he was a teenager.

Prior to being bed-ridden, Russell spent time traveling and saying goodbye to close friends and family. Jeff Whittier recalls meeting with Russell on the West coast at this time, and together they shared their interpretations of the *Bardo Thodol*, often with differences of opinion: "I think of it as being symbolic. But Arthur was thinking of preparing himself for the death process in light of this book. He definitely believed in reincarnation" (Lawrence, *Hold On* 317).

The *Bardo Thodol* is a Tibetan Vajrayana Buddhist text which offers advice and guidance for personal well being as well as for the preparation of death and reincarnation. It is sometimes emphasized that this book was written as much for the living, at all stages of life, as it is for those consciously nearing their death. A large part of the book is devoted to the colorful imagery and situations of deities, as they are represented in mandala form.

As Robert Thurman notes, it is the subjective imagining of these heavenly Buddha-lands, such as the Pure Land of Bliss, that is uniquely esoteric and in contrast to more exoteric and conservative religions who, through orthodoxy and dogma, "suppress the individual imagination of heavenly realms of pleasure" (Thurman, 52). Drawing heavily from the sutras, the *Bardo Thodol* uses mandala visualization, which allows the individual to engage with heavenly Buddhas, arising from various geometrical quadrants of the mandala. The primary aim is in facilitating the individual's imagination of the heavenly realm and to restrain impulsive thought and action. Other techniques involve the reading and recitation of sutras, yogic rituals of the body and breath, prostrations, ethical efforts reinforcing selflessness and compassion towards all, and various meditations on emptiness, on deities, on the five aggregates, or other attentional content. The aim of it all is to liberate one's self from negative karma and its samsaric cycle, so that upon dying one can be reincarnated as an ever more enlightened being, ideally, a Buddha.

Charles Arthur Russell Jr. took his final breath on April 4, 1992. Ginsberg, along with numerous friends and family, delivered reflective eulogies at Russell's funeral on April 12, 1992 at Experimental Intermedia, the venue that had presented so many of Russell's works over the years. At the eulogy Ginsberg recalled first meeting Russell in Berkeley, when Russell was performing with the Kailas Shugendo Mantric Sun Band; he closed with a recitation of the Heart Sutra, including the mantra, *gate gate pāragate pārasaṃgate bodhi svāhā*, which the Dalai Lama has translated as "Go, go, go beyond, go totally beyond, be rooted in the ground of enlightenment," or more concisely, "go to the other shore" (Dalai Lama, 131).

Since his passing, Russell has experienced a posthumous revival of interest. Following Soul Jazz Record's release of *The World of Arthur Russell* (2004), Steve Knutson began Audika Records, a label exclusively devoted to releasing Russell's music. Beginning with Audika's first release, *Calling Out of Context* (2004), several releases have since followed, including re-pressings and corrections of previous releases, as well as un-released material. In 2008 Matt Wolf released, *Wild Combination*, his video documentary on Russell; then, the following year, Tim Lawrence published a definitive biography of Russell, *Hold Onto Your Dreams*.

This outpouring of memorial culminated in the Arthur Russell Symposium, organized by Lawrence and taking place on October 9, 2009. The symposium featured lectures and performances by Russell's friends, collaborators, fans, and academes. Russell's Buddhism was referred to several times in these lectures--most notably in Joyce Bowden's "Impermanence and Non-Duality: Buddhist influence in the music of Arthur Russell," which I was unable to learn more of during the writing of this book. More recently the Brooklyn Academy of Music hosted a tribute concert of Russell covers by contemporary music icons like Devonté Hynes, Lonnie Holley, Sam Amidon, and Richard Reed Parry (of Arcade Fire).

Russell's stylistic fusion and technologically enhanced solo performances pre-figured much of what would come into the musical zeitgeist of the 21st century, as the accessibility and portability of recording technology and digital information became widespread through the aid of computer technology. Looking back, it can be alarmingly disconcerting to comprehend how Russell was unable to gain more attention during his lifetime. Lawrence's biography, however, shows time and time again the fact that Russell, through his stubbornness and perfectionism, could be hard to work with or hard-pressed to settle on a final version of a given project.

Nevertheless, the body of work that has manifested since his passing shows an artist who produced an enormous amount of music, works that continue to reveal themselves by ever new aspects and which continue to inspire contemporary listeners. Most of all, rather than view his work as "unfinished" or "abandoned" in the context of commercial music, we are better served to consider Russell's work according to the ephemerality and dynamism of Buddhist philosophy. While Russell had admired popular music and maintained an interest in nurturing his own popular success, his primary focus had not wavered since he was teenager at Kailas Shugendo. He was constantly drawn back into the creative process, which was at the same time his spiritual practice.

"A Simple Dog"

In the early 1970's Russell wrote the song "Eli" (a Biblical name meaning "[God is the most] high"). The lyrics describe an unwanted and unloved dog. I had this song in mind when one day I received an email from one of Russell's most long-standing friends, Alan Abrams, whom Russell had met during his days in California. Abrams was reflecting on the poor reception of Russell's music during the artist's own lifetime. In trying to understand and explain this phenomena, Abrams took recourse to Lama Govinda's treasured Vajrayana deity, Maitreya, whom in this story takes the form of an unwanted dog:

> [Russell's reception during his own lifetime] is very much like the story of Arya Asanga and his quest to see the Buddha Maitreya, who finally came as a mangy dog. When he revealed himself, Asanga was so excited he hoisted the Buddha on his shoulders and ran through the town shouting, "Maitreya is here!" Only one pious old woman could see a mangy dog on his shoulders. The rest of the town only saw a crazy old monk running around screaming. This is my take on Arthur's super perfection. Like making a needle by rubbing a piece of iron with a cloth, so was Arthur's desire to share his vision to people—who at best saw a mangy dog (Abrams, 2012).

In Abram's recounted story above, Asanga had struggled for years, through devout meditation, to encounter Maitreya face to face; but it was only by his humble attendance to an unwanted and diseased dog, that Maitreya showed himself to Asanga. After this humble relation, Maitreya brought Asanga to the full reception of Mahayana teachings, from which Asanga composed influential Buddhist writings. Since Russell's passing and the resurrection of his work, listeners have begun to know better, finding themselves able to see and hear his work through the unique artistry and spirit as it was unabashedly offered.

In Tibetan Buddhist tradition a *terma*, which literally means "hidden treasure," is a kind of tantric literature or teaching. These teachings are often hidden —buried in the ground, hidden in caves, secretly handed off to others—in order to be revealed at a later time. Russell's work was never intention-

Image 50. Page one of an early score of "Eli, Eli" one of Russell's earliest original songs (Russell, EWF)

ally hidden. But following his death and two decades without attention, the growing interest in his work since 2010 seems to offer the posthumous music of this "Buddhist pop star" as a musical *terma* of sorts, at least for those able or interested in receiving it as such. Having been respected, though largely ignored, as an "outsider" figure in New York's Downtown scene, Russell's works come to us now as a reflective, playful, and deeply spiritual music. Or, as frontman of the Ramones, Joey Ramone, once proclaimed after hearing one of Russell's songs: "That song is a prayer" (Lawrence, Hold On 348).

BIBLIOGRAPHY

BOOKS [PRINT]

Abé, Ryuichi. *The Weaving of Mantra: Kukai and the Construction of Esoteric Buddhist Discourse*. New York: Columbia UP, 1999.

Adamenko, Victoria. *Neo-Mythologism in Music: From Scriabin and Schoenberg to Schnittke and Crumb*. Hillsdale: Pendragon Press, 2007.

Asai, Susan Miyo. *Nomai Dance Drama: A Surviving Spirit of Medieval Japan*. Westport: Greenwood Press, 1999.

Ashkenazi, Michael. *Handbook of Japanese Mythology*. Santa Barbara: ABC-CLIO, Inc., 2003.

Beck, Guy L. *Sonic Theology: Hinduism and Sacred Sound*. Delhi: Jainendra Prakash Jain At Shri Jainendra Press, 1995.

Beer, Robert. *The Handbook of Tibetan Buddhist Symbols*. Chicago: Serindia Publications, Inc., 2003.

Benayoun, Robert. *Alain Resnais: arpenteur de l'imaginaire*. Paris: Ramsay, 2008.

Blacker, Carmen. *The Catalpa Bow: A Study of Shamanistic Practices in Japan*. Surrey: Japan Library/Curzon Press, 1999.

Brewster, Bill. *Last Night a DJ Saved My Life: The History of the Disc Jockey*. NYC: Grove/Atlantic, Inc., 2014.

Bucknell, Roderick S.; Stuart-Fox, Martin. *The Twilight Language: Explorations in Buddhist Meditation and Symbolism.* Surrey: Curzon Press Ltd., 1994.

Cashford, Jules. *The Moon: Myth and Image.* New York: Four Walls Eight Windows, 2002.

Dahl, Cortland. *Entrance to the Great Perfection: A Guide to the Dzogchen Preliminary Practices.* Ithaca: Snow Lion Publications, 2009.

Dalai Lama; Jinpa, Geshe Thupten [trans.]. *The Essence of the Heart Sutra: The Dalai Lama's Heart of Wisdom Teachings.* Somerville: Wisdom Publications, 2005.

---Berzin, Alexander [Ed.]. *The Gelug/Kagyu Tradition of Mahamudra.* Ithaca: Snow Lion Publications, 1997.

Dukes, Terence; Tomio, Shifu Nagaboshi. *The Bodhisattva Warriors: The Origin, Inner Philosophy, History and Symbolism of the Buddhist Martial Art within India and China.* York Beach: Red Wheel/Wesier, LLC., 1994.

Dylan, Bob. *Chronicles, Volume One.* New York: Simon & Schuster, 2004.

Ertan, Deniz. *Dane Rudhyar: His Music, Thought, and Art.* Suffolk: University of Rochester Press, 2009.

Fanthorpe, Lionel; Fanthorpe, Patricia. *Mysteries and Secrets of Numerology.* Toronto: Dundurn Press, 2013.

Fischer-Schreiber. *The Encyclopedia of Eastern Philosophy and Religion: Buddhism, Hinduism, Taoism, Zen.* Boston: Shambhala Press, 1989.

Fremantle, Francesca [Trans.]. *The Tibetan Book Of The Dead.*

Boston: Shambhala Publications, 1975.

Goodwin, Matthew Oliver. *Numerology: The Complete Guide.* Newcastle: Newcastle Publishing Company, 1981.

Govinda, Lama Anagarika. *The Way of the White Clouds: A Buddhist Pilgrim in Tibet.* Berkeley: Shambhala Press, 1971.

---*The Foundations of Tibetan Mysticism.* York Beach: Red Wheel/Weiser, LLC., 1969.

Green, Ronald S. *Kukai, founder of Japanese Shingon Buddhism: portraits of his life.* Madison: University of Wisconsin, 2003.

Hakeda, Yoshito S. *Kukai: Major Works.* New York: Columbia UP, 1972.

Hess, Linda. "The Cow Is Sucking at the Calf's Teat: Kabir's Upside-Down Language." *History of Religions.* Vol. 22, No. 4, Devotional Religion in India (May, 1983), pp. 313-337. Chicago: University of Chicago Press, 1983.

Holmes, Paul. *Gustav Holst.* London: Omnibus Press, 1998.

Hudson, Lee. "Poetics in Performance: The Beat Generation." Amsterdam: *Studies in Interpretation, Volume 1*. Editions Rodopi N.V., 1977.

Kanda, Christine Guth. *Shinzo: Hachiman Imagery and Its Development.* Cambridge: Harvard UP, 1985.

Khan, Ali Akbar. *The Classical Music of North India: The Music of the Baba Allaudin Gharana as taught by Ali Akbar Khan at the Ali Akbar College of Music.* Volume One: "The First Years Study." New Delhi: Munshiram Manoharlal Publishers Pvt. Ltd., 2009.

King, Richard. *Early Advaita Vedanta and Buddhism: The Ma-*

hayana Context of the Gaudapadiya-Karika. Albany: State University of New York Press, 1995.

Kolhatkar, Madhavi; Tachiwaka, Musashi. *Buddhist Fire Ritual in Japan*. Osaka: National Museum of Ethnology, 2012.

LaFleur, William R. *Awesome Nightfall*. Somerville: Wisdom Publications, 2003.

Lagerquist, Kay; Lenard, Lisa. *The Complete Idiot's Guide to Numerology*. New York: Amaranth Illuminare, 2004.

Lawrence, Tim. *Hold Onto Your Dreams: Arthur Russell and the Downtown Music Scene (1973-1992)*. Durham: Duke UP, 2009.

---*Love Saves the Day: A History of American Dance Culture, 1970-1979*. Durham: Duke UP, 2003.

Lewis, George. *A Power Stronger Than Itself: The AACM and American Experimental Music*. Chicago: The University of Chicago Press, 2008.
Lopez, Donald S. *Elaborations on Emptiness: Uses of the Heart Sutra*. Princeton: Princeton UP, 1996.

Merriam-Webster. *Merriam-Webster's Collegiate Dictionary*. Eleventh Edition. Springfield: Merriam-Webster, 2004.

Midal, Fabrice. *Chögyam Trungpa: His Life and Vision*. Boston: Shambhala Publications, 2004.

Miles, Barry. *In The Seventies: Adventures in the Counter-Culture*. London: Serpent's Tail/Profile Books Ltd., 2011.
Mishlove, Jeffrey. *Roots of Consciousness*. NYC: Random House, 1975.

Morgan, Bill. *The Beat Generation in San Francisco: A Literary Tour*. San Francisco: City Lights Books, 2003.

Nath, Samir. *Encyclopedic Dictionary of Buddhism*. Volume 4, Issue 4. Ceylon: Gunapala Piyasena Malalasekera. Government of Ceylon, 1989.

Neuman, Daniel. *The Life of Music in North India: The Organization of an Artistic Tradition*. Detroit: Wayne State UP, 1980.

Park, Jin Y; Kopf, Gereon [Eds.]. *Merleau-Ponty and Buddhism*. Plymouth: Lexington Book/Rowman & Littlefield Publishers, Inc., 2009.

Payne, Richard Karl. *Tantric Buddhism in East Asia*. Somerville: Wisdom Publications, 2006.

Power, Richard. *The Lost Teachings of Lama Govinda: Living Wisdom from a Modern Tibetan Master*. Wheaton: Quest Books. 2013.

Prabhupada, A. C. Bhaktivedanta Swami. *Chant and be Happy: The Power of Mantra Meditation*. Los Angeles: Bhaktivedanta Book Trust, 2010.

Reader, Ian. *Religion in Contemporary Japan*. Honolulu: University of Hawaii Press, 1991.

Rinchen, Geshe Sonam. *The Bodhisattva Vow*. Boston: Snow Lion Publications, 2000.

Rinpoche, Diglo Khyentse. *Guru Yoga: According to the Prelimi-*

nary Practice Longchen Nyingtik: an Oral Teaching by Dilgo Khyentse Rinpoche. Ithaca: Snow Lion Publications, 1999.

Suzuki, D.T. *Manual of Zen Buddhism*. NYC: Grove Press, 1994.

Sylvan, Robin. *Traces of the Spirit: The Religious Dimensions of Popular Music*. NYC: New York UP, 2002.

Ruckert, George. *Music in North India: Experiencing Music, Expressing Culture*. Oxford: Oxford UP, 2004.

Rudhyar, Dane. *The Moon: The Cycles and Fortunes of Life*. Philadelphia: David McKay Company, 1946.

Seager, Richard Hughes. *Buddhism in America*. NYC: Columbia UP, 2012.

Sherab, Khenchen Palden. *The Buddhist Path: A Practical Guide from the Nyingma Tradition of Tibetan Buddhism*. Ithaca: Snow Lion Publications, 2010.

Suzuki, Daisetz Teitaro. *Manual of Zen Buddhism*. NYC: Grove Press, 1960.

---*Studies in the Lankavatara Sutra*. Delhi: Motilal Banarsidass Publishers (Private Limited), 1999.

Terrel, Carroll Franklin. *William Carlos Williams: Man and Poet*. Orono: National Poetry Foundation, University of Maine at Orono, 1983.

Thurman, Robert [trans.]. *Tibetan Book of the Dead: Liberation Through Understanding in the Between*. NYC: Bantam Books, 1994.

Tomlinson, Gary. *Music in Renaissance Magic: Toward a Historiography of Others*. Chicago: University of Chicago Press, 1993.

Trungpa, Chögyam. *Smile at Fear: Awakening the True Heart of Bravery*. Boston: Shambhala Publications, 2009.

--*The Collected Works Of Chögyam Trungpa. Volume 6: Glimpses of Space; Orderly Chaos. Xxix*. Boston: Shambhala Publications, 2006.
---*The Collected Works of Chögyam Trungpa. Vol 7*. Boston: Shambhala Publications, 2004.
   ---*Myth of Freedom*. Boston: Shambhala Publications, 2001.
   ---*True Perception: The Path of Dharma Art*. Boston: Shambhala Publications, 1996.
   --- *The Lion's Roar: An Introduction to Tantra*. Boston: Shambhala Publications, 1992.
   ---*Crazy Wisdom*. Boston: Shambhala Publications, 1991.
   ---*First Thought, Best Thought*. Boston: Shambhala Publications, 1983.

Urban, Hugh B. *Tantra: Sex, Secrecy, Politics, and Power in the Study of Religion*. Oakland: University of California Press, 2003.

Wade, Bonnie C. *Khyal: Creativity within N. India's Classical Music Tradition*. Cambridge: University of Cambridge Press, 1984.

Waldman, Anne. *The Beat Book: Writings from the Beat Generation*. Boston: Shambhala Publication, 1996.

---[et al.] *Disembodied Poetics: Annals of the Jack Kerouac School*.

Albuquerque: University of New Mexico Press, 1994.

Whorf, Benjamin Lee; et al. *Language, Thought, and Reality: Selected Writings of Benjamin Lee Whorf.* Boston: MIT Press, 2012.

Wilke, Annette. *Sound and Communication: An Aesthetic Cultural History of Sanskrit Hinduism.* Berlin/New York: Walter de Gruyter GmbH & Co. KG, 2011.

Williams, William Carlos; Rosenthal, M.L. *The William Carlos Williams Reader.* NYC: New Directions Publishing, 1966.

Yamazaki, Taiko. *Shingon: Japanese Esoteric Buddhism.* Boston: Shingon Buddhist International Institute/Shambhala Publications, 1996.

JOURNALS/PERIODICALS [PRINT]

Chatham, Rhys; Wolff, Christian. "Figure Among Motifs: Rhys Chatham and Christian Wolff on Arthur Russell." New York: *Art Forum.* April 1, 2009.
Hiss, Anthony. "Talk of the Town: You Never Know." *The New Yorker.* April 11, 1977. Pgs. 29-31.

"Other Offerings." The Golden Nagas. *Berkeley Barb.* "Campus Underground" Series. Jan. 18-31, 1979. Berkeley, CA. Pg. 12.
Owen, Frank. "Echo Beach." *Melody Maker.* April 11, 1987. 36-37.

Simms, Robert. "Some Thoughts on the Meaning of Riaz in Hindustani Music." *Bansuri Magazine.* Volume 11, 1994. Pgs. 6-14.

Stubbs, David. "Arthur Russell: World of Echo." *Melody Maker*. April 11, 1987.

Toop, David. "The Flying Heart." *The Wire*. Issue 239. January, 2004. Pgs., 30-37.

ONLINE SOURCES [DIGITAL]

Benrido Co., Ltd., Tokyo. "Womb Realm." https://commons.wikimedia.org/wiki/File:Taizokai.jpg. Last accessed: August 22, 2015.

Braxton, Anthony. "A Conversation with Anthony Braxton" [online interview]. Restructures Music Forum. October 15, 1995. http://www.restructures.net/links/BraxtonConversation.html. Last accessed: August 22, 2015.

Cage, John. "John Cage on 'Empty Words' and the demilitarization of language" [online mp3 interview]. University of Pennsylvania. August 8, 1974. http://www.writing.upenn.edu/~afilreis/88v/cage-radio.html. Last accessed: August 22, 2015.

Chowka, Peter Barry. "Online Interviews with Allen Ginsberg." University of Illinois at Urbana Champagne. Modern American Poetry. April, 1976. http://www.english.illinois.edu/maps/poets/g_l/ginsberg/interviews.htm. Last accessed: August 22, 2015.

Dayal, Geeta. "Recalling Experimental Music in '70s New York" [online article]. NPR Music. October 20, 2010. http://www.npr.org/sections/therecord/2010/10/20/130698344/

new-york-in-the-70s. Last accessed: August 22, 2015.
Dawes, William. "Richard Maxfield" [online article]. Mela Foundation. 1989. http://www.melafoundation.org/rm00.htm. Last accessed: August 22, 2015.

Goodman, Steven. "Wisdom Crazy: An Interview With Steven Goodman." Inquiring Mind. Spring, 2005. http://www.inquiringmind.com/Articles/WisdomCrazy.html

Hall, Steven. "Steven Hall: It's Basically a Very Dirty Joke." Keep On [online interview]. Volume Two, Issue 1. July/August, 2005. Pgs. 16-17. http://web.archive.org/web/20060705083628/http://www.keeponmagazine.co.uk/features.htm. Last accessed: August 22, 2015.

Hallett, Nick. "Roses on the Disco Floor: Peter Gordon" [online interview]. Bomb Magazine. Oct 12, 2010. http://bombmagazine.org/article/3675/roses-on-the-disco-floor-peter-gordon. Last accessed: August 22, 2015.
Hassell, Jon. "Jon Hassell: There Was No Avant Garde." 2002. http://marcusboon.com/jon-hassell-there-was-no-avant-garde/. Last accessed: August 22, 2015.
Khan, Ali Akbar. "Indian Music and the Ali Akbar College of Music" [IM, PDF pamphlet]. Ali Akbar Khan [Digital] Library. http://aliakbarkhanlibrary.com/concert_experience/documents/Upper_Grades_Curriculum.pdf. Last accessed: August 22, 2015.

Khider, Ibrahim. "Phill Niblock is a happy man" [PDF article]. June 19, 2005. http://www.phillniblock.com/phillniblocksays.pdf. Last accessed: August 22, 2015.

Lauten, Elodie. "Singing Tractors, Hold onto Your Dreams" [online text]. Sequenza. September 9, 2009. http://www.sequenza21.com/lauten/2009/09/singing-tractors-hold-on-to-your-dreams/. Last accessed: August 22, 2015.

Leary, V.K. "Keisho." California Tendai Buddhist Monastery. March 3, 2008. http://vkleary.blogspot.com/2008_03_01_ archive.html. Last accessed: August 22, 2015.

Lee, Tom. Lee, Tom. "An Interview with Tom Lee, Partner of Arthur Russell" [online interview, 2008a]. Gothamist. December 5, 2008. http://gothamist.com/2008/12/05/tom_lee.php. Last accessed: August 22, 2015.

---"Q+A: Tom Lee On His Life With Arthur Russell" [online interview, 2008b]. The Fader. September 22, 2008. http://www.thefader.com/2008/09/22/q-a-tom-lee-on-life-with-and-without-arthur-russell. Last accessed: August 22, 2015.

Menist, Chris. "Arthur Russell." DJ Friendly Records. http://djfriendly.co.uk/more_arthur.php?PHPSES-SID=b85999859e6a03b077fbba7754af8ed8. Last accessed: August 22, 2015.

Riley, Terry. "Remembering Guruji" [online interview]. Otherminds. 1996. http://www.otherminds.org/html/Riley.htm. Last accessed: August 22, 2015.

Rogers, Damien. "Damien Rogers talks to Ann Waldman" [online interview]. Lemon Hound. March 8, 2011. http://lemonhound.com/2011/03/08/damian-rogers-talks-to-anne-waldman/. Last accessed: August 22, 2015.

Russell, Arthur. "The Music of Arthur Russell with Declan Kelly Part 1" [radio interview]. R-N-D.NET. http://www.r-n-d.net/fileadmin/audio/mixes/DKelly_AR_Pt.1.mp3. Last accessed: August 22, 2015.

---"Beats in Space." B.I.S. Radio. #440. Oct 28, 2008. http://

www.beatsinspace.net/playlists/440. Last accessed: August 22, 2015.

Sachdev, G.S. Hinduism Today [online interview]. Hinduism Today. Nov, 1989. http://www.hinduismtoday.com/modules/smartsection/item.php?itemid=672. Last accessed: August 22, 2015.

Schelling, Andrew. "Allen Ginsberg Death Notes" [online text archive]. Terebess Asia Online. April 9, 1997. http://www.terebess.hu/english/haiku/aginsberg.html. Last accessed: August 22, 2015.
"Gedatsu Church of America." SF Genealogy. 1963. http://www.sfgenealogy.com/san_francisco_directory/1963/1963_870.pdf.
Last accessed: August 22, 2015.
Sharp, Irene. "Margaret Rowell: An Introduction" [online article]. Internet Cello Society. 1984. http://www.cello.org/newsletter/articles/mrowell.html. Last accessed: August 22, 2015.
Uttal, Jai. "The Baba in the Stilt House" [comment on website]. Jai's Blog. October 9, 2009. http://jaiuttal.com/jais-blog-the-baba-in-the-stilt-house/. Last accessed: August 22, 2015.

Zummo, Peter. "Experimental Composers" [online interview]. Clocktower Radio. NYC, January 22, 2010. http://clocktower.org/show/peter-zummo. Last accessed: August 22, 2015.

AUDIO DOCUMENTS [MEDIA]

Ginsberg, Allen. "Ballad of the Lights" [liner notes]. NYC: Audika Records, 2010.

Russell, Arthur. *Ballad of the Lights* [vinyl e.p.]. Tokyo: Press-pop Music, 2010.
  ---*First Thought, Best Thought* [c.d.]. Audika Records. NYC, 2006.
  ---*World Of Echo* [c.d.]. NYC: Audika Records, 2005.

Zummo, Peter. *Experimenting With Household Chemicals* [Liner Notes]. NYC: Experimental Intermedia Foundation, 1995.

VIDEO DOCUMENTS [MEDIA]

Russell, Arthur. *Another Thought* [AT, press kit, online video]. NYC: Point Music, 1994. Via Red Hot: https://www.youtube.com/watch?v=y9Bt6G5psXw

Ruyle, Bill. "Arthurs Landing Discuss Their Album Project & The Late Arthur Russell" [online video interview]. Strut Records. April 6, 2011. http://www.youtube.com/watch?v=RFZ_VOdkHXU

Wilson, Robert. *Medea* [In Prologue and Five Acts, Washington Open Rehearsal, 1981-02-28; 6 sound discs (198 min.)]. NYC: New York Public Library.1981.

Wolf, Matt. *Wild Combination* [Video]. DVD Extras. NYC: Polari Pictures, 2009.

ARTHUR RUSSELL ARCHIVES

[N.B. The following bibliographic sources refer to particular folders or collections within Russell's physical estate. In the body of this dissertation, they are referenced by their abbreviations, for names that were given by Russell or myself. Russell's archive is now at the New York Public Library for the Performing Arts at Lincoln Center in New York City, NY.]

Allen Ginsberg Folder [AG]. Arthur Russell Estate. Portland, OR.

Black Notebook [BN]. Arthur Russell Estate. Portland, OR.

Dance Folder [DF]. Arthur Russell Estate. Portland, OR.

Early Works Folder [EWF]. Arthur Russell Estate. Portland, OR.

Grant Application [GA]. Arthur Russell Estate. Portland, OR.

Instrumentals Folder [IF]. Arthur Russell Estate. Portland, OR.

Notebooks [N], Arthur Russell Estate. Portland, OR.

Poster Folder [PF]. Arthur Russell Estate. Portland, OR.

Spiral Notebooks [SN]. Arthur Russell Estate. Portland, OR.

PERSONAL CORRESPONDENCES WITH AUTHOR

[N.B. This is the bibliography for all personal interviews, emails, or other forms of correspondence involving the author.]

Abrams, Alan. Email correspondence with the author. July, 2012.

Ahmed, Mustafa. Personal interview with the author. September, 2013.

Anderson-Harold, Beth. Email correspondence with the author. Jun 16, 2013.

Blank, Bob. Telephone conversation with author. February 9, 2011.

Brooks, Ernie. Personal interview with the author. 2012.

Franck, Andrew. Email correspondence with the author. December 24, 2010.

Gordon, Peter. Personal interview with the author. March 2, 2012.

Hazarika, Tej. Personal interview and email correspondence with the author. NYC, 2013

Kuivila, Ron. Email correspondence with the author. March 20, 2011.

Lauten, Elodie. Personal interview with the author. June, 2012.

Leary, V.K. Email correspondence with the author. February 17, 2012.

Moran, John. Personal correspondence with author via Facebook message. 2013.

Nagy, Paul. Personal interview with author. Brooklyn, New York. April 26, 2012.

Ruyle, Bill. Personal interview with author. Brooklyn, New York. July 11, 2012.

Zummo, Peter. Personal interview with author. Staten Island, NY. December 2010.

About the author

Matt Marble (b. 1979, MS) is an artist, author, and audio producer. Both creatively and through historical research, his work explores the inspired intersection of art and spirituality and the intuitive disciplines they mutually employ. He is the producer and host of Secret Sound, a podcast revealing the influences of esoteric spirituality and marginalized voices in American music history. Matt holds a Ph.D. in music composition from Princeton University and a totemic black rattlesnake from his dreams. Previous writings have been published in Abraxas Journal, Desert Suprematism, Ear_Wave_Event, and The Open Space magazine. To explore Matt's work further, please visit: www.mattmarble.net.

Printed in Great Britain
by Amazon

79148951R00156